A Radical Pluralist Philosophy of Religion

A Radical Pluralist Philosophy of Religion

Cross-Cultural, Multireligious, Interdisciplinary

Mikel Burley

BLOOMSBURY ACADEMIC
LONDON · NEW YORK · OXFORD · NEW DELHI · SYDNEY

BLOOMSBURY ACADEMIC
Bloomsbury Publishing Plc
50 Bedford Square, London, WC1B 3DP, UK
1385 Broadway, New York, NY 10018, USA

BLOOMSBURY, BLOOMSBURY ACADEMIC and the Diana logo are trademarks
of Bloomsbury Publishing Plc

First published in Great Britain 2020

Copyright © Mikel Burley, 2020

Mikel Burley has asserted his right under the Copyright, Designs and Patents Act,
1988, to be identified as Author of this work.

For legal purposes the Acknowledgements on p. xi constitute an extension of this
copyright page.

Cover design: Louise Dugdale
Cover image: Photo of the Deodhanī festival at Kāmākhyā temple,
Assam, by Pinku Haloi, 2017

A catalogue record for this book is available from the British Library.

A catalog record for this book is available from the Library of Congress.

ISBN: HB: 978-1-3500-9830-5
       PB: 978-1-3500-9831-2
       ePDF: 978-1-3500-9832-9
       eBook: 978-1-3500-9833-6

Typeset by RefineCatch Limited, Bungay, Suffolk
Printed and bound in Great Britain

To find out more about our authors and books visit www.bloomsbury.com
and sign up for our newsletters.

Contents

Part Two Exemplifying a Radical Pluralist Approach

4 'Compassion beyond Our Imagination': Radical Plurality in Buddhist Ethics 97

5 'Ways of Being Human': Cannibalism and Respecting the Dead 119

6 'Awe at the Terrible': Divine Possession, Blood Sacrifice and the Grotesque Body 135

Illustrations

Acknowledgements

My work on this book was assisted by the granting of a period of research leave from February to July 2018 by the School of Philosophy, Religion and History of Science at the University of Leeds. I am grateful both for this and for the productive and accommodating working environment that the School provides, not least in the form of its Centre for Philosophy of Religion and Centre for Religion and Public Life. I could not hope to be among colleagues more affable or intellectually stimulating than those who surround me.

Although none of the chapters in this book has previously been published in precisely the form that it appears here, some of them draw upon previous articles of mine. Chapter 1 combines elements from my 'Religious Pluralisms: From Homogenization to Radicality', *Sophia* (Springer, published online in January 2018) and 'Religious Diversity and Conceptual Schemes: Critically Appraising Internalist Pluralism', *Sophia* (Springer, published online in February 2018). Chapter 2 incorporates material from my 'Thickening Description: Towards an Expanded Conception of Philosophy of Religion', *International Journal for Philosophy of Religion* 83, no. 1 (Springer, 2018). Chapter 3 is based on my '"The Happy Side of Babel": Radical Plurality, Narrative Fiction and the Philosophy of Religion', *Method and Theory in the Study of Religion* 29, no. 2 (Brill, 2017). Chapter 5 is a revised version of my 'Eating Human Beings: Varieties of Cannibalism and the Heterogeneity of Human Life', *Philosophy* 91, no. 4 (Cambridge University Press, 2016). Chapter 6 adapts material from my 'Dance of the *Deodhās*: Divine Possession, Blood Sacrifice and the Grotesque Body in Assamese Goddess Worship', *Religions of South Asia* 12, no. 2 (Equinox Publishing Ltd, 2019). And Chapter 7 is a modified version of my '"A Language in Which to Think of the World": Animism, Indigenous Traditions, and the Deprovincialization of Philosophy of Religion', published in two parts in *Religious Theory: E-Supplement to the Journal for Cultural and Religious Theory* (Whitestone Foundation, October and November 2018). For these permissions, I thank the respective editors and publishers of the journals concerned. I am also indebted to more than a dozen anonymous referees who provided comments on my articles during the various journals' review processes.

Ideas and material that have contributed towards this book were tried out in papers presented at several conferences and research seminars from 2016 to 2018. In addition to the University of Leeds, venues of these events include Charles University in Prague, Durham University, the University of Edinburgh, University of Macau, University of Oxford, University of Wales Trinity Saint David and the University of Zurich. I thank the organizers of each of these events and the respective audiences for their comments and questions. Also deserving of thanks are several people who assisted me prior to, during or subsequent to a two-week research trip to Guwahati, Assam, in August 2017. These include Rajib Sarma (Foundation for History and Heritage Studies, Guwahati), Maniraj Baruah, Gopal Das, Prasanta Kalita, Nirmal Mandal and staff at the Kamakhya Tourist Information Office. Patricia Dold and Jayashree Athparia provided helpful information, and Hugh Urban generously shared some of his recent published and unpublished work on animal sacrifice, Hindu nationalism and the Kāmākhyā temple. I am especially indebted to Pinku Haloi for permission to use two of his photographs of the Deodhanī festival, one of which is featured on this book's front cover and the other of which is figure 6.4 in Chapter 6. For the right to reproduce other photographs and illustrations elsewhere in the book, I thank Alamy, Bridgeman Images, the British Library Board, Dinodia Photos, Getty Images, Robbie Jack, Paul Kennedy, Dan Kitwood, Trustees of the British Museum and Wikimedia Commons.

It is gratifying to be working in the philosophy of religion at a time when a number of colleagues both in the United Kingdom and elsewhere are moving this field of inquiry in directions roughly congruent with the aims of this book. This common purpose was palpable during a conference that I convened on the theme of *Philosophy of Religions: Cross-Cultural, Multi-Religious Approaches* at the University of Leeds, 3–4 July 2018. I wish to thank the delegates who attended that conference for their lively participation, especially the speakers, who included Arif Ahmed, Richard Amesbury, David Cheetham, Jessica Frazier, Victoria Harrison, Ian James Kidd, Tim Knepper, Kevin Schilbrack and Tasia Scrutton. The present book has undoubtedly benefited from many fruitful conversations with these and other colleagues. Although our philosophical approaches differ considerably, there is general agreement among us – and also among many who were unable to attend the conference – about the need to expand both the methods and the content of philosophy of religion. A special issue of the journal *Religious Studies* comprising articles based on papers presented at the conference is to be published by Cambridge University Press in 2020.

With regard to the present book, Brian Clack, Christopher Hamilton and Kevin Schilbrack offered insightful and encouraging comments on an early proposal. Kevin Schilbrack also commented on a draft of the full manuscript, as did an anonymous reader for the publisher. Several colleagues at the University of Leeds generously commented on one or more chapters, including Ben Kirby, Rachel Muers, Tasia Scrutton, Stefan Skrimshire, Adriaan van Klinken and Mark Wynn. And Colleen Coalter, Helen Saunders, Becky Holland and their colleagues at Bloomsbury Publishing, along with the production team at RefineCatch, have been as cordial, meticulous and efficient as ever in seeing the work through to publication.

Finally, to Sue Richardson: for her love and unstinting support of my philosophical obsessions, I owe a debt of gratitude far beyond my capacity to repay.

Mikel Burley

Introduction

Contemplative attention to radical plurality is not a retreat from life, a lack of interest in the fray, but a certain kind of interest in human life, born of wonder at it.

(D. Z. Phillips 2007b: 207)

Introducing a radical pluralist approach

This book is a contribution to the task of expanding and diversifying philosophy of religion both methodologically and with regard to its range of subject matter. Taking inspiration from the 'contemplative conception of philosophy' formulated by D. Z. Phillips[1] – a conception that was itself modelled on an interpretation of the philosophical methods of Ludwig Wittgenstein – my own work seeks to build upon, embellish and further that conception. It does this both by developing stronger engagement between philosophy and other disciplines involved in the study of religion and by widening the horizon of the resulting interdisciplinary enterprise in cross-cultural and multireligious directions. The emergent approach is thus

---

[1] See, e.g., Phillips (1999, 2001b), Sanders (2007).

radically pluralist in at least two senses: first, it actively promotes a plurality of methods, unconstrained by conventional disciplinary demarcations; and second, it aspires to do conceptual justice to the radically plural character of religious phenomena themselves, aiming to deepen understanding of the variegated nature of religious – and indeed nonreligious – forms of life without rushing to evaluate them in terms of some supposedly universal standard of truth or rationality.

An increasingly common and thoroughly understandable complaint about much contemporary philosophy of religion is that its scope remains abysmally restricted. While professing to investigate religion in general, most of what goes by the name of philosophy of religion has been, and continues to be, fixated on a small cluster of questions pertaining to an ahistorical and decontextualized 'theism'. The resultant limitation is twofold. For one thing, the obsession with a homogenized theism militates against consideration of the full diversity of religions, both theistic and nontheistic; and for another, it encourages an exclusive preoccupation with matters of beliefs about God – narrowly construed in terms of 'propositional attitudes' – at the expense of a more capacious appreciation of what human religiosity consists in. The recent movement known as analytic theology, which purports to apply the methods of analytic philosophy to 'the explication of core doctrines in Christian theology' (Rea 2009: 1), is, for the most part, only accentuating these limitations.[2]

Calls for a more expansive approach are far from new. Figures such as Ninian Smart and John Hick, for example, were pioneering in their advocacy of attention to religious ideas from outside the Abrahamic traditions.[3] Smart in particular spotlighted what he called the multiple 'dimensions of the sacred', including the ritual, mythic, experiential, ethical, legal, social, material and political as well as the explicitly doctrinal aspects of religion (Smart 1996). Recent decades have seen several other philosophers of religion taking up the challenge to not only incorporate a wide array of religious traditions into the conversation,[4] but also engage philosophically with dimensions of religious life beyond the standard repertoire of beliefs.[5] Questions persist, however, about how to make philosophy of religion

---

[2] For a critical appraisal of so-called analytic theology from a theological perspective, see Oliver (2010).

[3] See, e.g., Smart (1960, 1998), Hick (1973, 1976).

[4] See, e.g., Clayton (2006), Griffith-Dickson (2005), Kessler (1999) and the series of books by Arvind Sharma taking different perspectives on the philosophy of religion, such as Sharma (1995, 2006).

[5] See, e.g., Cottingham (2005), Schilbrack (2002, 2004b), Wynn (2005, 2009).

genuinely reflective of the diversity that obtains amid the religious lives of humankind in general, as opposed to only a small portion of it. These questions are of the utmost importance for philosophy of religion, for they bear upon the extent to which practitioners of this field of inquiry may legitimately claim to have gained a firm grasp of the very phenomenon they profess to be studying. For that same reason, the questions are also important for anyone wishing to understand the complex and ramified phenomenon of religion in the contemporary world, given that philosophy has a prominent place among the disciplines engaged in the study of religion more broadly. While it would be unreasonable to expect any philosopher to acquire a thorough understanding of even a modest subset of the vast assortment of religious orientations and modes of belief and practice that have characterized the cultural lives and histories of human beings, there remains an onus on those who wish to speak about religion in general to explicitly recognize the diversity.

One way of conceptualizing the problem is in terms of abstraction. When philosophers of religion speak of theism – or of 'bare theism', 'standard theism', 'restricted theism', 'broad theism', etc. – what they are often trying to do is enable their arguments to apply to more than one sect, denomination or religion.[6] They may presume, for example, that Judaism, Christianity and Islam, notwithstanding the multiple differences between these religions and the sectarian divergences within them, are all 'theistic' – which, in a sense, they are.[7] On this account, to speak of theism rather than more specifically of Judaism, Christianity or Islam is a move in the direction of inclusivity. Some philosophers have taken this abstractive approach a stage further, by replacing talk of theism with talk of something that is supposedly common to all religions – or, at any rate, to all the 'great world religions', be they theistic or nontheistic. For Hick, the unifying principle is 'the Real' – a principle that no religion explicitly recognizes but which, according to Hick, all the 'great religions' are implicitly directed towards (see esp. Hick 2004: xix *et passim*). Thus, although Hick was indeed a trailblazer in promoting a more encompassing conception of religion, his conception could be regarded as unhelpfully homogenizing insofar as it presumes all major religions to have a single object of reverence. While calling his approach 'pluralism', he ends

---

[6] For instances of the term 'bare theism', see Swinburne (2008: 23) and Philipse (2012: 145); for 'standard theism' and 'restricted theism', see Rowe (1984: 95) and (2004: 4) respectively; for 'broad theism', see Davis (1989: 191).

[7] See, e.g., Swinburne (2004: 7): 'The claim that there is a God is called theism. Theism is, of course, the core belief of the creeds of Christianity, Judaism, and Islam.'

up with a diminished appreciation of what, following D. Z. Phillips, we might call the *radical* plurality of religious and nonreligious perspectives on the world.

Although greater inclusivity is a laudable objective, a hazard of any abstractive attempt to achieve this is the loss of contact with the real-life phenomena to which one's discussion was intended to have relevance in the first place. If the god of the philosophers – let alone some noumenal, 'transcategorial Real' (Hick 2004, esp. xx–xxxiii) – is not a god to whom anyone wittingly prayed or bowed down in worship, then a problem arises for the whole enterprise of an abstractive philosophy of religion. To the extent that it loses touch with people's actual religious lives, philosophy risks leading us away from rather than towards a deeper understanding of religion. As an antidote to this problem, a radical pluralist approach, without simply eschewing generalizations altogether, endeavours not to succumb to the *craving* for generality, seeking instead to give due attention to particular cases[8] – assembling illustrative reminders for the purpose of bringing out complexity and diversity where these obtain.[9] The present book comprises both methodological proposals for how this can be done in philosophically innovative and fruitful ways and also extensive examples of these methodological proposals being put into practice. Integral to the approach deployed is the inclusion of photographs and other images in several of the book's chapters. It is hoped that these illustrations complement the text in ways that remind us of religion's highly visual – and visually variegated – elements. Philosophizing about religion all too frequently drifts away into overly rarefied spheres of argumentation, whereas pictures can, among other things, help to keep the discussion grounded in the bodily realities of human life.

The remainder of this introduction summarizes the chapters that are to come.

Chapter summaries

The book is divided into two main parts. Part One, 'Critique and Methodology', comprises Chapters 1–3 and performs two principal tasks. First it critically engages with a representative sample of approaches to philosophy of religion

---

[8] For the phrase 'craving for generality', see Wittgenstein (1969: 17–18).

[9] 'The work of the philosopher consists in assembling reminders for a particular purpose' (Wittgenstein 1958: §127).

– and especially to the philosophy of religious diversity – from which a radical pluralist approach strives to differentiate itself. Second, it expounds the methodological elements constitutive of the radical pluralist approach that I am envisaging. Part Two, 'Exemplifying a Radical Pluralist Approach', comprises Chapters 4–7 and, as its title indicates, serves to demonstrate what a radical pluralist approach looks like. The book ends with a concluding chapter. Below I shall summarize each of the eight chapters in turn.

Chapter 1, 'Religious Pluralisms', examines the theoretical response to the phenomenon of religious diversity that has come to be known as religious pluralism. As many commentators have observed, several variant theories of religious pluralism have been proposed. Of these, I select three for particular attention, namely those put forward by John Hick, John Cobb and Victoria Harrison respectively. In the case of Hick and Cobb, I conclude that, despite these theorists' pluralist pretensions, each of them ends up advancing a homogenized conception of religious traditions as opposed to one that does justice to the genuine plurality that exists. Harrison, meanwhile, seeks to acknowledge this plurality by characterizing religions or 'faith stances' as distinct conceptual schemes. While avoiding homogenization, this approach risks exaggerating the extent to which religions are discrete and incommensurable with one another. What is needed instead, I propose, is not another *theory* of religious pluralism, but careful philosophical attention to the particularities of religious and nonreligious forms of life – the sort of approach that I am calling radical pluralism.

Chapters 2 and 3 are methodologically focused, expounding central elements of the philosophical approach for which this book is endeavouring to make conceptual space. Chapter 2, 'Radical Plurality and Critical Description', concurs with Kevin Schilbrack that much contemporary philosophy of religion remains locked into a mould that is 'narrow, intellectualist, and insular' (2014b: 3). Having identified some notable exceptions to these tendencies, along with certain residual limitations to those exceptions, I then take issue with the common assumption – typified by Schilbrack himself among many others – that an inquiry must go beyond description if it is to be properly philosophical. Through arguing that this assumption underplays description's critical potential, and by drawing an analogy with the notion of 'cultural critique' in anthropology (à la Marcus and Fischer 1999), I present a conception of philosophy of religion that is cross-cultural, interdisciplinary and radically pluralist in scope, facilitating critical reflection on the contingency of culturally rooted assumptions about what religion is or 'must' be.

Chapter 3, 'Narrative Fiction and Philosophical Inquiry', considers the extent to which works of narrative fiction – whether literary, cinematic or theatrical – can constitute not merely resources for philosophical reflection but also, in certain instances, examples of pluralistic philosophizing themselves. Debates concerning the possibility of narrative fiction *as* philosophy are discussed and, elaborating a suggestion by Phillips, an analogy is drawn between the role of the contemplative philosopher and that of a playwright who places multiple voices in juxtaposition to one another. To illustrate the sense in which works of narrative fiction can provide thickly described scenarios with philosophical and religious significance, attention is given both to Dostoevsky's *The Brothers Karamazov* and, at greater length, to Wole Soyinka's play *Death and the King's Horseman*. Each of these works makes available to readers and audiences a plurality of religious and nonreligious perspectives on the world as well as the conflicts that can arise within individuals who experience divergent impulses.

Chapters 4–7, which constitute Part Two of the book, carry forward the methodological recommendations propounded in Chapters 2 and 3, aiming thereby to do conceptual justice to religious diversity in ways that are neglected by the sorts of purportedly pluralistic approaches discussed in Chapter 1. Chapter 4, '"Compassion beyond Our Imagination": Radical Plurality in Buddhist Ethics', assembles a multiplicity of examples for the purpose of disrupting overgeneralizing assumptions about the centrality and nature of compassion in religious traditions. By showing how varied the acts that get called compassionate can be within Buddhist ethics in particular, I argue not that it is straightforwardly false to affirm that compassion is the core or essence of Buddhism or of other religions, but rather that we should be cautious about assuming in advance of a nuanced investigation that such affirmations have a clear sense.

Chapter 5, '"Ways of Being Human": Cannibalism and Respecting the Dead', continues the theme of disrupting assumptions, this time in relation to the notion of what it is to be human. Responding to a contention from Cora Diamond that the very concept of a human being involves a prohibition against consuming human flesh, the chapter draws upon ethnographic accounts of the Wari' of western Brazil to consider how cannibalism can have an intelligible place among a community's funerary rituals. By coming to see this, we are enabled to enlarge our understanding of possible ways both of respecting the dead and of being human.

Chapter 6, '"Awe at the Terrible": Divine Possession, Blood Sacrifice and the Grotesque Body', takes as its starting point the marginalization of ritual practices in the philosophy of religion. A detailed exposition is then provided of ritual practices involving divine possession and animal sacrifice, especially in the context of traditions of Goddess worship in the Northeast Indian state of Assam. The exposition is based in part on direct observations that I made of a Hindu festival in August 2017, thus exemplifying an instance of philosophically oriented fieldwork. Noting the virtual absence of existing debates in the philosophy of religion with which to bring these observations into productive engagement, the chapter invokes imagery from analyses of 'the grotesque' to develop a vivid descriptive elucidation of sacrificial rites of possession.

Chapter 7, "'A Language in Which to Think of the World": Animism, Philosophy and Indigenous Traditions', addresses the problem of the lack of attention to, accompanied by occasional facile dismissals of, small-scale indigenous traditions in the philosophy of religion. Examining the concept of animism in particular, the chapter discusses how this concept has regained acceptability in recent anthropology and has received some, albeit limited, attention from philosophers. While endorsing proposals to look beyond a crude dichotomy between literal and metaphorical ways of interpreting animistic discourse, I highlight the danger of missing the complexity in such discourse – and in the forms of life with which it is interwoven – when an over-romanticized picture of indigenous spirituality is adopted. By expounding salient aspects of the so-called 'ecologically noble savage debate', with particular reference to studies of Native American peoples, the chapter accentuates the importance for philosophy – yet also the difficulty – of remaining alert to relevant contributions from other disciplines. Such alertness can help philosophers of religion to avoid replacing one set of simplistic conclusions with a different but no less simplistic set.

Finally, the concluding chapter seeks to capture a central motif of the entire book by borrowing from Wittgenstein the idea of philosophical investigation into religion as a means to 'loosen up' one's life (2003: 83),[10] in the sense that the investigation invites one, and one's readers, to perceive in diverse perspectives on the world genuine possibilities of human life. By prioritizing the recognition of heterogeneity and nuance over the rush to pigeonhole and evaluate, in both religious and nonreligious matters, a radical pluralist approach enables us to loosen up our lives and loosen up our minds to possibilities that had previously been neglected or underappreciated. Far

---

[10] The phrase occurs in one of Wittgenstein's diary entries, dated 6 May 1931.

from losing or softening its critical edge, the approach sharpens and radicalizes that edge, but does so by focusing it upon the presuppositions we bring to the inquiry. Though by no means the only way of expanding philosophy of religion, both methodologically and with regard to its subject matter, this approach, I maintain, constitutes one effective instrument for doing so.

Part One

Critique and Methodology

1

Religious Pluralisms

The context in which philosophizing about religion takes place in the contemporary world is one characterized by a plurality of worldviews and forms of life, both religious and nonreligious – a 'polyphony' (Bakhtin 1984a, esp. Ch. 1) or 'hubbub of voices' (Phillips 2001b: 135, 322; 2004a: 22). Some philosophers of religion continue to pretend that this hubbub or polyphony can be largely ignored, and that philosophical inquiry into religion can carry on as though Christianity were the paradigm case from which the largely theoretical invention known as *theism* may be distilled. But most philosophers now recognize that religious diversity is a reality that unsettles past assumptions about how to proceed in philosophy of religion.

To the question of how to proceed, various responses are evident in the literature. Some of these derive from thinkers who are more commonly identified as theologians than as philosophers, but the disciplinary boundaries are fluid in this discursive area. A well-known threefold typology of theoretical positions is that which comprises exclusivism, inclusivism and pluralism. Initially devised by Alan Race in the early 1980s,[1] the typology has been enthusiastically endorsed and appropriated by many participants in the debate, albeit not by all.[2] My purpose in this chapter, and in the book as a whole, is not to enter into the dispute over the viability of the typology. Rather, my interest here is to critically examine the position known as religious pluralism in particular, since, on the face of it, this comes closest to recognizing the kind of radical plurality with which my own project is concerned. As we shall see, religious pluralism is itself really a cluster of positions. Indeed, there have now been too many versions of religious pluralism proposed by philosophers and theologians for it to be feasible to survey them all here. As Gavin D'Costa has put it, '"pluralism" is Hydra-like in its growth' (2016: 137).[3] I shall thus be selective in my focus, though not arbitrarily so. My principal exemplars of religious pluralism will be the respective variants proposed by three authors – namely John Hick, John Cobb and Victoria Harrison – each of whom, while self-identifying as a proponent of religious pluralism, brings out different aspects of the purportedly pluralistic project. These aspects will provide useful points of contrast with the radical pluralism that is to be developed and exemplified in this book.

My procedure will be to begin with Hick, who from the 1980s until his death in 2012 became 'the best known as well as the most controversial representative of the pluralist position' (Meacock 2000: 3),[4] the locus classicus of his *pluralistic hypothesis* being his comprehensive work, *An Interpretation of Religion: Human Responses to the Transcendent* (2004, esp. Ch. 14), which was based on his 1986–87 Gifford Lectures and first published in 1989.[5] Though much admired and celebrated, this work, and Hick's pluralist position more generally, have been the target of extensive criticism. My own appraisal, too, will be largely critical, my main complaint being that, despite styling itself as pluralistic, Hick's position really amounts to a highly reductive and homogenizing account of religion. Far from doing justice to the genuine diversity that has characterized modes of religiosity throughout history and across the world, Hick's theory proposes that 'all the great traditions' pursue the same ethical ideal and are directed towards a single

---

[1] See esp. Race (1993 [1983]).
[2] For objections to the typology, see D'Costa (1996, 2016). For a defence, see Schmidt-Leukel (2005).
[3] For a variety of pluralist perspectives, see Knitter (2005).
[4] For comparable descriptions of Hick, see Hedges (2010: 115) and Oppy (2014: 11).
[5] See also Hick (1995: Ch. 1).

metaphysical principle, which Hick designates 'the Real'. Those forms of religion that diverge from this normative paradigm are relegated to the subordinate category that Hick variously terms 'pre-axial', 'primal', 'archaic' or 'tribal' religion, instances of which may possess 'some dim sense of the Real' but have yet to evolve to the heights of 'developed monotheism' (Hick 2004: 275 n. 2). A consequence of this homogenization of the 'great traditions', combined with a hasty and condescending dismissal of smaller religions, is that what began by claiming to be an interpretation of religion in general ends up being, at best, a one-sided distortion.

My second exemplar, John Cobb, has been especially influential within the field of process philosophy and theology, a movement that draws its inspiration from the work of Alfred North Whitehead.[6] Cobb has himself been critical of Hick's brand of pluralism. Rather than supposing all religions, or even all the 'great' ones, to be promoting the same values and revering (albeit indirectly) the same metaphysical reality, Cobb admits that there are 'ontologically distinct' realities towards which different religions are directed (Cobb 1993). His position has been dubbed *complementary pluralism* because he regards the claims of diverse religions as, on the whole, 'complementary rather than contradictory' (Cobb 1990b: 14; see also Griffin 2005a). Thus, like Hick, he sees no ultimate incompatibility between the major religions. But unlike Hick, Cobb wishes to distance himself from any suggestion that those religions have 'a common characteristic' underlying them (Cobb 1990a: 81). The compatibility and complementarity, Cobb maintains, are found not in commonality or sameness, but in dialogue and the potential for mutual 'creative transformation'.[7] However, despite Cobb's sometimes referring to his position as 'radical pluralism' (1990a: 88, 92), I shall argue that it ends up becoming another form of homogenization. This is because, while recognizing some degree of current diversity, Cobb nevertheless adopts a limiting threefold categorization of religions that labels them as 'cosmic', 'acosmic' or 'theistic' depending on their conception of divinity (Cobb 1993). Moreover, the transformation that Cobb wishes to promote consists in 'a movement toward greater resemblance' (1999: 59), his own theological ideal being a global religious convergence in which diversity is diminished.

---

[6] See esp. Whitehead (1978 [1929]), based on Whitehead's Gifford Lectures of 1927–28.
[7] Cobb borrows the term 'creative transformation' from Wieman (1946) and says it can be used interchangeably with 'the creative event' (Cobb 2002: 194 n. 5).

What we see, then, both in Hick's pluralistic hypothesis and in Cobb's complementary or professedly radical pluralism, are two varieties of homogenization. The third exemplar whose work will be discussed in this chapter, Victoria Harrison, has sought to avoid the homogenization of different religious perspectives by developing a theory that she calls *internalist pluralism*. This theory is intended to do justice to the diversity of religious and nonreligious worldviews while at the same time serving to 'underwrite the appropriateness' of interreligious toleration and respect (Harrison 2008: 109). The theory contends that apparent disagreements between members of different religions are not, at least for the most part, genuine disagreements at all; they are instead mere differences that emerge from distinct conceptual schemes, a conceptual scheme being the 'general system of concepts with which we organize our thoughts and perceptions' (Blackburn 1994: 72, quoted in Harrison 2008: 98 n. 4). In this context, 'we' and 'our' may refer either to human beings in general or, more relevantly to Harrison's thesis, to some particular community or group. As will become evident, I am doubtful about the coherence of Harrison's proposal, both as a theory and as a means of purportedly advancing interreligious tolerance or respect. I am also concerned that the perfunctory manner in which Harrison discusses underdescribed examples in her argument typifies a common tendency in philosophy that has afflicted the philosophy of religion; this is the tendency to overlook alternative interpretive possibilities that, if attended to, may help us to avoid overgeneralizing conclusions.

The purpose of this chapter is, therefore, largely critical rather than constructive. It is to bring out some of the ways in which positions that go by the name of religious pluralism often end up overlooking or misdescribing the diversity that exists in their hurry to devise a general theory of religion. In many cases, including those examined in this chapter, the devising of a theory is motivated by a specific theological or otherwise irenic agenda – a desire to foster greater harmony among religions. There is, of course, nothing wrong with wishing to promote harmony rather than discord. But even if the theories were apt to be successful in this aim – which is doubtful – a harmony based on theoretical illusions is unlikely to be enduring. If our priority is clarity and understanding, then alternative methods will need to be sought – methods that enable attentiveness to nuance and particularity and hence to the overall complexity that those particularities betoken.

John Hick's pluralistic hypothesis

As I have acknowledged in the introduction to this book, John Hick was a pioneer in the philosophy of religion who was one of the first to take seriously the need for philosophical scrutiny of (in principle) 'the religious experience and thought of the whole human race' (2004: xiii). Unlike philosophers who pay lip service to the desirability of cross-cultural and multireligious understanding but then politely excuse themselves from making the effort, Hick in several of his works devotes sustained attention to non-Abrahamic religious and philosophical traditions, especially certain strains of Buddhism and Vedāntic Hinduism.[8] With regard to the issue of religious diversity, Hick's name is strongly associated with his 'pluralistic hypothesis', according to which 'the great world faiths' (or 'great world traditions') 'constitute different conceptions and perceptions of, and responses to, the Real from within the different cultural ways of being human' as well as providing methods for transforming 'human existence from self-centredness to Reality-centredness' (2004: 240, 376). The hypothesis thus comprises both a metaphysical and an attitudinal or ethical dimension. It contends that there is a metaphysical something, 'the Real', towards which all the 'great' religions are directed, and that the ethical attitudes and behaviour of religious adherents are able to be moved along a path of increasing selflessness through participation in the religious life.

Despite calling it merely a hypothesis, Hick evidently considered the hypothesis to be true. Yet his overall argument for its truth is easy neither to discern nor to summarize, not least because much of it relies heavily on ideas from the epistemology of Immanuel Kant while, at the same time, drastically and self-consciously revising those ideas. The principal Kantian 'insight' that Hick appropriates consists in the thesis that rather than passively perceiving the world as it is 'in itself' (*an sich*), human beings, by means of our cognitive apparatus, play an active part in constructing how the world appears to us, and hence that a fundamental distinction must be made between things as they merely appear and things as they really are in themselves.[9] Hick is not, for his purposes, interested in the implications of this thesis for our understanding of our everyday experience of the spatiotemporal world. Instead, he wishes to transpose the thesis into the

---

[8] See esp. Hick (1976: Chs 16–19; 1993: Part III *et passim*).
[9] See esp. Hick (2004: 240–6); cf. Kant (1998 [1787]: A42/B59, B69).

domain of religious experience while also augmenting it by adding the contention that a person's cultural background affects his or her modes of cognition in the religious case. What we end up with, then, is a distinction between the object of religious experience as it is in itself and that same object as it appears to those who encounter it experientially. It is the former that Hick calls 'the Real', whereas the latter – the Real as it appears (or 'manifests') to religious experiencers – takes as many forms as there are religious conceptions of either a personal deity or an impersonal absolute. To say that Hick provides an argument, in support of either the general Kantian view of ordinary experience or his extension of that view to the religious sphere, would require a generous understanding of what counts as an argument. What Hick really gives us is an exposition of the Kantian view followed by an affirmation of the plausibility of extending and modifying it. It is as though Hick, by putting forward his hypothesis, imagines himself to have argued for its veracity.

The ethical dimension of his pluralism emerges out of a perceived need on Hick's part to find a criterion for distinguishing an authentic from an inauthentic 'manifestation of the Real' (2004: xxvi, 338 *et passim*). His view is that, since only authentic or truthful manifestations will possess salvific or liberative efficacy, the authenticity of a given tradition's conception of divinity (or, in the case of a nontheistic religion, its conception of some other esteemed principle) is indicated by the 'soteriological effectiveness' of the tradition in question (2004: 248, 373). Soteriological effectiveness, according to Hick, is disclosed by the extent to which the tradition promotes a certain set of ethical values, which Hick lists as comprising such qualities as 'generosity, forgiveness, kindness, love, compassion' (314). These, Hick proposes, are 'epitomised in the Golden Rule', some rendition of which is taught in the scriptures of 'all the great traditions' (316). Their progressive embodiment in a religious believer's life is what, on Hick's account, constitutes a transformation from self-centredness to Reality-centredness.

Hick's evaluative procedure is thus to seek out pronouncements of something approximating the Golden Rule in the primary textual sources associated with the traditions in which he is interested, while downplaying the presence of counterexamples. Having found a suitable number of instances, he then declares it to be the case that 'all the great traditions' do indeed champion this ethical ideal, and that any tradition espousing values incompatible with it ought to be rejected as morally deficient along with any conception of the divine that the tradition in question propounds (2004: 311, 339).

These central components of Hick's position – notably the unargued-for postulation of a single metaphysical 'Real' behind the diverse conceptions of divinity affirmed by the major religious traditions, plus the demarcation of 'authentic' from 'inauthentic' religions on the basis of a particular ethical ideal – have implications for the study of religious diversity that are both reductive and homogenizing. I shall elaborate some of the important implications in the following section.

Reductive and homogenizing implications of Hick's approach

Of the various objections that could be raised to Hick's position, I here focus on the following three. First I point out how Hick's binary distinction between 'the great traditions' on the one hand, and all the rest on the other, impedes a well-rounded and suitably nuanced comprehension of religious diversity. Second, I argue that Hick's instrumental or pragmatic conception of religious doctrine is a distraction from the task of understanding the doctrines themselves and the roles that they have in the religious forms of life at issue. And third, I contend that Hick's ethical criterion for distinguishing authentic from inauthentic religions encourages a distortedly narrow appreciation of the forms that religious life can take. In short, then, I argue that Hick's position, far from enabling a full recognition of religious diversity, in fact engenders a reductive and homogenized picture.

In distinguishing 'the great traditions' from those that are, by implication, not so great, Hick draws heavily upon the theory of an 'Axial Age' or 'Axial Period' first proposed by Karl Jaspers (see Jaspers 1953).[10] Jaspers had differentiated between 'Pre-Axial cultures' and those that emerged during the Axial Period. The former, which include 'Babylon, Egypt, the Indus valley and the aboriginal culture of China', despite having possibly 'been magnificent in their own way', nevertheless 'appear in some manner unawakened' in comparison with the Axial cultures, which arose during the first millennium BCE primarily in China, India, Iran, Palestine and Greece (Jaspers 1953: 2, 6–7; see also Eisenstadt 1986). According to Jaspers' thesis, failure to undergo

---

[10] Jaspers cites certain intellectual forerunners such as Ernst von Lasaulx (1856) and Victor von Strauss (1870), but it was Jaspers himself who coined the term 'Axial Period' (*die Achsenzeit*). For critical appraisal of the theory of an Axial Period, see Tsonis (2012, 2014).

the spiritual and intellectual transformations characteristic of the Axial Period is indicative of a people's 'primitive' and 'unhistorical' stage of development; upon coming into contact with Axial civilizations, such peoples tend to either die out or be assimilated into the new, historically apposite cultural environment (Jaspers 1953: 7–8).

Hick appropriates Jaspers' conception of a transnational Axial awakening in order to distinguish two types of religion, which he often calls 'pre-axial' and 'post-axial' respectively. He also uses terms such as 'primal' and 'archaic' interchangeably with 'pre-axial' and equates 'post-axial religion' with 'the great world traditions'. Following Jaspers, Hick associates pre-Axial religion with the absence of a concern for individual salvation: instead, this type of religion strives merely to keep 'communal life on an even keel' (Hick 1995: 109; see also, inter alia, Hick 2004: 12, 23, 28).[11] Post-Axial religion, by contrast, is 'concerned with salvation/liberation as the realisation of a limitlessly better possibility' (2004: 12). As with Jaspers' use of this vocabulary, Hick's talk of pre- and post-Axial religion has more than merely chronological implications. The contention is not that Axial or post-Axial religion universally replaced that which preceded it, for it is admitted that pre-Axial religion has continued to exist up to the present day, albeit only in relatively small pockets. Hick's deployment of the distinction is one of the principal means by which he separates the type of religion in which his pluralist project is interested from that which falls outside the project's remit, excusing his relative lack of attention to 'archaic' or 'primal' religion by noting that his aim has not been to devise a definitive theory (2004: xiii; see also 1990: 3).

Although, as Hick rightly observes, it would be impossible for any single project to be fully comprehensive in its treatment of forms of human religiosity, it is for this very reason that any attempt to provide an interpretation of religion tout court needs to proceed with caution. The interpretation that Hick offers us, however, is one that treats as normative for religion in general a set of dominant religious traditions, narrowly construed in terms of a simplified and largely decontextualized nexus of ethical factors, while excluding from its purview the multifarious small-scale or indigenous traditions that have been a pervasive presence throughout history. The inevitable result is an unduly homogenized and one-sided picture of religion.

With regard to Hick's treatment of religious doctrine in particular, this may be objected to on the grounds that it reduces doctrine to something

---

[11] Cf. Jaspers (1953: 12): 'They also have in common a magical religion destitute of philosophical enlightenment, devoid of any quest for salvation'.

purely functional, where the function in question is itself understood in narrow ethical terms. Hick's reason for interpreting religious doctrine, and indeed religion *simpliciter*, in functional (or instrumental or pragmatic) terms is that he needed to find some way of accounting for the obvious doctrinal divergences between different religious traditions. If all the 'great' religions are equivalent inasmuch as they are directed towards the Real, why, we might ask, do they profess discrepant teachings? For Hick, the solution is to claim that the discrepancies are merely at the level of myth: the religions communicate their teachings through diverse mythologies, but the mythologies are all 'true' in a functional or pragmatic sense insofar as they advance the transformation of religious practitioners' lives from self-centredness to Reality-centredness (see, e.g., Hick 2004: 375).

A problem with this functional analysis is not only that it misrepresents the practitioners' relationship to the doctrines they espouse, but that it also homogenizes doctrine by compressing it all into a single 'mythic' mould. Mythology is in fact a broad and variegated phenomenon that is capable of fulfilling multiple purposes in relation to religious traditions. For example, the epic tales of Rāma and Sītā in Indian mythology may be utilized to, among other things, provide part of the narrative backdrop to the annual Diwali festival, epitomize a vision of the victory of righteousness over evil, depict an ideal of uxorial loyalty and vindicate Hindu nationalist claims that India is a Hindu nation. But our understanding of such myths is hampered rather than enhanced by collapsing all forms of religious doctrine into a single category and by reducing the functions of myth to that of expediting the transformation from self- to Reality-centredness. In place of Hick's homogenizing account, what is needed is a more fine-grained analysis that recognizes the multiple roles of doctrine in the lives of religious believers. These roles, as Paul Griffiths has usefully articulated, include: providing community rules and defining community boundaries; expressing and informing spiritual experience; forming members of the community through imbuing them with a catechism; and enunciating propositions that aid soteriological development, not merely by recommending particular modes of action but also by making 'claims about the nature of human persons and the world in which they live' (Griffiths 1990: 167). In short, doctrines are constitutive of the very worldview within which a religion has the sense that it does. It is thus unlikely to be interpretively illuminating to presuppose that doctrinal differences between religions amount merely to variations on a common ethically inflected theme.

Finally in this critical appraisal of Hick's style of religious pluralism, I should reiterate the reductive implications of Hick's privileging of the capacity to foster a certain mode of ethical transformation as the principal criterion of a religion's authenticity. When considering the issue of whether religion can be defined, Hick is favourable towards a 'family resemblance' account of the concept of religion, according to which the correct application of the term 'religion' does not depend on there being any single property or set of properties that all the things that are called religions have in common: it is enough that these things exhibit 'a network of similarities overlapping and criss-crossing like the resemblances and differences ... among the members of a natural family' (Hick 2004: 4).[12] In the light of such a flexible and expansive account, Hick is able to admit that traditions as diverse as Christianity, Theravāda Buddhism and the ancient worship of Moloch (which allegedly involved human sacrifice) are all religions (2004: 5). When it comes to distinguishing between 'authentic' and 'inauthentic' religions, however, Hick's family resemblance principle goes out the window. It gets replaced by the essentializing and narrowly prescriptive 'ethical criterion' that Hick claims to find in the scriptures of 'all the great traditions'.

As noted in the previous section, Hick's procedure for arriving at his ethical criterion is to inspect scriptural sources associated with the religions in which he is interested, and to select key passages expressive of what he identifies as the Golden Rule – roughly, the principle that one ought to treat others as one would wish to be treated oneself. While admitting that even the 'great world traditions' have been sources of suffering and conflict as well as of healing and beneficence (Hick 2004: 337), Hick is quick to regard this as merely an indication that, in practice, the adherents of the religions have not lived up to the ideal that is common to all of them. When expounding the modes of action and forms of life enjoined by the traditions in question, it is as though Hick has already decided in advance what is to count as properly ethical, and it is this *a priori* decision that determines which textual passages are to be treated as normative for each tradition as a whole – and indeed for the traditions considered collectively. Thus, for example, with reference to the Brahmanical Hindu scripture known as the *Bhagavad Gītā*, Hick quotes a 'description of the good person' in which characteristics such as generosity, honesty, gentleness, compassion, humility and forbearance are praised (Hick 2004: 317, citing *Bhagavad Gītā* 16.1–3). What Hick does not pause to mention is the overall context of the quoted passage, located within a dialogue between the warrior-prince Arjuna and the divine incarnation, Lord Kṛṣṇa, in which Kṛṣṇa is ostensibly seeking to convince Arjuna that the

---

[12] Hick is here explicitly paraphrasing Wittgenstein (1958: §66). See also Hick (1990: 2–3).

right course of action is that of fulfilling his military duty by entering resolutely into an internecine battle, which, as Arjuna recognizes, threatens to tear the society apart. The deep ethical ambivalence and complexity of the text, and the multiple interpretations and appropriations to which it is amenable, are set aside in Hick's eagerness to find fodder to support a general thesis about an ethical ideal allegedly shared by all the great traditions.

With regard to doctrines that, on a natural interpretation, come into conflict with the ethical ideal in question, Hick's strategy is to treat them as aberrations that ought to be amended or expunged through a process of critical purification internal to the traditions concerned. To illustrate his point, Hick cites examples such as the version of the doctrine of karma that maintains that a person's present disadvantages are natural repercussions of sins committed in a former life, the Judaic doctrine that Israel is God's chosen people, the Islamic conception of *jihād* as a holy war against infidels and the doctrine of double predestination in its Augustinian and Calvinist forms (2004: 339–40). Disapproving of all these doctrines, Hick recommends that they be reformed to enable the respective traditions to more consistently embody the ethical ideal that each of them, according to Hick, espouses. It is by embodying that ideal that the religions bring themselves into 'alignment with the Real' (2004: xxiii *et passim*). Regardless of the extent to which one might concur with Hick's own moral preferences, a consequence of this privileging of a certain evaluative agenda is that the intricacies and particularities of diverse religious traditions are glossed over. Some religions are summarily precluded from the inquiry on the grounds that their respective conceptions of the divine 'are clearly morally defective' (2004: 339), while those religions that are deemed worthy of consideration are shoehorned into a constricted ethical framework. Once again, the inevitable result is far from an enriched understanding of religious diversity. On the contrary, what we get is a homogenized and sanitized caricature of diversity, with any incongruities demoted to the status of anomalies that require cleansing through doctrinal reform. In view of this consequence, we might follow D'Costa in characterizing the sort of pluralistic hypothesis offered by Hick as being itself a kind of mythology.[13]

---

[13] 'Since "pluralistic theology" ironically often seems to hinder rather than aid a proper recognition of religious plurality, despite its literal intention, it seemed appropriate to deem it mythical' (D'Costa 1990: xi). Compare Mark Heim's characterization of Hick's pluralism as a specifically modern and Western 'mythos' that, rather than promoting an appreciation of the diversity of existing religions, in fact enters into competition with them (Heim 1995: 214).

John Cobb's vision of creative transformation

John Cobb has characterized his own position as one that, 'for the sake of a fuller and more genuine pluralism' (Cobb 1990a: 81), rejects what often goes by the name 'pluralism', including the type advocated by Hick. In expounding the difference between the sort of pluralism to which Cobb is opposed and the sort that he commends, David Ray Griffin refers to the former as *identist* and to the latter as *differential* or *complementary* pluralism (Griffin 2005b: 24).[14] Here, 'identist' means something close to what I have been meaning by 'homogenizing'. Identist pluralism homogenizes in both an ontological and a soteriological sense. By maintaining that 'all religions are oriented toward the same religious object' and that they all 'promote essentially the same end (the same type of "salvation")', it really constitutes only a 'pseudo-' or 'superficial' pluralism (Griffin 2005b: 24, 29; cf. Heim 1995: 7). Differential pluralism, meanwhile, accepts that religions favour different salvific ends and allows for the possibility that they are 'oriented toward different religious objects' (Griffin 2005b: 24).

Borrowing concepts from John Hutchison, Cobb draws a threefold distinction between 'theistic, cosmic, and acosmic' religions (Cobb 1993: 78),[15] proposing that each of these is typified by a different mode of religious experience through which a distinct object is encountered. Though tempted to regard these objects as together constituting 'a plurality of "ultimate realities"', Cobb opts instead to refer to them as three 'aspects' or 'features' of reality (1993: 79–80, 81). His contention is that while cosmic reality is a multiplicity of entities, acosmic reality is the 'common ground or source' of that multiplicity and theistic reality, or God, is 'a Worldsoul' – 'the unity of experience that contains all the multiplicity of events and interacts with them' (80). Thus, Cobb distinguishes his own position from that of Hick by claiming that Hick's account ultimately falsifies all religions whereas his own account allows 'that all may be correct in their fundamental positive beliefs, even if they are often wrong in their negations of others' (81). In other words, while it follows from Hick's account that any religion that treats its own

---

[14] A comparable distinction is made by Perry Schmidt-Leukel between 'monocentric' and 'polycentric' pluralism (Schmidt-Leukel 2017: 29), though Schmidt-Leukel does not attach to 'monocentric' the pejorative associations that Griffin attaches to 'identist'.
[15] Cf. Hutchison (1991: 15–18), in which the terms used are 'cosmic', 'acosmic' and 'historical'.

conception of the divine as absolutely true is in fact mistaken because the Real is beyond the power of human conceptualization, on Cobb's account there is room for different conceptions of the divine to all be true: given that reality possesses cosmic, acosmic and theistic features, religions that accept one or other of these characterizations are mistaken only insofar as they suppose the other characterizations to be false.

We might wonder, however, about the extent to which Cobb's account is really doing justice to the traditions concerned. The schema of cosmic, acosmic and theistic types is, at best, a starting point for a more refined analysis of the specificities of particular religions. It risks getting in the way of that analysis if distinct forms of religion are forced into the same category without further qualification. With regard to the category of acosmic conceptions of reality, for example, Cobb treats this as encompassing such contextually heterogeneous notions as Paul Tillich's sense of God as 'being-itself',[16] Advaita Vedānta's 'Brahman without attributes' (nirguṇa brahman), the ultimate 'emptiness' (śūnyatā) of all things propounded by Mahāyāna Buddhism and also the 'creativity' proposed by Alfred North Whitehead (see, e.g., Cobb 1993: 80, 82; Griffin 2005a: 49).[17] Considered at a high level of abstraction, there are undoubtedly affinities between these notions, but to avoid the danger of the label 'acosmic' obscuring more than it illuminates, one would need also to give close attention to the contexts in which these notions are articulated. In some cases one would need in particular to examine places where advocates of one of these notions have tried vigorously to differentiate it from another, such as is the case with disagreements between Advaita Vedāntins and Mahāyāna Buddhists (see Ingalls 1954, Biderman 1978, Whaling 1979). Upon examining these debates one sees that they hinge as much upon sectarian rivalries and adherence to particular doctrinal lineages as they do upon technical philosophical exposition of the concepts of Brahman and emptiness. It is these broader parameters of the disputes that are liable to be lost sight of when traditions such as Advaita Vedānta and Mahāyāna Buddhism are lumped together in the same 'acosmic' religious category.

We should also not overlook the significant shift from understanding and interpretation to revision and imposition that occurs when a commentator such as Cobb declares that the religions he is discussing have failed to see that their own conception of reality is merely partial. When Cobb

---

[16] See, e.g., Tillich (1951: 235).
[17] For critical discussion, see Schmidt-Leukel (2017: 238–9, esp. 239 n. 86).

recommends, for instance, that the God of Israel, the Holy Trinity of Christianity, Allāh of Islam and other notions of the divine be reconceptualized as a 'Worldsoul', and that this be understood as 'the unity of experience that contains all the multiplicity of events and interacts with them' (1993: 80), his proposal is no less revisionary than is Hick's contention that all the great traditions are really, regardless of their own self-conceptions, oriented towards a 'transcategorial Real'. Just as Hick does violence to the concepts of (for example) Allāh and *śūnyatā* when he imagines that these could usefully be thought of as 'manifestations' of the same transcendent reality, so Cobb does comparable violence to these concepts when he asserts that it would be mistaken to regard them as mutually incompatible. While it would, no doubt, be possible to find a place for aspects of both Islam and Mahāyāna Buddhism in a single religious life, it is unlikely that doing so would leave intact the worldviews of each, including the concepts of Allāh and *śūnyatā*. The presumption that Abrahamic monotheism is compatible with the Buddhist doctrine of emptiness seriously underplays the extent to which religious worldviews are often defined as much by what they exclude as by what they encompass. On this matter, we should again take notice of remarks about religious doctrine made by Paul Griffiths, to which I referred in the previous section.

In short, then, it is evident that, in common with Hick, Cobb's main interest is not in the rigorous explication of religious worldviews and forms of life. Instead, he is intent on promoting a particular theological agenda, one which encourages interreligious dialogue in the hope of engendering mutual 'creative transformation'. Speaking explicitly from what he regards as a Christian point of view, Cobb seeks to transform Christianity through the selective appropriation of elements from other religions. The aspects of religion into which he enquires are selected not for their intrinsic interest or because they promise to expand our appreciation of religious diversity, but rather on the grounds that they may have something of value to contribute towards Christianity's self-improvement. As Cobb puts it in a book exploring Christian–Buddhist dialogue, 'The research into the traditions which the dialogue should stimulate will be for the sake of participating more effectively in the present engagement' (Cobb 1982: xi). Elsewhere, Cobb urges his fellow Christians to appropriate and interiorize imagery from Asian traditions, such as the *yin* and *yang* symbolism of Chinese Daoism, to help 'purify the Christian imagination of the divine from its masculine sexism' (1975: 264). Recognizing, however, that the Daoist imagery itself may not be immune from bias in its binary gendered associations, Cobb regards it as an advantage that these associations will be unknown to many Christians; such ignorance enables the images 'to be appropriated in abstraction from their full connotations in their own traditions' (264). Not only, then, is careful contextualized analysis of religious phenomena not the primary goal: such analysis can in some instances be detrimental to Cobb's real purpose, which is to expedite the formation of a 'global theology' – a progressive convergence in which Christianity and other religions evolve 'toward greater resemblance' (1999: 59).

The desire for greater religious resemblance, and hence greater homogeneity, of the sort that Cobb advocates is itself a religious preference. As such, we might, when speaking for ourselves, feel sympathetic or antipathetic towards that preference, but neither these feelings nor the preference itself has anything to do with developing a deeper understanding of religious diversity as it obtains in the world around us. Similarly, in the case of Hick's 'hypothesis' pertaining to a mysterious 'Real' that no one can experience or conceptualize directly and yet which is somehow 'manifested' in the religious visions of 'all the great traditions': this hypothesis is itself the expression of a religious or theological impulse – a yearning for harmonization between religions that, ironically, characterizes all existing religions as deluded despite their ethical merits. Thus, in the case of both the formulations of religious pluralism that we have considered so far, what purports to involve the recognition of religious diversity is really a highly selective defence of a personal theology. In each case, ethical criteria are deployed to differentiate acceptable forms of religiosity from those that are deemed to be beyond the pale. For both Hick and Cobb, the criteria of appraisal are ones upon which, they assume, representatives of all the major religions would concur. Hick, as we have seen, privileges the Golden Rule; Cobb, similarly, maintains that teachings inciting destructive behaviour towards a religion's own members or towards others 'would count against it' (Cobb 1993: 83). Rather than striving to enrich our comprehension of the diversity of religious ethics by deliberately seeking out instances of 'destructive' religions, the approaches pursued by Hick and Cobb eschew such broad-ranging inquiry. Owing to the specific theological aspirations guiding these approaches, the religious outlooks judged to be unethical are thereby also excluded from further investigation.

As we shall see later in this book, a properly radical pluralist approach to the study of religion does not condemn or turn away from forms of religiosity that may be deemed by many to be morally unsettling; rather, it seeks a comprehensive understanding of religion in all its roughness and moral complexity. Before completing this chapter, however, there is a further philosophical formulation of religious pluralism to be considered, namely what Victoria Harrison has termed *internalist pluralism*. A critical examination of this will disclose further pitfalls to be avoided when developing a radical pluralist approach.

Victoria Harrison's internalist pluralism

The prevalent obsession with Hick's pluralistic hypothesis in discussions of religious pluralism has tended to divert attention away from other formulations of pluralism, which differ from Hick's – and also from Cobb's – to a greater or lesser extent.[18] Of particular novelty among these others is work by Victoria Harrison, who has advocated her theory of internalist pluralism in several publications from 2000 onwards (see esp. Harrison 2000, 2006, 2008, 2012).

Harrison appropriates the term 'internalism' from Hilary Putnam, who, in what is sometimes referred to as his middle period, championed a theory called internal realism.[19] Notwithstanding Putnam's own subsequent modifications and partial disavowals of internal realism (Putnam 1994a: 242–54; 1994b), Harrison treats it as a live theoretical option. Although internal realism is itself a metaphysical theory, Putnam defines it in opposition to what he calls 'metaphysical realism', the latter comprising the following three theses: first, that 'the world consists of some fixed totality of mind-independent objects'; second, that '[t]here is exactly one true and complete description of "the way the world is"'; and third, that '[t]ruth involves some sort of correspondence relation between words or thought-signs and external things and sets of things' (Putnam 1981: 49). The perspective of metaphysical realism can, Putnam proposes, be designated 'the *externalist* perspective, because its favorite point of view is a God's Eye point of view' (ibid.). This is to be contrasted with 'the *internalist* perspective', according to which the question '*what objects does the world consist of?*' makes sense only '*within* a theory of description' (ibid., Putnam's emphasis).

---

[18] A concise comparative overview of some of these theories is presented in Ruhmkorff (2013).
[19] For talk of Putnam's 'middle period', see, e.g., Norris (2002, esp. Chs 3 and 4) and Cormier (2015: 803–5). Putnam later came to refer to this internal realism as 'pragmatic realism' (1987: 17) and as 'realism with a small "r"' (1992a: 26–9).

Interchangeably with the term 'theory of description', Putnam also uses the term 'conceptual scheme'. He remarks, for example, that on the internalist view, 'a sign that is actually employed in a particular way by a particular community of users can correspond to particular objects *within the conceptual scheme of those users*' (52, Putnam's emphasis) – but not outside it. Indeed, on this view, it makes no sense to suppose that objects could exist *as objects* independently of any conceptual scheme, for it is the conceptual scheme (or 'theory of description' or 'scheme of description') that divides up the world into distinguishable objects. While some commentators would construe this as a form of nonrealism or antirealism, Putnam calls it internal *realism* because it maintains that the objects we, as individuals, perceive and think about do really exist independently of our own thoughts and perceptions, albeit not independently of the conceptual scheme from within which our perceiving and thinking are occurring.

Taking up Putnam's internal realism, Harrison applies it to religions. Central to this appropriation of the theory is Harrison's contention that if 'there is no way of intelligibly discussing what exists in a manner that is conceptual-scheme neutral', then 'the existence of purported religious realities can only be meaningfully discussed within a particular conceptual scheme or, what we might call, a "faith-stance"' (Harrison 2006: 292). The use of the term 'faith-stance' enables Harrison to avoid committing herself to the view that religions themselves constitute distinct conceptual schemes. She prefers instead to regard religions as being 'composed of overlapping conceptual schemes' (2012: 76), and the term 'faith-stance' allows this measure of flexibility. From the claim that intelligible talk of religious realities is always internal to a conceptual scheme or faith-stance, it follows that the very concepts of certain religious realities are untranslatable from one faith-stance to another. In other words, different religious communities, insofar as they assume different faith-stances and hence operate with different conceptual schemes, will not be able to understand one another's religious beliefs. Thus, Harrison contends, this theory gives us a form of religious pluralism – internalist pluralism – that avoids both eliminativism and reductivism (2015: 267). The theory is non-eliminativist inasmuch as it eschews the denial of there being any objective reality corresponding to the beliefs and concepts of the various religions. And it is non-reductive in that it does not assert that the beliefs and concepts of all religions, or of all faith-stances, correspond to the *same* objective reality; rather, the theory allows for a plurality of such realities, albeit that they are objective only in the sense that, internal to a given conceptual scheme, their reality is not dependent on any individual member of the community that operates with that scheme. There is still, however, a sense in which the reality of anything, including objects of religious faith and worship, is dependent upon a given conceptual scheme, and on the face of it this is likely to strike many religious believers as an unacceptable implication of the theory. It is likely to appear unacceptable because it seems to suggest that objects of religious faith are mere conceptual constructs. To deal with this issue, Harrison introduces a technical distinction between 'conceptual-scheme targetability' and 'successful conceptual-scheme targeting' (2008), which I shall outline below.

If I have understood Harrison correctly, for an object to be conceptual-scheme targetable is merely for it to be conceptualized within the conceptual scheme in question. It is its conceptualization – that is, the fact of there being a concept of that object – that makes the object a possible target for belief. Thus, for example, the concept of nirvāṇa has a place within the conceptual schemes of various Buddhist traditions, thereby making nirvāṇa a possible object – a targetable object – of belief for people who operate with (or 'subscribe to', as Harrison often puts it) one or other of the Buddhist conceptual schemes. For an object to be successfully targeted within a given conceptual scheme, meanwhile, is for it to be the case that not only does the conceptual scheme in question have a concept of that object, but there is in fact – in reality – an object to which the concept corresponds. To illustrate the point, Harrison adduces a simplified nonreligious imaginary example. She invites us to envisage 'a world in which there are three large plants' (Harrison 2008: 102). Someone employing a conceptual scheme that possesses the concept of a tree but lacks any distinction between elm trees and beech trees, 'would see a world containing three trees, which he regards as large plants'. By contrast, someone whose conceptual scheme includes a distinction between elms and beeches 'would see a world containing, for example, one elm and two beeches'. Harrison then adds the following remarks:

> The question of whether, along with the first person, we subscribe to a conceptual scheme that just identifies trees or, along with the second person, we subscribe to a conceptual scheme that identifies elms and beeches is quite distinct from the question of whether or not there are any large plants. The latter is, in this example, not simply conceptual-scheme dependent in the way in which the question of whether there are just trees or whether there are elms and beeches is wholly a matter of the choice of conceptual scheme.
>
> Harrison 2008: 102

Harrison's point appears to be that, despite the differences between their respective conceptual schemes, both of the individuals in the example can be regarded as having successfully targeted the objects that Harrison describes as three large plants. The success consists in the fact that the concepts with which each of the individuals is operating apply to the objects in question and, furthermore, the objects in question – the three large plants – really are there to be targeted, independently of the concepts being applied to them from within specific conceptual schemes. So, in other words, each of the conceptual schemes represented in the example contains concepts that make the three large plants targetable, and the application of the concepts to the plants, coupled with the fact that the plants themselves are not dependent on the conceptual schemes in question, results in both individuals having successfully targeted the objects. There is, however, a difficulty in making this part of the theory consistent with Harrison's overall commitment to internalist pluralism. I shall discuss that difficulty in the next section before turning to a more general issue with the way in which Harrison works with illustrative examples.

A difficulty with the internalist picture

A brief recap: Harrison intends her theory of internalist pluralism to be acceptable to religious believers. Indeed, she intends it to be a useful intervention in debates over religious diversity, for she maintains that its acceptance would promote tolerance and even respect between different religious communities. Harrison is aware, however, that internalist pluralism is hardly likely to be accepted by religious believers if it is interpreted as portraying the very existence, or reality, of objects of religious faith and worship as being a mere artefact of conceptual schemes. The 'three large plants' analogy is intended to show how internalist pluralism can avoid that interpretation. But how is the analogy supposed to relate to a specifically religious, or multireligious, context? Harrison sketches the following example concerning Christian, Muslim and Hindu conceptions of the divine.

The Christian in Harrison's example believes in a triune God and also in the existence of angels and human beings. The Muslim, similarly, believes in angels and human beings, but believes Allāh to be unipersonal. The Hindu, too, believes in angels (or in beings at least comparable to angels) and in humans, but believes the ultimate divine principle to be Brahman, which is 'projected' as multiple deities, including the three divine forms (*trimūrti*) popularly known as Brahmā, Viṣṇu and Śiva (Harrison 2008: 105–6). According to Harrison, the respective conceptual schemes of these three religious believers are what determine the differences between the three sets of beliefs, but it is not the case that the conceptual schemes determine whether the beliefs are true. 'For if', Harrison writes, 'irrespective of which conceptual scheme is employed and what range of entities that scheme deems targetable, only human agents are in fact successfully targeted, the substantive religious claims of Muslims, Christians and Hindus are false' (2008: 106). A difficulty here is that of understanding what, on an internalist account, it means to speak of something's being 'in fact successfully targeted' by a certain concept or set of concepts. In the light of the 'three large plants' example expounded above, Harrison here appears to be asserting that if, independently of the respective conceptual schemes of the Christian, the Muslim and the Hindu, there are no divine or angelic 'agents', then there is no God or supreme divine principle and neither are there any angelic beings, and hence regardless of what any of the three religious conceptual schemes at issue deems to be targetable, the concepts pertaining to anything divine or angelic will miss their target – because there is no target for them to hit.

Harrison might wish to qualify this interpretation by insisting that 'irrespective of which conceptual scheme is employed' does not mean independently of all conceptual schemes. She might reiterate that it makes no sense to suppose that a given being or type of being exists or does not exist independently of conceptual schemes in toto, for 'the existence of purported religious realities can only be meaningfully discussed within [some] conceptual scheme' (Harrison 2006: 292). To spell out what is meant by 'irrespective' in this context, Harrison might then appeal to the notion of a 'meta-conceptual scheme', which is what in one place she identifies her internalist pluralist theory as being (2006: 299–300). This appeal would enable Harrison to say that 'irrespective of which conceptual scheme is employed' should be understood to mean 'irrespective of which *first-order* conceptual scheme is employed'; if the objects or agents in question exist within, or from the perspective of, a meta- (i.e. second-order) conceptual scheme, such as internalist pluralism, it is precisely this fact that enables us to declare that they exist 'irrespective of which [first-order] conceptual scheme is employed'. According to this interpretation of Harrison's view – which she does not herself state explicitly – it would be the existence of human agents combined with the non-existence of any divine or angelic beings within a meta-conceptual scheme that would make it the case that 'only human agents are in fact successfully targeted' by Muslims, Christians and Hindus.

There are, however, two main problems with this attempt to make sense of Harrison's position. One problem derives from Harrison's recommendation that conceptual schemes be regarded as faith-stances. Since a philosophical theory such as internalist pluralism is not itself a faith-stance, such theories appear to fall outside of Harrison's category of conceptual schemes. This problem would be relatively easy to rectify: Harrison could merely replace her stipulation that conceptual schemes be thought of as faith-stances with the alternative stipulation that faith-stances are one type of conceptual scheme and philosophical theories are another. The second problem is harder to resolve. It is that the interpretation of Harrison's position that I offered above fails to clarify why, for any given class of objects or beings, it should be the fact that this class is deemed to exist from within a meta-conceptual scheme that determines whether members of that class are 'successfully targeted' by the concepts of the first-order conceptual schemes that are under examination by someone operating with the meta-scheme.

The upshot of my discussion in this section could be expressed in terms of a dilemma for internalist pluralism. Either (a) the notion of a concept's failing to successfully target anything 'irrespective of which conceptual scheme is employed' means that, irrespective of all first-order conceptual schemes, there exists no such target in a given meta-conceptual scheme (such as the theory of internalist pluralism), or (b) 'irrespective of which conceptual scheme' means, in this context, simply 'independently of any conceptual scheme'. If we opt for '(a)', then we face the problem of its being unclear why any meta-conceptual scheme should be deemed capable of determining whether certain things do or do not exist for first-order conceptual schemes. But if we opt for '(b)', then it looks as though what began as internal realism has collapsed into the very externalism, or metaphysical realism, that Harrison wanted to abjure. This is because, according to '(b)', the issue of whether the concepts – including, of course, the specifically religious concepts – of a religious community (or of those who adopt some particular faith-stance) succeed in 'targeting' anything real is dependent on what is 'in fact' the case, where facts of the matter are supposed to be independent of all conceptual schemes.

In the light of my discussion above, it is pertinent to observe that, were we to opt for the second horn of the dilemma that I have identified, the resulting picture would be comparable to the one advocated by Hick, which Harrison terms 'transcendental pluralism' (Harrison 2006: 295–301; 2013: 484–7). She calls it transcendental because the 'Real' that it postulates is supposed to transcend human conceptual capacities. By Hick's lights, this transcendent or transcategorial Real eludes description by any conceptual scheme and yet is that towards which every major religion's conception of a divine or other supreme principle is directed. Although Harrison's talk of 'agents' is at a lower level of abstraction than Hick's talk of 'the Real', what option '(b)' would give us is closely resemblant of Hick's realism. In other words, it gives us the view that what makes it possible to deny that conceptions of the divine – such as the Trinity, Allāh, Brahman et al. – must be purely conceptual constructs is the fact that their truth or falsity is determined by their targeting, or failing to target, something that is not itself dependent on the conceptual scheme to which they belong. This, as I have contended, appears to be the picture we are offered when Harrison is defending internalist pluralism against the charge that it allows the existence of objects of religious faith and worship to be determined solely by the conceptual schemes themselves. However, when Harrison is presenting examples to illustrate how internalist pluralism enables apparent religious disagreements to be reconstrued as mere religious differences, we get a very different picture.[20] As will become clear in the next section, I consider Harrison's way of working with examples to be unsatisfactory both for substantiating her particular position and as an argumentative strategy more generally. In this respect, however, she is by no means alone in contemporary philosophy.

Working with examples

There is a tendency within analytic philosophy in general, from which analytic philosophy of religion is far from immune, to illustrate arguments with examples that are thinly sketched and poorly contextualized. Discerning readers of such arguments, if they can make any sense of the examples at all, could be excused for wondering what purpose the examples are serving and whether, in the absence of thicker description, they really serve any useful purpose whatsoever. Unfortunately, the examples adduced in Harrison's arguments on behalf of internalist pluralism, though ostensibly intended to show how the theory facilitates the dissolution of interreligious disputes, are

---

[20] I am borrowing the terminology of a difference versus a disagreement from Harrison herself, who repeatedly affirms that her internalist theory can 'acknowledge the genuine differences between religious [or moral] traditions' (2006: 300; see also 2012: 86) while regarding these as 'mere' differences rather than competing truth claims (e.g. 2012: 79). The implication here is that a 'mere difference' does not amount to a real disagreement.

of the thin and under-contextualized variety. Examining the weaknesses of a selection of them will, I propose, provide a helpful starting point for reflecting on alternative ways of proceeding in the philosophy of religion – ways that invoke and dwell with examples long enough to learn what they have to teach us, as opposed to treating them as mere decoration for a line of argument that owes little if anything to the examples' particularities.

Among the relatively few examples that Harrison deploys to illustrate apparent interreligious disagreements are the following two. First is the case of Śaivite Hinduism vis-à-vis Roman Catholicism. Within the Śaivite conceptual scheme Śiva 'is a real, objectively existing God', whereas in the Catholic scheme God is the Trinity comprising Father, Son and Holy Spirit. Observing that internalist pluralism allows us to acknowledge these differences, Harrison adds that what the theory does not allow us to do is to 'intelligibly discuss the qualities of, for example, Śiva from within a conceptual scheme, such as a Christian one, in which Śiva occupies no place' (2006: 293).[21] What this is supposed to illustrate is that, from the perspective of internalist pluralism, the Catholic is in no position to oppugn the god of Śaivism and neither is the Śaivite in a position to oppugn the god of Roman Catholic Christianity. The conceptual-scheme dependence of these respective conceptions of God is considered by Harrison to facilitate a sense in which both might be true – that is, true within the relevant conceptual scheme – and to thereby delegitimize any denunciation of one or the other as false.

The second of Harrison's examples is that 'of a Christian asserting that Jesus is the Son of God, and a Muslim replying: "No, he isn't!"' Despite appearances, the two may in fact not be in disagreement, 'but merely talking past each other' (2006: 293; 2012: 80). Harrison notes that the situation may be compared to that in which one logician describes three atoms as a set of three objects while another logician describes the same atoms as a set of seven objects. Although the logicians appear to be disagreeing, what is really the case is that the second logician's conceptual scheme allows pairs and trios (and other mereological sums) as well as single atoms to count as objects in their own right, whereas the first logician's conceptual scheme counts only single atoms as objects.[22]

---

[21] Virtually the same example occurs in Harrison (2012: 79). I have, incidentally, amended the transliteration of the name Śiva in the quotation.
[22] Harrison borrows the three-atoms example from Putnam (1987: 18, 32–5; 1992b: 120).

Harrison's treatments of both the Śaivite and Catholic case and the Christian and Muslim case raise more questions than they address. Why, for example, should we suppose that it would be unintelligible to discuss the qualities of Śiva from within a non-Śaivite conceptual scheme? If I, or Harrison herself, were to be teaching a class on Hindu representations of the divine, then among the topics we would be discussing are the qualities that are typically attributed to Śiva by Śaivite Hindus. The fact that an academic course within a secular educational institution is operating with a conceptual scheme other than that of religious Śaivism need not vitiate all attempts at discussing Śiva's qualities within that context. Harrison concedes that 'genuinely entering into' another's belief system or conceptual scheme would open up the possibility of intelligible interreligious dialogue, and hence also of interreligious dispute, about issues such as the objectivity and truth of their respective claims (2006: 293 n. 28). This seems right. There are many ways in which one may learn about the concepts of another religion, including concepts relating to the religion's deity or supreme principle; and there are many degrees of learning. Clearly, it would be surprising if a Roman Catholic were to speak of Śiva with the air of reverence that a Śaivite might, but given a little instruction in Hindu theology, there would be nothing to stop the Catholic from conversing intelligibly about Śiva's qualities. So the force of Harrison's initial claim about the impossibility of discussing those qualities from 'within', say, a Christian conceptual scheme becomes hazy. If all it means is that one could not intelligibly discuss something without having at least some understanding of that thing, the claim is at risk of banality.

With regard to the Christian who affirms the divinity of Christ and the Muslim who denies this, on what grounds are we to say whether they are disagreeing with each other? Since, on the face of it, they do appear to be disagreeing, the onus is on those who deny that this is what is going on to show how it could be the case that the apparent disagreement is anything other than it seems. Harrison's analogy with the two logicians does not get us very far, for a difference in criteria for determining how many objects are constituted by three physical atoms is radically different from a dispute between two people over whether a certain human being is God incarnate. To even begin to clarify what the latter dispute amounts to, we would have to gain some understanding of what it means for a Christian – and perhaps what it means for the particular Christian involved in the dispute – to believe in the divinity of Christ. For many Christians, this belief will be inextricable from the attitude of veneration that goes along with regarding Christ as one's lord and saviour. To see what this means, one would have to look to the lives of those who proclaim it. It may turn out to mean many things, depending on who the proclaimer is. Describing the situation in terms of a distinctive conceptual scheme need not be entirely misleading in this context, for the belief in Christ's divinity is indeed enmeshed in a rich conceptual network: what Wittgenstein in one place refers to as 'a system of reference' or 'system of coordinates' (1980: 64e; 1998: 73e). 'Hence', Wittgenstein continues, 'although it's belief, it is really a way of living, or a way of judging life. Passionately taking up *this* interpretation' (1998: 73e). In short, one might say, the conceptual scheme is inseparable from the form of life that is being lived.

Pertinent to this issue is Wittgenstein's distinction between agreement in opinions and agreement in form of life (Wittgenstein 1958: §241). Deep religious disagreements are among the most obvious cases in which a divergence between forms of life is paramount. They are disagreements that could not, even in principle, be resolved by appeal to facts or evidence that both parties would readily accept. In his 'Lectures on Religious Belief', Wittgenstein gives the example of someone who believes in the Last Judgement and someone else who expresses doubt about it by saying 'Well, I'm not so sure. Possibly.' In such a case, Wittgenstein proposes, 'an enormous gulf' would exist between the speakers, whereas in a case where two people disagreed merely about the nationality of an aeroplane that was flying overhead, the conceptual distance between them would be relatively meagre (Wittgenstein 1966: 53). Wittgenstein's point may be understood in terms of the distinction between agreement (or disagreement) in opinions and agreement (or disagreement) in form of life. The disagreement over the nationality of the aeroplane is a matter of opinion, and it is not hard to imagine what evidence might be gathered in order to resolve the issue. The disagreement over the Last Judgement, however, is more categorical: persuading one party or the other to change his or her view would require far more than merely gathering evidence of a sort that would, *ab initio*, be acceptable to both parties. Rather, what would be required is something as thoroughgoing as a religious conversion: coming to see the sense in a form of life that had previously been opaque to one.

So if we think of what Harrison means by different conceptual schemes in terms of what, in Wittgenstein's vocabulary, we might call different forms of life, there is certainly a sense in which the disagreement between a Christian and a Muslim over the divinity of Christ is apt to be thought of as such a difference. But to assert that it is therefore not really a disagreement at all is to go too far. How the disagreement is likely to unfold is impossible to say on the basis of the thin description that Harrison offers. The Muslim may have an incisive understanding of what it means to regard Jesus Christ as God incarnate and to live one's life in accordance with that commitment; it may be precisely *that commitment* that the Muslim is rejecting, in which case the disagreement would be one about how to live one's life. If that were the case, then it would certainly be a disagreement that goes deeper than a difference of opinion over an everyday matter of fact, but there is no reason to suppose that the two individuals would merely be talking past each other. Most puzzling is why Harrison thinks that by identifying it as a difference arising from disparate conceptual schemes, we somehow ease the path towards mutual toleration and respect. Toleration and respect may be present, but not because the divergence between forms of life has been shown to be insignificant. That divergence – and hence the deep religious disagreement – remains in place.

To take further these considerations about how to work with examples, let us now turn to another of the examples adduced by Harrison, which in this instance she borrows from D. Z. Phillips.

Conceptual schemes, incomprehensibility and respect

It is central to Harrison's argument that 'the meanings of statements differ according to which conceptual scheme they are employed within' and that 'statements made within one conceptual scheme can thus be incomprehensible to those within another conceptual scheme' (2012: 82). Worth noting immediately is Harrison's use of the word 'can' here: that statements *can* be incomprehensible to someone operating with a different conceptual scheme implies that they are not necessarily incomprehensible. So mutual understanding across conceptual schemes is not being ruled out. But to illustrate the point that incomprehension does sometimes occur, Harrison borrows a passage from Phillips that is worth quoting in full:

> If I hear that one of my neighbours has killed another neighbour's child, given that he is sane, my condemnation is immediate. (There are exceptions. See Faulkner's *Requiem for a Nun*.) But if I hear that some remote tribe practises child sacrifice, what then? I do not know what sacrifice means for the tribe in question. What would it mean to say that I condemned it when the 'it' refers to something I know nothing about? If I did condemn it I would

be condemning murder. But murder is not child sacrifice. 'The ethical expression of Abraham's action is that he wished to murder Isaac: the religious expression is that he wished to sacrifice him.'

Phillips 1970: 237[23]

Though the example is poignant, it is not immediately obvious how it relates to Harrison's point about the incomprehensibility of statements. In order to bring out the relevance, we might imagine that within the society where human sacrifice is practised, someone states or makes an inscription to the effect that the sacrifice of children is required to propitiate the gods. It is not far-fetched to suppose that declarations of this kind have been made in some societies, such as those of the Aztecs and Mayans of pre-Conquest Mesoamerica for example (Fig. 1.1).[24] One might then, following Phillips

Figure 1.1 Depiction of human sacrifice from a pre-Columbian manuscript, Central Mexico. Codex Laud (MS. Laud Misc. 678, Bodleian Library, Oxford), folio 8. Wikimedia Commons.

---

[23] Most of this passage is quoted in Harrison (2012: 82 n. 33), though Harrison omits the final sentence, which is itself a quotation from Kierkegaard (1939: 34). The very next clause of Kierkegaard's sentence, which is quoted neither by Harrison nor by Phillips, reads: 'and it is precisely here, in the contradiction of the two expressions of his desire, that lies dread, which may well rob one of one's sleep.'

[24] On Mayan sacrificial practices, see Siegel (1941: 65): 'Human sacrifice played a significant role among the "endless rites and ceremonies" required to supplicate and propitiate the gods. Besides sacrifice by tearing out the heart, men and girls were flung into pools of water to "propitiate the rain gods."'

and Harrison, wonder whether, from one's present position in contemporary modernity, one could readily understand this statement. If one cannot understand it, then one might, as Phillips does, feel at a loss to know how to form a moral evaluation of the sacrificial practices at issue.

It is important to recognize that it is by no means self-evident that an intimate understanding is impossible to achieve in this case. Achieving it may require time and effort. Sustained study of the historical and anthropological literature may be needed to acquaint oneself with the forms of life of the people who carried out the sacrifices and of those, including children, who were sacrificed. Also instructive might be reflection upon the ritualistic dimensions of one's own life and of the lives of people in cultures with which one is already familiar – paying particular attention to the 'deep and sinister' aspects of certain ritual practices, as Wittgenstein does in some of his 'Remarks on Frazer's *Golden Bough*' (1993, esp. 147). As noted in the previous section above, Harrison allows for this kind of intercultural and interreligious understanding across conceptual schemes: 'internalist pluralism', she acknowledges, 'is not committed to the claim that one must become an adherent of a particular religious belief system before one can understand it' (2006: 293 n. 28). So, again, the 'can' in the assertion that 'statements made within one conceptual scheme can ... be incomprehensible to those within another conceptual scheme' should certainly not be read as a 'must'.

Nor should we assume that the process of learning about and familiarizing oneself with a particular society or culture would lead inevitably to a specific moral judgement. After coming to an enhanced understanding of what it means within the culture (or conceptual scheme or faith-stance) of the Mayan priesthood to hold child sacrifice to be necessary for propitiating the gods, some may feel that condemnation is inappropriate, whereas others may feel even more compelled than they did before to denounce the practices as morally repugnant. A response of this latter kind might be fortified by the knowledge that the people who were sacrificed were very far from being willing victims, having normally, in both the Mayan and the Aztec cases, been taken captive during warfare (Sharer and Traxler 2006: 751–4; Purdum and Paredes 1989: 143). In cases where adults who were sacrificed appear to have volunteered, having regarded a sacrificial death as an honour and privilege, a different set of moral responses may be elicited.[25] My point here

---

[25] The topic of voluntary human sacrifice is controversial. For claims about voluntary sacrifice among the Aztecs, see Prescott (1873: 87) and Bakk (1989: 49). For perspectives on other cultural locales, see Wu (1983: 44), Law (1985: 59), Willerslev (2009)

is not to suggest that the moral judgements ought to go one way rather than the other, for the picture in almost any culture we care to examine is liable to be complicated. But the essential point is that there is no reason to assume that differences in form of life – differences between conceptual schemes – invariably constitute an insuperable barrier to mutual understanding.

The purpose behind each of the examples of Harrison's that I have discussed, including the one borrowed from Phillips, appears to be to support the contention that where a high degree of incomprehension obtains, condemnation of or hostility towards the uncomprehended statement or practice is out of place. In the case of the Śaivite and the Roman Catholic, they must, on Harrison's account, refrain from trying to discuss each other's god unless they are somehow able to enter into the other's conceptual scheme. Whatever they do, however, they should respect each other. In the case of the Christian and the Muslim who appear to disagree about Christ's divinity, they should, it seems, accept that they do not really understand what the other is saying. If they were to gain more insight into each other's conceptual scheme, they would see that their apparent disagreement is really nothing more than a mere difference. Again, regardless of whether they see this, they should respect each other. And in the case of Phillips' reluctance to make any moral judgement about child sacrifice in a distant culture, it appears that on Harrison's interpretation this reluctance is the appropriate response. It shows that Phillips has recognized the holistic nature of linguistic and perhaps other forms of expression: without knowing a good deal about the surrounding cultural and conceptual context, one cannot be sure what the act, which one hazards to call 'child sacrifice', means for the people involved.

What remains unclear is how the attitudes of toleration and respect are supposed to follow from the appreciation of the diversity of conceptual schemes that Harrison wishes to encourage. One way of reading Harrison's argument would be as advocating the view that incomprehension of another's conceptual scheme is, or ought to be, sufficient in itself to motivate a respectful attitude towards the other's religious beliefs and practices. That, however, would be a surprising claim to make. Indeed, one might presume that incomprehension precludes respect as much as it precludes rebuke. Is Phillips, for example, displaying respect or even tolerance when he says that he would not know what to say about child sacrifice performed in a distant society? He is certainly refraining from condemnation, but so too is he refraining from approval or condonance. None of these attitudes would be apropos in the absence of a clear understanding of what is going on in the other society – of what the behaviour amounts to and of what it means for the participants. Only once one has learnt a good deal more about the society under consideration – and thence, at least to some extent, entered into or gained a familiarity with their conceptual scheme or schemes – will one be in a position to express either toleration and respect on the one hand, or reprobation on the other. That, I think, is the only plausible way of interpreting the point that Harrison is making. To interpret it that way, however, does not give us the conclusion that internalist pluralism necessarily or inevitably promotes 'equal respect' (Harrison 2012: 84). It gives us merely the conclusion – perhaps the obvious conclusion – that developing some degree of understanding of another's point of view, and of the conceptual system through which that point of view is articulated, is a necessary condition for either respecting or not respecting the view in question.

Concluding remarks

Inevitably, there is much more that could be discussed in relation to each of the versions of religious pluralism that have been considered in this chapter. But enough has been said to indicate both the variety and the predominant tendencies of pluralist approaches in recent and contemporary philosophy of religion. In Hick's pluralist hypothesizing we see a contention that all the 'great' religions already share a nexus of common values and are, despite their apparent theological differences, really directed towards the same metaphysical reality. In Cobb's purportedly more radical position we see an affirmation of threefold complexity in the supreme reality – which is held to comprise cosmic, acosmic and theistic aspects – combined with a hope and aspiration that the major religious traditions will advance towards ever greater theological convergence through dialogue and 'inward appropriation of other traditions' (1975: 60). The respective visions of both Hick and Cobb thus amount to variants of homogenization. We might call Hick's position *actual* religious homogenization inasmuch as it emphasizes that religions are already directed towards the same reality and the same soteriological goal; and we might call Cobb's position *aspirational* religious homogenization inasmuch as convergence towards a common goal is precisely what he wishes to promote.

In Harrison's internalist pluralism we see an apparent attempt to break out of the homogenizing paradigm typified by Hick and Cobb – an attempt indeed to accentuate the particularities of different religions or faith-stances. But by initially portraying faith-stances as mutually incommensurable,

Harrison saddles herself with an implausible theory. It is implausible because we know that one does not have to participate in a given religion in order to come to understand important features of it. Although it might be the case that a practitioner's understanding will differ from a non-practitioner's, this cannot be determined once and for all across all possible scenarios. The details of specific cases would have to be examined. Harrison thus concedes that it is possible for a faith-stance to be entered into by someone from outside that stance, and that mutual intelligibility between faith-stances or between religious and nonreligious conceptual schemes can thereby be facilitated. So it is unclear where the theory of internalist pluralism leaves us. On the one hand, intelligibility is 'internal' to each faith-stance or conceptual scheme, but on the other hand, intelligibility across faith-stances or conceptual schemes can be cultivated. Again, what is needed is attention to particular examples. But the examples offered by Harrison are thin and hastily interpreted. This is a common tendency in contemporary analytic philosophy.

The radical pluralist approach that I explore and recommend in this book is one that takes examples seriously. To mitigate the risk of drawing impetuous or overgeneralizing conclusions, counterexamples to any general thesis should be rigorously sought out rather than neglected or glossed over. And where understanding what an example has to teach us demands sustained attention, we should be willing to devote such attention, or to at least ensure that the ambitiousness of our conclusions is proportionate to the degree of attention that we have had the time and space to expend. In the next chapter, in addition to reiterating some of the shortcomings of much contemporary philosophy of religion, I begin to delineate more fully the form that a genuinely radical pluralist approach would take, especially with regard to its critically descriptive dimension. That approach will then be elaborated further in Chapter 3 before being more fully deployed in Part Two of the book.

2

Radical Plurality and Critical Description

The issue of how to expand the scope of philosophy of religion is inextricably bound up with matters of methodology. Finding ways of engaging philosophically with traditions and modes of religiosity from outside the standard repertoire of concerns is not straightforward. Philosophical inquiry tends to take the form of an ongoing conversation with the work of other philosophers, and hence if a high degree of conservatism has prevailed in the past, there is liable to be a residual temptation to be drawn back into formulaic debates. Innovative and adventurous steps will need to be taken if the field of inquiry is to be diversified. To this end, the approach being developed and exemplified in this book comprises two main interrelated methodological dimensions. One of these is *attentiveness to heterogeneity*; the other is the *thickening of description*.

In a comment that has been widely cited, Wittgenstein differentiates his own approach to philosophy from that of Hegel by observing that while Hegel is the kind of philosopher who treats different-looking things as 'really the same', Wittgenstein seeks to show 'that things which look the same are really different.' To encapsulate the point, Wittgenstein adds that he considered using as a motto for the book that was to become the *Philosophical Investigations* the phrase 'I'll teach you differences' from Shakespeare's *King Lear* (see Wittgenstein, quoted in Drury 1984: 157).[1] Although the two contrary tendencies highlighted by Wittgenstein – to view apparently different things as really the same and to view apparently identical things as really different – no doubt come in many guises, we might, as a starting point, call them the *homogenizing* and the *heterogenizing* tendencies respectively. Each tendency is vividly discernible in the study of religion. We have, in Chapter 1, already seen versions of the homogenizing tendency exemplified in the thought of John Hick and John Cobb. Illustrative of this tendency is a well-worn image that likens religions to separate paths ascending a single mountain. As Huston Smith puts it: 'At base, in the foothills of theology, ritual, and organizational structure, the religions are distinct. Differences in culture, history, geography, and collective temperament all make for diverse starting points. . . . But beyond these differences, the same goal beckons' (1991: 73). The heterogenizing tendency, meanwhile, is one that, without overlooking similarities where they exist, strives not to play down differences but to see them for what they are. If doing so prevents our picture of religion from acquiring the smooth edges that the homogenizers would prefer, then – from this point of view – so much the worse for the homogenizers' preferences. 'What's ragged should be left ragged', as Wittgenstein was apt to say (1998: 51).[2]

Attention to heterogeneity, and the willingness to leave ragged edges as they are, is complemented and facilitated by the cultivation of careful methods of description. In some instances, descriptions of religious phenomena may be concise, provided they bring out the features that are relevant to the issue being discussed. But in many instances a more sustained and comprehensive description will be required to adequately contextualize and identify the particularities of a given phenomenon. Yet description is routinely undervalued in philosophy. It is perceived as a mere preliminary exercise: something that has to be done in order to set the scene for philosophy's proper task to get underway. That purportedly proper task is generally characterized in terms of critical evaluation. What I argue in this chapter, however, is that description itself can be critical, for it can disclose the dubiety of endemic assumptions that philosophers and other theorists

---

[1] The phrase is spoken by the Earl of Kent in *King Lear*, Act 1, Scene 4.
[2] See also Phillips (1986: ix), who identifies the desire of many philosophers 'to tidy things up' as a 'refusal to recognise, with Wittgenstein, "that what is ragged must be left ragged"'.

have been prone to hold. By complexifying and enriching our descriptions, we are doing more than mere scene-setting: we are doing philosophy in a descriptive and contemplative mode. Rather than hastily rushing to evaluate the phenomena under discussion in terms of some supposedly universalizable set of normative criteria, we dwell longer with the radical plurality of phenomena themselves, allowing our attention to be drawn to salient characteristics that might unsettle expectations about what religion is or 'must' consist in.

In this largely methodologically oriented chapter I begin with some reminders, borrowed from Kevin Schilbrack, about the shortcomings of much contemporary philosophy of religion. Next I concisely survey a number of potentially transformative innovations in this area of philosophy while also outlining my reservations about some of them. Citing Schilbrack himself as an instance of someone who underestimates the critical potential of philosophical description, I develop a more thoroughgoing account of that potential. In doing so, I draw an analogy with notions of defamiliarization and cultural critique in anthropology and elaborate the notion of thick description that, though devised by the philosopher Gilbert Ryle, has been taken up most prominently in anthropology and other disciplines that deploy ethnographic methods. As will become evident, the conception of a critically descriptive and radically pluralist approach to philosophy of religion that I am developing in this book is one that views itself as having much to learn from ethnographic studies, albeit that ethnography is not the only source of thickly described religious examples; other sources, as we shall see in Chapter 3, may include works of narrative fiction.

Shortcomings of contemporary philosophy of religion

A pertinent way of capturing what several commentators have perceived as prevalent deficiencies in contemporary philosophy of religion is to borrow some critical vocabulary from Kevin Schilbrack. In his book *Philosophy and the Study of Religions: A Manifesto*, Schilbrack accuses what he calls 'traditional philosophy of religion' of exhibiting three cardinal faults, namely 'narrowness, intellectualism, and insularity' (2014b: xii). By 'narrowness', Schilbrack means that philosophy of religion has generally been preoccupied with only a narrow selection of the world's religious traditions and that, even within that selective category, the focus has been overwhelmingly upon a particular conception of God that is liable to exclude how God is understood even by many believers (xi). By 'intellectualism', Schilbrack means to indicate the fixation on beliefs, construed narrowly as the giving of intellectual assent to specific propositions, typically concerning the existence or defining characteristics of God. Borrowing a turn of phrase from the anthropologist Thomas Csordas, Schilbrack has quipped that philosophers tend to study religion only 'from the neck up' (Schilbrack 2016).[3] Finally, by 'insularity', Schilbrack means the inclination of philosophers of religion to remain preponderantly confined to their own subdisciplinary silo, failing to cultivate connections between their own pursuits and those of other areas of philosophy and other disciplines involved in the study of religion.

Careful not to disparage 'traditional' philosophy of religion as wholly misguided, Schilbrack denies neither that its questions are important nor that its methods are rigorous and appropriate as far as they go. His call is for a broadening or expansion of the discipline so that it may 'become a fully global form of critical reflection on religions in all their variety and dimensions, in conversation with other branches of philosophy and other disciplines in the academic study of religions' (2014b: xi).

Some might wish to take issue with Schilbrack's characterization of philosophy of religion in its 'traditional' or contemporary guise. William Wood, for example, has contended that a quick glance at the content of an esteemed analytic philosophy of religion journal such as *Faith and Philosophy* reveals an assortment of interests extending far beyond 'the rationality of bare theism' (2015: 248). Moreover, Wood maintains that Schilbrack's charge of insularity is beside the point because '[t]he value of philosophy of religion in no way depends on its usefulness to other kinds of inquiry' (251). While the latter observation may be well taken, Schilbrack's concern about insularity is not merely that a less insular philosophy of religion could be of benefit to other disciplines; he is equally emphatic that a philosophy of religion that engages with other branches of philosophy and with other disciplines is apt to be enriched through this engagement, developing new questions and new methods for addressing them. As for Wood's observation about the content of *Faith and Philosophy*: while it may be true that this and other philosophy of religion journals cover a wider spectrum of topics than that of whether it is rational to believe in God, the predominant focus

---

[3] Cf. Csordas (1999: 150–1) on the need to go beyond studying 'culture from the neck up'.

remains the rationality of theism more broadly construed. In fact, as Schilbrack points out in a reply to Wood, the topics specifically cited by Wood – namely, 'whether God can be tempted, whether petitionary prayer is pointless, whether Christian and non-Christian religions worship the same God, whether Molinism can solve the problem of moral luck, and whether theism and the theory of "emergent individuals" are really rivals' (Wood 2015: 248) – could all be described as exercises in Christian apologetics (Schilbrack 2015: 258).

Ultimately, the question of whether Schilbrack's picture of philosophy of religion ends up painting the current scene with an overly broad and pessimistic brush remains secondary to the question of whether more could be done to increase the scope and inclusivity of the subject, in terms of the variety both of religious traditions and of religious phenomena discussed. Schilbrack is far from alone in insisting that there is indeed more that could be done in this regard and that moving in the direction of a more encompassing and outward-looking subdiscipline would do much to justify its claim to be the philosophy of *religion* as opposed to the philosophy of merely a small subset of religious elements.

Expansive innovations and residual limitations

There are undoubtedly exceptions to the tendencies Schilbrack identifies in the philosophy of religion. As I acknowledged in the introduction to this book, John Hick and Ninian Smart were early pioneers who sought to enlarge the pool of religions of which philosophers are apt to take notice. Hick's attention to Buddhism and Vedānta, especially in his speculations about soteriology and eschatology (e.g. Hick 1976), was a significant development at the time, contributing to his advocacy of a historically and geographically commodious conception of the proper range of philosophy of religion. As we have seen in Chapter 1, however, Hick's commitment to a particular model of religious pluralism ends up being less accommodating, for it involves demarcating 'authentic' from 'inauthentic' religions on the basis of an 'ethical criterion'. A consequence of this is that philosophical scrutiny is averted from religions that fail to conform to the ethical criterion in question, while those religions that are deemed ethically respectable are forced into a homogenizing mould. By contrast, Smart's encouragement of the extensive study of both religious and secular 'worldviews' (1999), combined with his recognition of multiple 'dimensions of the sacred' (1996), offers a relatively non-homogenizing starting point for an expanded conception of philosophy of religion.

Comparable to Smart's accentuation of the multidimensionality of religious worldviews have been recent efforts by philosophers such as John Cottingham and Mark Wynn to move away from an exclusive fixation on epistemological questions concerning theism's rational credentials and towards what Wynn identifies as 'the embodied, action-orienting, perception-structuring, and affect-infused character of religious understanding' (2009: back cover). By developing a more holistic picture of the 'spiritual life' (Wynn 2013) or the 'spiritual dimension' (Cottingham 2005), the work of these philosophers offers a valuable counterweight to the intellectualist bias that, as Schilbrack observes, has predominated in philosophy of religion. '[I]t is', Cottingham remarks, 'in the very nature of religious understanding that it characteristically stems from practical involvement rather than from intellectual analysis' (2005: 6), and hence philosophy of religion ought not to privilege the intellectual or theoretical over the practical aspects of religious life.

A limitation both of Cottingham's and of Wynn's work is a degree of one-sidedness with regard to the breadth of religious examples, which repeatedly gravitate towards a Christian paradigm. Cottingham, for instance, turns to distinctively Christian imagery such as that of the Trinity when discussing 'connections between religious, theological, and moral thought' alongside the reciprocal responsiveness between self and other that, on Cottingham's view, religion ought to promote (2005: 168–70).[4] Wynn, meanwhile, admits that his most recent book 'is an apologetic work of a kind', aiming not merely to articulate but also to defend the vision of the spiritual life that it presents (2013: 12). While apologetics need not be excluded from the philosophical academy, its pursuit does militate against a broad palette of religious examples, with those that contravene the preferred vision tending to be downplayed or neglected. There thus remains a need to build upon and expand the approaches exemplified by Cottingham and Wynn if the narrowness of scope that Schilbrack highlights is to be overcome.

A rare instance of a scholar who has engaged critically with a variety of styles of philosophy of religion, including those pursued in the Continental

---

[4] For further critical discussion of Cottingham's work, see Oppy (2015) and Burley (2018a).

European as well as those in the Anglo-American tradition, is Timothy Knepper. Having pointed out the tendencies of each of these philosophical traditions to neglect historical, hermeneutical and cross-cultural particularities, Knepper proposes five criteria of an approach that he envisages as being 'historically grounded and religiously diverse' (2013: xiii; see also Knepper 2014). Such an approach would aim to: first, inquire into a diverse range of religious objects or phenomena; second, promote the pursuit of the approach among a heterogeneous community of inquirers; third, describe 'religious reason-giving with thick and critical sensitivity'; fourth, compare religious reason-giving across different traditions 'with methodological and categorical awareness'; and fifth, deploy 'a plurality of resources and criteria' in the task of explaining and evaluating religious reason-giving (2013: xiii).

Although there is much to be commended both in Knepper's overall proposal and in the five criteria that he advocates, the privileging of reason-giving as the principal, or perhaps even exclusive, object of investigation risks our slipping again into an intellectualist groove and thence neglecting aspects of religion that do not involve the giving of reasons at all. The examples that Knepper offers to illustrate what he means by 'religious reason-giving' are certain arguments presented by philosophers or theologians, such as the arguments advanced by the Indian philosopher Śaṅkara in support of the contention that there is no ultimate difference between *brahman* and *ātman* and, in Mahāyāna Buddhism, 'Nāgārjuna's argument that *saṃsāra is nirvāṇa*' (Knepper 2013: 80–1). While these are no doubt worthwhile arguments to be examined, there is a danger that by focusing as closely as Knepper does upon reason-giving and argumentation, the need for a more fundamental level of investigation might be overlooked – a level at which one asks simply what is *meant* when terms such as *brahman*, *ātman*, *saṃsāra* and *nirvāṇa* are used. Instances of reason-giving will be among the discursive contexts in which these terms occur, but they are not the only such contexts. A fixation on reason-giving, especially when the exemplary cases are assumed to be specimens of philosophical or theological argumentation, is liable to delimit the benefits that the kind of historically and cross-culturally ambitious project championed by Knepper may yield.

Finally in this summary of innovative developments, let us turn to Schilbrack himself, who argues for 'a post-secular, post-colonial, cross-cultural, comparative, global philosophy of religions' or, more concisely, simply a philosophy of religion that lives up to its name (rather than one that restricts its purview to issues concerning theism's epistemic standing)

(2014b: 14). Schilbrack's proposals involve three principal axes, each of which is intended to tackle one of the three problems that he identifies with philosophy of religion as traditionally conceived. To tackle narrowness, Schilbrack proposes widening the philosophical net to embrace religions beyond the standard Christian-centric and monotheistic domain. To tackle intellectualism, he proposes that due regard be paid to the embodied character of religious ways of being-in-the-world and to questions concerning the extent to which religious activities (such as pilgrimages) and material religious objects (such as murals depicting scenes from religious narratives) might constitute 'opportunities for cognition' and tools with which to extend one's thinking and learning.[5] And to tackle the problem of insularity, Schilbrack proposes and indeed exemplifies how philosophers of religion might draw upon and critically engage with other areas of philosophy and other disciplines involved in the study of religion.

For those who wish to make room for a more cross-cultural, interdisciplinary and radically pluralist approach to philosophy of religion, there is little in Schilbrack's work with which to disagree. However, when characterizing what he regards as philosophy's role in relation to other disciplinary approaches to the study of religion, Schilbrack, in common with many other philosophers, privileges a certain notion of evaluation, which he contrasts both with the predominantly explanatory role of social scientific approaches and with the descriptive role of 'phenomenological–hermeneutical' approaches. While acknowledging that these roles are not mutually discrete, there is a tendency on Schilbrack's part to assume a somewhat oversimplified view of what can be achieved by means of description. In particular, he leaves seriously underdeveloped what we might call description's critical potentiality. And since similar assumptions – amounting to a prejudice against 'merely' descriptive approaches – are highly prevalent among philosophers, the prospect of a critically descriptive orientation deserves further discussion here. In the next section I elaborate what I mean by the claim that Schilbrack's view of description's critical potential is underdeveloped. In subsequent sections I then offer a more well-rounded account of how that potential could be actualized in a radically pluralist direction.

---

[5] For the phrase 'opportunities for cognition', see Schilbrack (2014b: 44). Interchangeably with this phrase, Schilbrack also describes religious practices as 'opportunities for inquiry' (44–5), by which he means occasions for 'learning and exploration' on the part of the practitioner (45), as opposed to objects to be inquired into by someone external to the practice.

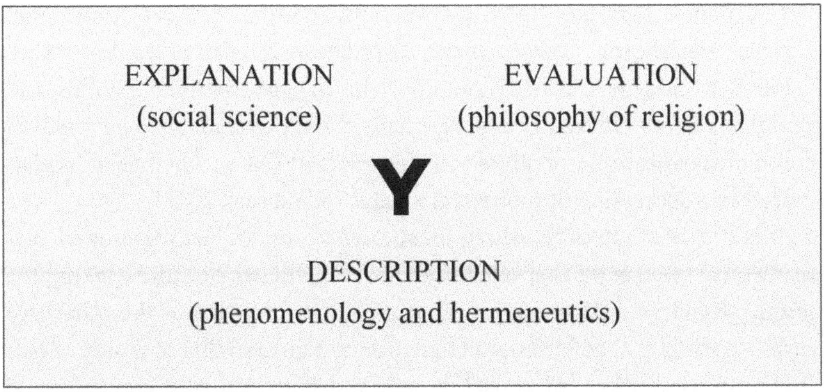

EXPLANATION
(social science)

EVALUATION
(philosophy of religion)

DESCRIPTION
(phenomenology and hermeneutics)

Figure 2.1 Schilbrack's 'tripartite model'. Diagram by Mikel Burley.

Description's critical potential

As part of his strategy for addressing the problem of insularity, Schilbrack devises a 'tripartite model' to show how the philosophy of religion relates to other disciplines involved in the study of religion (Fig. 2.1). Inviting his readers to picture the model as a Y-shape, Schilbrack places the 'phenomenological–hermeneutical stage', which he equates with the describing of religious phenomena, at the base of the Y, and he conceives of the Y's two 'arms' as, respectively, the task of explanation, performed by social scientific approaches, and the task of evaluation, which is what philosophers of religion ought to undertake (2014b: Ch. 7). As Schilbrack sees it, 'the distinctive contribution of philosophy of religion has to do with the evaluation of truth claims, which means the assessment of reason-giving and arguments' (25). In view of the lengths to which he goes elsewhere in the book to coax us away from an over-intellectualized conception of religion, the foregrounding of 'reason-giving and arguments' in Schilbrack's characterization of the aspects of religion on which philosophy ought to focus is surprising.

To illustrate what he means by 'the evaluation of religious reasons', Schilbrack adduces two examples (2014b: 192). One of these consists in examining the vow to become a bodhisattva, as articulated by the Buddhist philosopher-monk Śāntideva, and appraising the vow's moral value by determining whether it fulfils the universalizability requirement propounded in Kant's moral philosophy. Schilbrack's other example is the assessment of whether Śaṅkara's arguments for a monistic metaphysics suffer from the logical inconsistencies of which the twentieth-century American philosopher Charles Hartshorne accuses them (Schilbrack 2014b: 192).[6] Elsewhere, Schilbrack cites as a further example 'the debates between Hindus and Buddhists about consciousness', especially the disagreements over whether consciousness is to be attributed to a permanent self or whether it consists merely in a succession of momentary states (Schilbrack 2017).

It is notable that, of the three illustrative examples just mentioned, it is really only the second that would require the philosopher undertaking the inquiry to adopt a particular evaluative position. In each of the other two cases – namely that of Śāntideva in relation to Kant and that of Hindu versus Buddhist conceptions of consciousness and the self – the inquiry could proceed with a purely comparative or elucidatory purpose in mind: to establish whether Śāntideva's ethics is consistent with Kant's in the one case, and to elucidate Hindu–Buddhist debates in the other. These are perfectly respectable philosophical tasks, yet neither of them requires 'the evaluation of truth claims' in the sense of arriving at a view about whether the claims under examination are true in some purportedly absolute sense. The case of assessing whether Śaṅkara's arguments are susceptible to the objections raised by Hartshorne is a little different, inasmuch as concluding that Hartshorne's objections are successful would amount to judging Śaṅkara's arguments to be defective, at least by the standards of logical consistency that Hartshorne shared with numerous other modern philosophers in the Anglo-American tradition. But, even so, it is misleading of Schilbrack to imply that all three of the aforementioned examples illustrate what the evaluative task of philosophy of religion consists in, given that two of them – while being nonetheless philosophical tasks – need not involve any overt evaluative judgement on the substantive issues by the investigator herself.

The assumption that evaluating truth claims is philosophy's 'distinctive contribution' to the study of religion is liable to compound an already widespread disparagement and oversimplification of the descriptive dimension of philosophy of religion. A common conception of description among philosophers is that it amounts, at most, to a preliminary exercise that may be necessary as a starting point but then needs to be transcended if the proper task of philosophy is to get underway, this supposedly proper task being a critical analysis and evaluation of the phenomena that have been described. A possibility that is thereby neglected is that of descriptive work

---

[6] For Hartshorne's position, see esp. Hartshorne (1988).

itself serving a critical function by, for example, drawing to our attention aspects of the phenomena under investigation that call into question certain general assumptions that we were previously inclined to hold.

Schilbrack speaks of philosophy of religion as comprising two distinguishable stages: 'a descriptive stage that includes phenomenology, along with hermeneutics, and then a critical stage of evaluating the religious phenomena according to the normative criteria of the philosopher' (2014a: 386). Were we to remain at the descriptive stage, Schilbrack contends, we would not be avoiding evaluation, or indeed explanation, entirely; rather, we would be implicitly accepting the correctness of the participants' perspective.[7] Two substantial assumptions underlie this view of Schilbrack's. First is the assumption that 'the goal of description is to provide an accurate account of what participants understand themselves to be doing [or believing or experiencing]' (2014b: 183); second is the assumption that providing such an accurate account amounts to implicitly accepting the participants' view of things. This latter assumption is strongly implied when Schilbrack remarks of evaluation that, like explanation, its task 'is a form of critical inquiry, in the sense that it does not assume that the practitioners' perspective is correct' (186). Since Schilbrack is here contrasting evaluation and explanation on the one hand with description on the other, the insinuation is that description *does* assume the correctness of the practitioners' perspective. Questions can be raised in response to both of the assumptions underlying Schilbrack's account.

We might begin by invoking Wittgenstein's injunction to remember 'how many different kinds of thing are called "description"'; for example: 'description of a body's position by means of its co-ordinates, description of a facial expression, description of a sensation of touch, of a mood', and so on (2009: §24). Accordingly, we have no reason to assume that describing religious phenomena is merely a single kind of activity that consists in providing accurate accounts of the participants' understanding of their own behaviour. Wittgenstein subsequently adds that 'What we call "*descriptions*" are instruments for particular uses'; if we think exclusively 'of a description as a word-picture of the facts', then we may be tempted to overlook the purposiveness of the activity of offering a description (§291). While

---

[7] A comparable view is asserted by J. Samuel Preus, who maintains that 'even when one only "describes" religious traditions, the self-understandings and self-justifications of these traditions are inevitably included in any adequate description. The result is that a subtle form of apologetic may result' (Preus 1987: xx). For objections to this assertion, see Phillips (2001b: 6–8).

Schilbrack has clearly not overlooked the purposiveness of descriptions, there is a danger that if we pay heed to his discussion we are liable to adopt an unduly constrained conception of what the purposes of description in the philosophy of religion can be.

A further layer of complication is added by the fact that the sort of description with which Schilbrack is chiefly concerned is that which involves interpretation. This is why he refers to it as a hermeneutical as well as a phenomenological task. But 'hermeneutics' itself has various meanings, as indeed does 'phenomenology'. In the mid-1960s Paul Ricoeur introduced a distinction between the 'hermeneutics of recollection' and the 'hermeneutics of suspicion' (see esp. Ricoeur 1965, 1970, 1971).[8] For Ricoeur, the former is concerned with 'the restoration of meaning' by means of a 'phenomenological analysis' of religious rituals, myths and beliefs. Going beyond what earlier figures such as Edmund Husserl understood phenomenology to involve, Ricoeur maintains that 'the philosopher cannot and must not avoid the question of the absolute validity of his object', by which Ricoeur means that rather than 'bracketing' the question of whether the objects of religious belief and worship are real, this is precisely what philosophical inquiry should be interested in (1970: 29–30). It is, Ricoeur adds, the possibility of discovering the truth towards which religious discourse is directed that motivates his investigation.[9] In this respect, it is to Schilbrack's conception of evaluation rather than to his conception of description that Ricoeur's preferred approach to phenomenological hermeneutics is closest.

Meanwhile, what Ricoeur terms 'the school of suspicion' comprises a melange of methods of inquiry that have in common the aim of demystifying religion by exposing its objects as mere constructions out of secular materials (1970: 32). As the three patriarchal 'masters of suspicion', Ricoeur cites Marx, Nietzsche and Freud, each of whom articulates in his own way a conception of much of what human beings think and do as products of delusion or false consciousness, including what is thought and done in the name of religion. For these suspicion-mongers, interpreting religion consists in dissolving the mirage of its object and identifying the underlying sources, whether these are deemed to be political and economic relations, power struggles or pathological neuroses. Hence what Ricoeur calls the hermeneutics of

---

[8] It is in Ricoeur (1971) that the specific phrase 'hermeneutics of suspicion' first occurs, though the concept is present in the earlier book.

[9] 'It is this expectation, this confidence, this belief, that confers on the study of symbols its particular seriousness. To be truthful, I must say it is what animates all my research' (Ricoeur 1970: 30).

suspicion is in this instance close to what Schilbrack conceives of as explanation, or more specifically as explanation of a reductive sort (cf. Schilbrack 2014b: 184).

By contrast with both the hermeneutics of recollection and the hermeneutics of suspicion, D. Z. Phillips devised an approach to the philosophy of religion that he terms the 'hermeneutics of contemplation' (2001b), which is itself a facet of his 'contemplative conception of philosophy' (see esp. Phillips 1999; Sanders 2007). On the face of it, Phillips' contemplative hermeneutics might seem to fit Schilbrack's category of the descriptive stage of philosophy of religion fairly neatly, since Phillips characterizes his approach as attempting neither to explain nor to evaluate religious beliefs and practices in the name of some supposedly universal standard of rationality; it aims instead to contemplate 'the world in all its variety' – including, of course, the world of religious phenomena – and to describe it in a way that 'does conceptual justice' to that variety (2001a: 174; Phillips 2004b: 54–5). For Phillips, to do conceptual justice to a phenomenon is to elucidate its meaning in relation to the forms of life and forms of discourse wherein it has its natural place. Thus, to do conceptual justice to a religious practice would be to describe how it connects with other strands of a religious form of life – and perhaps to nonreligious forms of life as well. Again, this could be construed as entirely consistent with Schilbrack's notion of the descriptive stage of philosophy of religion.

However, a crucial feature of Phillips' approach that is not captured by the sort of exposition of description offered by Schilbrack is the emphasis it places on disclosing not so much 'an accurate account of what participants understand themselves to be doing' (as Schilbrack puts it), but rather 'possibilities of sense' or 'possibilities of meaning' that are discernible *in* what the participants do and say.[10] Speaking of possibilities instead of actualities effects a subtle shift in the orientation of the inquiry. Rather than one's trying to provide a description that constitutes what Wittgenstein calls 'a word-picture of the facts', the emphasis is redirected towards the untying of certain knots in one's own thinking[11] – knots that risk foreclosing the recognition of what *might* be going on in the practice or form of life being observed. On

---

[10] See, e.g., Phillips (2001b: 23): 'For that is what I am interested in – possibilities of sense – it is these which inspire the wonder which is an essential part of philosophical enquiry'. See also Phillips (2001b: 157) on the need to avoid stipulating what religious activities '*must* mean' and thereby 'obscuring possibilities of meaning'.

[11] Cf. Wittgenstein (1981: §452): 'Philosophy unties knots in our thinking; hence its result must be simple, but philosophising has to be as complicated as the knots it unties.'

this matter, Phillips is strongly influenced by the philosophical procedure of his friend and colleague Peter Winch, as exemplified for instance in Winch's treatment of certain practices of the Azande people of southern Sudan (see Winch 1964). Phillips remarks that although Winch believed that his discussion had succeeded in elucidating the significance that the practices actually have for the Azande,

> the main thrust of his [i.e. Winch's] argument would not be affected even if he were factually mistaken in this instance. The citing of such *possibilities* would still be of logical importance in weaning us away from the idea that what *we* find important, the ways in which *we* make sense of our lives, are underpinned by a necessity, such that this is all that *could* be important or make sense to anyone.
>
> Phillips 1990: 216–17

It is in remarks such as this that we see the critical potential of the kind of descriptive approach pursued by Phillips and by Winch. Bringing out the possibilities of sense within the practices of a society other than one's own serves a double purpose. Not only does it deepen one's understanding of at least what may be going on in the other society, but it also places one's own assumptions and values and ways of doing things in a new light, revealing (or reminding one of) the contingency of those aspects of one's life.

Moreover, the search for possibilities of sense rather than word-pictures of the facts reminds us that 'what participants understand themselves to be doing' – and hence also what they *are* doing – is unlikely to be capturable in a single description. There may be many ways of describing what is going on and how the participants understand what they are doing, depending on what the purpose of the description is. And different participants may understand their situation in different ways: taking a different view, holding different attitudes and different beliefs. By contemplating these possibilities, the philosopher stands a chance of doing justice to the complexities – the radical pluralities – of actual life, instead of painting an artificially uniform and ossified picture.

None of this shows that the sort of account of description exemplified by Schilbrack must be confused. But it does indicate the need for a more nuanced appreciation of the variety of purposes that a descriptive philosophical approach might serve. What I have suggested in this section is that Phillips and Winch illustrate a descriptive approach that facilitates the recognition of cultural contingencies. In this sense, the approach may be capable of destabilizing or 'defamiliarizing' our ordinary culturally embedded assumptions. In the next section I develop this suggestion further by drawing an analogy between philosophy of religion and the notion of anthropology as cultural critique.

Defamiliarization and cultural critique in anthropology

In their book *Anthropology as Cultural Critique: An Experimental Moment in the Human Sciences* (1986; second edition, 1999), George Marcus and Michael Fischer characterize social and cultural anthropology in terms of two illuminating promises that the discipline offers its audience. One of these is 'the salvaging of distinct cultural forms of life from a process of apparent global Westernization' (1999: 1). By this, the authors do not mean necessarily the actual protection and preservation of the cultural forms in question; though that is a project to which an anthropologist *might* contribute, its fulfilment would depend on multiple factors, not the least of which would be substantial political influence and resources. Rather (if I have understood them correctly), what Marcus and Fischer mean is that anthropologists can encourage the recognition of the distinctiveness of diverse cultural forms while also discouraging the expectation that all cultures inevitably drift towards a homogenized Western paradigm. Meanwhile, anthropology's other illuminating promise is that of providing a form of cultural self-critique. 'In using portraits of other cultural patterns to reflect self-critically on our own ways', Marcus and Fischer submit, 'anthropology disrupts common sense and makes us reexamine our taken-for-granted assumptions' (1999: 1).

I wish to argue that analogues of each of the promises just outlined could profitably be pursued in the name of a revitalized philosophy of religion as well as in that of anthropology. That is, among the worthwhile functions of philosophy of religion is, or ought to be, the 'salvaging' (in the sense of articulating and drawing attention to) the distinctive features of diverse religious traditions and varieties of religious belief and activity. And this attentiveness to distinctions and plurality can itself shine a critical and fruitfully disruptive light upon certain taken-for-granted assumptions that we – producers and audiences of philosophy of religion – commonly harbour concerning what religions are or 'must' be like.

Marcus and Fischer elaborate the second of the abovementioned promises by invoking the notion of *defamiliarization*. Of this, they identify two main variant strategies, namely 'defamiliarization by epistemological critique' and 'defamiliarization by cross-cultural juxtaposition' (137–8). Epistemological critique involves bringing oneself and one's readers into encounter with unfamiliar ways of thinking and behaving; by doing so, an anthropological study is able to unsettle assumptions that are culturally given, exposing the fact that our own values and norms, far from being natural and inevitable, are no less culturally conditioned than those of other societies (138). There is a sense in which the term 'defamiliarization' applies both to the process and to the result of this mode of anthropological inquiry: the process is one of taking oneself, and one's readers, into unfamiliar – hence 'defamiliarized' – cultural surroundings; the result is a more pronounced awareness of the contingency of the ways of being human with which one had formerly felt at home.

What Marcus and Fischer call 'cross-cultural juxtaposition' moves the defamiliarization process a step further by deploying more directly targeted comparisons. 'The idea', they write, 'is to use the substantive facts about another culture as a probe into the specific facts about a subject of criticism at home' (138). An illustration of such cross-cultural juxtaposition is Margaret Mead's classic study of Samoan adolescence (see Mead 1928). Beyond merely building up an ethnographic picture of life among adolescent Samoans, Mead went on to draw direct comparisons with Western childrearing practices and adolescent life. Even though questions have been raised about the reliability of Mead's ethnography (see Freeman 1983, 1999), her work nevertheless exemplifies a particular methodological strategy. By contrasting the apparent contentment of her Samoan subjects with the teenage rebellion and moodiness prevalent in the United States, Mead sought to undermine the assumption that the situation in the United States is one that is natural and unavoidable. By this means, the appropriateness of American ways of doing things is placed in doubt even if not explicitly denounced.

According to Marcus and Fischer, what Mead's work illustrates is a relatively weak variety of cultural critique: 'weak' insofar as its direction of critique is merely one way. She uses the example of Samoan society to shine a critical light on Western, or more specifically twentieth-century North American, society. 'A more powerful version of the technique of criticism by juxtaposition', Marcus and Fischer submit, 'would depend upon a dialectical, reciprocal probing of *both* ethnographic cases, using each as a probe to further stimulate questions about the other' (1999: 160). Marcus and Fischer propose that the optimal critical investigation would be one in which detailed ethnographic research were carried out by the same researcher both in her own society and in a substantially different one. Aspects of the two societies could then be juxtaposed in ways that 'engage the reader in a prolonged, dialectic discourse about the open-ended nature of similarities and differences' (161).

By introducing the notion of 'dialectic discourse' – and indeed by speaking of cultural critique more generally – it seems that Marcus and Fischer do not mean that the anthropologist and her readers ought to be chiefly interested in appraising the societies that are being compared and contrasted. That is, they are not, or at any rate are not explicitly or primarily, advocating that anthropologists and readers should be trying to establish which society is to be preferred with regard to particular practices and ways of thinking. They recommend, for instance, that the inquiry should not become 'overpowered by simplistic better-worse judgments about two cultural situations being juxtaposed' (139). Rather, the primary sense of 'critical' and 'critique' in this context is one that centres on the understandings and interpretations of the anthropologist and readers themselves. The investigation is critical precisely insofar as it destabilizes and problematizes assumptions; and it is an instance of strong critique by means of cross-cultural juxtaposition when it challenges our assumptions not only about our own cultural values and practices and so forth but also about those of the other culture involved in the comparison – and does so in a way that avoids regarding either of the two (or more) societies as static and monolithic. Thus, for example, in order for Mead's study to shift from the category of weak to the category of strong critique, it would need to incorporate a 'critical probing' of Samoan as well as American cultural norms and institutions – a probing that consists in an ongoing 'reassessment' of one's 'interpretations' of the societies under examination (160).

There are, no doubt, nuances and possible alternative interpretations of the notions of defamiliarization and cultural critique in relation to anthropology that my brief summary in this section has left underexamined. But my purpose here has been merely to place these ideas on the table in a way that makes them available for application in the philosophy of religion – or indeed in philosophy more broadly. My contention is that an approach to philosophy of religion that is descriptively oriented and radically pluralist can not only retain a critical edge but can deepen and reconfigure our understanding of criticality, turning the critique back upon the assumptions or presuppositions of the inquirer and the culture of inquiry in which he or she is operating. Space is thereby opened up for critical engagement consisting not in moralistically identifying types of religion that conform to one's own ethical and theological preferences, but in the active excavation of examples that confront those preferences with vivid reminders of divergence and discrepancy.

If the sort of critically descriptive orientation that I have been outlining is to be a live option, then philosophers of religion need also to be open to cultivating methods of describing religious phenomena that are sufficiently 'thick' for the nuances and complexities of the phenomena at issue to be appreciated. Thinly described thought experiments of the sort to which analytic philosophers habitually appeal are unlikely to suffice, though this is not to say that concisely described examples assembled for specific purposes cannot also provide poignant reminders. The remainder of this chapter elaborates what is meant by 'thick description' in the contexts of philosophical and other modes of inquiry into human forms of life.

Thickening description

The term 'thick description' has had a long and complicated history since its initial use by Gilbert Ryle in two papers first published in 1968. Ryle's purpose in introducing the term was to distinguish between different degrees of complexity and richness with which a description of someone's behaviour may be imbued. Although many commentators have tried to capture Ryle's distinction in terms of a general account of what thin and thick descriptions consist in respectively, it is doubtful that any such general account can be successful, since the terms are relative both to each other and to the subject matter of the description. Thus it is advisable to think in terms of thicker and thinner – or more and less thick – descriptions, as opposed to descriptions that are, categorically, either thin or thick.

To illustrate the distinction, Ryle adduces several examples, the best known and most thoroughly worked out of which is that of the winking boys. Ryle begins the example by inviting us to suppose that two boys each do something that could, in the thinnest terms, be described as contracting their right eyelids. But one of the boys is merely twitching involuntarily whereas 'the other is winking conspiratorially to an accomplice' (2009: 494). This conspiratorial winking, Ryle reminds us, is a single action comprising several elements. Hence to describe it fully – to describe it thickly – one should mention that it is a deliberate act intended to impart, without anyone else noticing, a particular message to a specific person in accordance with a previously agreed code (495). Ryle subsequently imagines a third boy who wishes to parody the conspiratorial winker. In practising the parody, this third boy's action could be described in terms of multiple nested forms of trying: he is trying to prepare to try to entertain his friends by imitating someone trying to convey a secret message to an accomplice by trying to contract his eyelids in the form of a wink (496). As Ryle remarks, 'The thinnest description of what the rehearsing parodist is doing' would be approximately equivalent to that of 'the involuntary eyelid twitch; but its thick description is a many-layered sandwich, of which only the bottom slice is catered for by the thinnest description' (496–7).

We can see, then, that for Ryle there is no blanket answer to be given to the question of whether a thicker or a thinner description is appropriate, for appropriateness will depend, minimally, upon what is being described. Thus if someone has rapidly closed and opened her eye as a consequence of a habitual twitch, a thin, uncomplicated, description is likely to suffice. But in other instances there may be several descriptive layers required to capture what the action is that is being performed. Nor would it be unduly stretching Ryle's point to add that the appropriateness of a thicker or a thinner description will also hinge, in part, upon the purpose for which the description is being offered – or requested. ('What we call "*descriptions*" are instruments for particular uses', to quote Wittgenstein again.) For example, if one friend asks another what she was doing last night, and the second friend replies that she went out for a walk, the description may be adequately thick for the purpose at hand, whereas if the same person is being interviewed by police as a crime suspect, the interviewing officers are apt to be hoping for more detail, more thickness.

Despite its having been coined by Ryle, the term 'thick description' has become most closely associated with the anthropologist Clifford Geertz – the veritable 'mahatma of "thick description"' (Shweder 2005: 1) – who invokes it to define what he understands the research method known as ethnography to consist in. Notwithstanding the contrived nature of Ryle's example of the winking boys, Geertz proposes that it 'presents an image only too exact of the sort of piled-up structures of inference and implication through which an ethnographer is continually trying to pick his way' (1973: 7). Several commentators have argued that there are considerable differences between Ryle's and Geertz's uses of the term 'thick description'. Indeed, it has been claimed that Geertz conflates description with interpretation and thereby turns the term's meaning 'on its head' (Descombes 2002: 439; Bazin 2003: 432 n. 22). According to this contention, Ryle is concerned to explicate an order of complexity that is strictly logical: to describe someone as winking is, as it were, a first-level description, whereas to describe that person as winking *conspiratorially* brings in a second level – it combines verb with adverb in a logical structure that, in principle, could be added to indefinitely; Geertz, by contrast, is declaring that for any situation or occurrence in which more than one agent is involved, there will be multiple interpretations that the respective agents have of what is going on, and thick description consists in the ethnographer's attempt to build a determinate picture – to 'construct a reading of' the relevant situation out of the available data, including the agents' respective interpretations (Geertz 1973: 10). There is thus a sense in which ethnography is a thoroughly interpretive endeavour: 'explicating explications', as Geertz puts it – 'Winks upon winks upon winks' (9).

Against those who accuse Geertz of misunderstanding and hence of misappropriating Ryle's notion of thick description by conflating description with interpretation, it could be argued that the difference between, on the one hand, presenting a contrived though culturally familiar and entirely plausible example, and, on the other hand, describing real-life occurrences in cultures very different from one's own (and with which most of one's readers are unlikely to be familiar), is of considerable importance. Ryle and his readers can readily understand what it means to wink conspiratorially, and to imitate someone winking conspiratorially, and to practise imitating someone winking conspiratorially and so on; and Ryle, as the author of the example, has no need to interpret for his readers what is going on: he simply describes it, as would the author of a novel. For this reason, plain description, albeit adverbially or logically 'thick', accomplishes its task of conveying the requisite information relatively straightforwardly. In the ethnographic context, however, the researcher often encounters difficulties in simply understanding *what* the agents are doing. Figuring this out will commonly involve attending to an extensive range of contextual factors that include what the various agents say about what they are doing. While these latter accounts will not differ from one another in terms of logical order, a description that draws upon all or several of them will nevertheless comprise a certain layering or thickness, in something like the way in which the sound of a choir, or even of a cocktail party, exhibits a thickness that is lacking in a single voice. It is, then, possible to view Geertz's appropriation of 'thick description' as an extension or adaptation – or recontextualization – of Ryle's original coinage without our needing to disparage it as a 'misinterpretation' (*pace* Bazin 2003: 432 n. 22).

What Geertz's appropriation made possible was an explosion of further appropriations of thick description within the social disciplines and humanities more generally. Instrumental in this popularization of the term, and of the various descriptive methods to which it has been attached, is work by Norman Denzin, whose expositions of qualitative methods of data collection and analysis have influenced generations of qualitative researchers since the 1970s.[12] Among Denzin's innovations is the devising of a typology of eleven different forms that thick description can take (Denzin 2001: Ch. 6). It would not be a profitable use of the space remaining in this chapter to provide even short summaries of all eleven of these, but there are a few recurrent characteristics that are worth mentioning. These characteristics include the capturing and recording of 'the voices of lived experience' – what Denzin, borrowing from Merleau-Ponty (1973), terms the 'prose of the world' – thereby creating 'verisimilitude, a space for the reader to imagine his or her way into the life experience of another' (Denzin 2001: 99). Thus not only voices in the literal sense, but also the 'feelings, actions, and meanings of interacting individuals are heard, made visible' (100).

Ironically, by Denzin's explicit criteria Ryle's original examples would count only as 'typified, thinly veiled thick description' as opposed to 'actual thick description', since the latter, according to Denzin (2001: 106), must describe experiences or actions of real-life individuals rather than of concocted characters. Denzin is, however, inconsistent on this point, since he has no trouble with invoking passages from literary fiction to illustrate what he means by 'biographical thick description' (108), which he appears to treat as genuine rather than as merely 'thinly veiled'. Given that descriptions of fictive scenes can be just as rich in such features as contextual detail and verisimilitude as can descriptions of real-life scenes, there seems little justification for regarding fictitiousness as precluding a description from being genuinely thick. But if we are thinking in typological terms, there are certainly good, and obvious, reasons for distinguishing between fictive and non-fictive descriptions, even if we acknowledge that in many instances the distinction is liable to become blurred.

For my purposes in this chapter, I am content to refrain from stipulating a tight definition of thick description. The impression one is likely to glean from a survey of the literature on this topic is that 'thick description' is or has become a highly ramified concept with, as Wittgenstein might put it, an assortment of family resemblances across its uses but no characteristics that are necessarily common to all. The concept remains, however, a serviceable

---

[12] His early work includes Denzin (1978 [1970]); his influential edited volumes include Denzin and Lincoln (2017), now in its fifth edition.

one, convenient for characterizing certain modes of description in comparison with others. As I have suggested above, it is unlikely to be very informative to propose that a description is either thick or thin *simpliciter*. But it does not follow from this that it cannot be informative to describe one description of a given phenomenon as thicker than another, perhaps while also noting the particular aspects in which its relative thickness resides. Even those who contend, polemically, that the term 'thick description' embodies a kind of anthropological hubris because ethnographic description never really succeeds in being anything other than thin (e.g. Jackson 2013) would have to admit that not all ethnographic descriptions are *equally* thin; and once this has been admitted, space has been opened up for distinguishing less from more thin – and hence thicker from thinner – modes of description.

Notwithstanding its Rylean derivation, 'thick description' is not a term that receives much recognition from philosophers these days, whether in the philosophy of religion or in any other branch. There has, in recent years, been considerable attention devoted in metaethics to the notion of thick *concepts*, and it has occasionally been observed that this notion, originated by Bernard Williams (1985), was probably influenced by Ryle's exposition of thick description (Kirchin 2013: 60; Väyrynen 2013: 1). But discussions specifically of thick description are few and far between in the philosophical literature. Aside from an article of my own, upon which the present section of this chapter is based (Burley 2018b), rare exceptions include work by Knepper (2013, 2014) to which I referred earlier. As we have seen, however, when Knepper offers examples of topics that call for thickly descriptive investigation, he foregrounds occasions of reason-giving that take the form of philosophical or theological arguments. This, we might think, is a reasonable approach for a philosopher to take, given that philosophers are trained specifically in methods of appraising arguments, normally in the form of written or spoken discourse, rather than in gathering descriptive information about the lives and daily interactions of complex sociocultural communities. Philosophers, after all, typically do their research at their desks and in the library rather than 'in the field'.

However, the fact that philosophers are not usually well equipped to undertake fieldwork themselves need not preclude their adopting approaches to the study of religion that exceed the mere analysis of arguments. Nor need it entail that the only thick description in which a philosopher can engage is the devising of imagined scenarios of the sort offered by Ryle. Among the other options available to philosophers is that of drawing upon existing published material that provides thick description of religiously relevant human phenomena. Such material, as I shall propose in the next chapter, could be in the form of insightful works of narrative fiction, including literature, films and plays; it might also include biographical or autobiographical accounts. So, too, could it comprise ethnographic studies by professional anthropologists. Indeed, familiarizing oneself with a wide variety of ethnographic material is one means of breaking out of the prevalent philosophical obsession with, precisely, the aspects of religion that involve reason-giving and argumentation, and thereby avoiding the over-intellectualized understanding of religion that commonly results from a restricted palette of examples. All of the sources of richly textured descriptive or narrative material to which I have just referred may be productively drawn upon in the effort to expand the philosophy of religion beyond its traditional limitations. Being open to expansion of this sort inevitably invites a methodological shift that brings philosophical ways of thinking into closer engagement with those of other disciplines, such as anthropology, literary studies and the broad field of religious studies. That is why I have included the term 'interdisciplinary' in the characterization of the approach I am pursuing in this book.

The viability of attentiveness to heterogeneity, combined with thick and critically oriented description, as a means of revitalizing and diversifying philosophy of religion can hardly be demonstrated in abstraction from illustrative examples. It is thus only in the light of subsequent chapters in this book that the approach's merits – as well as its potential weaknesses – can be judged. The subtitle of the book by George Marcus and Michael Fischer to which I referred earlier is 'An Experimental Moment in the Human Sciences'. The current period is, we might say, an experimental moment in the philosophy of religion. As knowledge of multiple religions and cultures becomes ever more readily accessible, and as the recognition grows that parochialism and cultural myopia in philosophy is no longer an option, exploration of alternative methods is urgently needed. The methods explored and implemented in this book do not constitute the only or even necessarily the best way of proceeding in philosophy of religion. But they constitute, I am arguing, a promising approach that offers the potential to do conceptual justice to the radical plurality of human forms of life, both religious and nonreligious, and to thereby substantially overcome the problems of narrowness, intellectualism and insularity to which Schilbrack and others have called attention.

3

Narrative Fiction and Philosophical Inquiry

[I]n appealing from philosophy to, for example, literature, I am not seeking illustrations for truths philosophy already knows, but illumination of philosophical pertinence that philosophy alone has not surely grasped – as though an essential part of its task must work behind its back. I do not understand such appeals as "going outside" philosophy.

(Cavell 2002: xxiv–xxv)

This chapter continues the theme of thick description that was introduced in Chapter 2. It takes its inspiration from debates in recent decades among philosophers, and to a lesser extent among theorists of film and literature, over whether narrative art forms – literary, aural, performative and cinematic – may reasonably be regarded as not merely illustrative of particular philosophical viewpoints but as, in some sense, doing philosophy themselves.[1]

---

[1] The number of contributions to this debate is now legion, but prominent among them are, on literature and philosophy, Nussbaum (1992), Lamarque and Olsen (1994) and Skilleås (2001); and

Whether one calls it philosophizing is not necessarily the crucial matter. What I shall argue is that narrative art forms can, and sometimes do, constitute conceptual environments in relation to which philosophers and other scholars of religion may develop an enriched comprehension of religion in its lived, embodied and highly variegated manifestations – a comprehension that is distinct from, though complementary to, the modes of understanding arising from the study of doctrinal or theoretical sources. In short, one could say that narrative fiction, in some of its instances, is itself a mode of philosophically illuminating thick description with the capacity to deepen its audiences' philosophical understanding of religion. Hence, as Stanley Cavell proposes in the epigraph to this chapter, looking to literature and to other narrative art forms need not be regarded as 'going outside' philosophy.

Following this introduction, the chapter examines debates over whether or to what extent it makes sense to treat works of narrative fiction – most notably works of literature or film – as instances of philosophical reasoning. Next I address the question of whether a condition of philosophy is that the types of reasoning deployed involve advocating or rejecting something, such as a specific thesis or something more like a view of life or moral outlook. Building upon the exposition that has already been provided in this book of D. Z. Phillips' contemplative conception of philosophy and his notion of the radical plurality of religious and nonreligious perspectives, I reiterate the view that philosophy need not be fixated on advocacy and evaluation. Phillips likens the philosopher to a dramatist who stages a play comprising characters with diverse perspectives on life, some of which conflict with one another. Like the dramatist, Phillips maintains, the philosopher need not strive to resolve disagreements, but to make them more visible, more intelligible – to underscore the variety of possible meanings in human forms of life (Phillips 2007b: 207–9). With this conception of philosophizing in mind, I then turn the analogy around and consider whether, if a philosopher can resemble an author of narrative fiction, a work of narrative fiction might itself constitute philosophy – with an eye on philosophy of religion in particular. Taking Stewart Sutherland's discussion of Dostoevsky's *The Brothers Karamazov* as an initial focus, I subsequently move to my principal – theatrical – example, namely Wole Soyinka's play *Death and the King's Horseman* (1975), a work that poignantly elucidates several religiously inflected and secular perspectives within the context of mid-twentieth century Nigeria. By doing so, I argue, the

---

on film and philosophy, Read and Goodenough (2005), Wartenberg (2007) and Livingston and Plantinga (2009: Part 4).

play exemplifies, among other things, a way in which narrative fiction can philosophize about religion – a way that avoids the frequently homogenizing and essentializing tendencies of standard academic philosophical analyses.

The upshot of my argument is not that philosophers of religion should stop writing academic articles or monographs and start writing plays or other works of narrative fiction instead. Rather, it is that philosophers have much to learn from certain works of narrative fiction about the nuances and complexities of human religiosity. It is amid the richly described interactions between individual characters, replete with varying perspectives on life and the world, that those nuances and complexities can be illuminated in ways commonly neglected by more abstracted philosophical treatments that are eager to evaluate truth claims. Without simply disparaging approaches that prioritize such evaluation, I seek throughout this book to make room for alternative conceptions of philosophizing, most notably a conception that by emphasizing attentiveness to heterogeneity and to the intricacies of particular cases, calls into question overgeneralizing assumptions or theories about what being religious must amount to and about the boundaries between religion and non-religion.

Narrative fiction and competing conceptions of philosophical reasoning

One way of giving focus to the question of whether narrative fiction can legitimately be regarded as participating in philosophy is to consider a disagreement that arose in the 1980s between Onora O'Neill and Cora Diamond, and which has subsequently been commented upon by others, notably Stephen Mulhall. What prompted the disagreement was O'Neill's taking issue, in a review of Stephen Clark's *The Moral Status of Animals*, with what she sees as a lack of properly philosophical argumentation in the case that Clark makes in defence of animals. If such a case is to do more than appeal merely to those readers who are already sentimentally inclined in its favour, O'Neill contends, it must engage with the debate over 'the metaphysical grounds that determine who or what may have moral standing' (O'Neill 1980: 446). In other words, it must seek to ground moral considerations on something more real or fundamental than themselves by first pointing to some non-moral feature of living beings, such as their sentience or capacity for reason, and then arguing that possession of this feature suffices to warrant a certain moral status. Instead of doing this, Clark had appealed primarily to the notion of kinship between humans and animals: not so much in the sense that we have a common ancestry with them, but rather in the sense that we do in fact share, and have shared throughout history, large portions of our lives with animals in environments that encompass a wide variety of species. In short, Clark advocates an expanded vision of our sense of community, in which animals are appreciated as members of that community who are worthy of greater respect than is customarily displayed in most contemporary societies. 'Not a community formed in myth or history by a signed contract between adult and autonomous persons', Clark writes, 'but a community, a biocoenosis which has evolved its own regulating factors, its own enormously varied ways of life over several thousand million years' (1977: 31).

O'Neill's review elicited a vigorous riposte from Diamond (1982), who takes O'Neill's criticisms of Clark as a point of departure for exploring the more general question of what count as legitimate methods of convincing someone to revise his or her attitudes, especially moral attitudes, in a particular direction. A major concern of Diamond's is that if we were to adopt criteria as narrow as those stipulated by O'Neill for what constitutes a bona fide way of convincing, we would be forced to concede that works of narrative fiction, even works of the highest literary standing, cannot be legitimate means of transforming their readers' sensibilities, for they contain nothing that would fit O'Neill's conception of a genuine argument. Far from making this concession, Diamond contends that many works of literature, including the lyric poetry of William Wordsworth and the novels of Charles Dickens, *do* constitute such means. While nowhere in them do we find arguments of the form that O'Neill privileges, they are nonetheless cogent attempts 'to lead their audience to new moral responses ... to enlarge the reader's moral and emotional sensibilities' (1982: 30). With reference to certain of Dickens' novels in particular, Diamond proposes that central to their aim is the changing of social attitudes towards children by enabling readers to more fully recognize children as possessors of a particular outlook on the world. According to Diamond, what Dickens, along with many other great authors, provides is 'paradigms of a sort of attention' – forms of description with the power 'to enlighten the understanding and ameliorate the affections' (32).

In a subsequent article, O'Neill (1986) responds to what she perceives as a general and dismaying tendency of 'Wittgensteinian writers' – among whom she counts Cora Diamond – to cite literary and sometimes hypothetical examples as objects for moral reflection rather than engaging with universalizing moral theories. Noting that Wittgensteinian authors speak of the possibility 'of coming to see the sense or point of a mode of life in a different way' and of undergoing 'an "education of the heart" towards enlarged and deepened moral sympathies',[2] O'Neill complains that such authors neglect the equally likely possibility that appeals to the heart will lead one's moral sympathies to be contracted and debased (1986: 15). In discussing this contention, Mulhall observes that it hardly counts against the sort of claim that Diamond is making concerning the morally and emotionally expansive potential of literary works. If we were to dismiss this potential on the grounds that literature can also engender contrary results, we should by parity of reasoning also reject the very forms of argumentation that O'Neill valorizes, given that formally valid philosophical arguments may be deployed just as readily in support of morally constricting conclusions as in support of morally edifying ones (Mulhall 2009: 13).

This debate involving O'Neill, Diamond, Mulhall and others could be elaborated at length. For my present purposes, however, its most salient aspect is the way in which it raises the issue of whether, or how, works of literature in general and of narrative fiction in particular can play a role in philosophical discourse. While there is no disagreement between the interlocutors I have mentioned over whether literature can instigate changes in a reader's attitudes and convictions, there is pronounced disagreement over whether the means by which literature achieves these changes is properly rational and hence properly philosophical. Although Diamond herself is not explicitly arguing that works of literature, such as certain of Dickens' novels, are in fact doing philosophy, she is arguing for an augmented conception of what constitute legitimate means of convincing someone of something – a conception that would allow the kinds of appeals to sentiment and to feelings of kinship that are evinced in Clark's case for the better treatment of animals to count as philosophical. Mulhall, for his part, does explicitly argue for the capacity of narrative fiction, in the media both of literature and of film, to philosophize – or, as he sometimes puts it (following Cavell), to be 'in the condition of philosophy' (Mulhall 2016: 88).[3] Since this

---

[2] Cf. Diamond's talk of 'the education of the emotions and . . . the development of moral sensibility' (1982: 36–7).

[3] Cf. Cavell (1979 [1971]: 14): 'Art now exists in the condition of philosophy'.

claim is important for my contention that narrative fiction can *be*, or *do*, philosophy of religion in particular, let us pursue Mulhall's line of thought a little farther.

Although Mulhall has written extensively on both film and literature in relation to philosophy, his most focused treatment of the question of whether narrative fiction can philosophize comes in his writings on film.[4] Rather than trying to develop an *a priori* theoretical account to justify the contention that films can – and some films do – philosophize, Mulhall's strategy is for the most part to discuss specific examples that demonstrate films philosophizing. In defending his contention against objections, however, Mulhall adduces some more general considerations in support of the capacious conception of philosophical reasoning that is essential to the case he is building. Following Diamond, Mulhall wants to interrogate the assumption that when it comes to reasoning, the emotions and imagination ought, as far as possible, to be kept out of the picture. In the face of the temptation to regard 'the imagination and the heart' as entirely separate from reason, Mulhall contends that these various faculties 'might in fact be internally related', in the sense not only 'that imaginative and emotional responses are themselves answerable to the claims of reason' but also 'that reason without imagination and feeling would be, morally speaking, dead' (2016: 93).

Taking issue with the objection that while films may be capable of presenting us with imaginative visions of the world, they are not capable of offering reasons for supposing those visions to be 'accurate', Mulhall proposes that, in many instances, coming to view the world differently may be precisely the film's point – or one of its points (2016: 90–1). It may, for example, be an articulation of 'different visions of what matters in human life, different conceptions of human flourishing' (92), in which case it is far from obvious what application the concept of accuracy would have. More appropriate, Mulhall suggests, would be notions of coherence and comprehensiveness – how readily a reconceptualization of an ethically infused situation can accommodate and connect with other aspects of human life. 'Giving reasons' would then take the form of showing how the vision of life at issue opens up fresh possibilities of understanding and of engaging with the world, rather than, more narrowly, of 'giving reasons for and against an opinion' (Mulhall 2016: 91).

It is noteworthy that, notwithstanding the significant divergences between O'Neill's adherence to a particular model of philosophical argumentation on

---

[4] Most notably Mulhall (2016: Ch. 5), which itself is largely derived from Mulhall (2007).

the one hand, and the more generous conceptions of philosophy's possibilities exemplified by Diamond and Mulhall on the other, these interlocutors share an underlying assumption that philosophy's business consists in certain modes of advocacy. While O'Neill envisages philosophy as an activity ideally uncontaminated by emotion or imagination, Diamond and Mulhall want these latter components of human reality to be recognized as having a legitimate place in philosophical reasoning. It is when – and perhaps *only* when – this more encompassing understanding of philosophy is adopted that, on Mulhall's account, works of narrative fiction, in the media of film and literature, become appreciable as existing in the condition of philosophy. However, for Mulhall and Diamond as well as for O'Neill there is an operative assumption that philosophy's task is to militate for a change in one's audience: for a change of opinion or judgement, in O'Neill's view, or – as Mulhall, following Diamond, prefers to emphasize – for a change in 'prevailing inclinations and assumptions' (2009: 8; 2016: 93). There are, though, alternative conceptions of philosophy, one of which is Phillips' contemplative conception, which is concerned not with advocating either specific conclusions or specific shifts in sympathies and inclinations, but with 'doing conceptual justice to the world in all its variety' (Phillips 2003: 182; 2007b: 207). I shall now turn to that conception, elaborating it in relation to the question of narrative fiction's philosophical capabilities.

Philosophers and dramatists

The way in which Phillips inherits a Wittgensteinian approach to philosophy differs from that of Diamond and Mulhall. For Phillips, the philosophical point of contemplating diverse aspects of human life – whether they be to do with morality, religion or anything else – is to bring out the possibilities of sense within them but not to either appropriate or reject them. Inevitably, *qua* human being, one will have certain preferences and aversions that manifest in one's thoughts and behaviour: there will be views and practices that one would advocate and others that one would wish to prevent. Phillips is not denying that. What he is denying is that these preferences and aversions should interfere with one's philosophical pursuits.

There is, Phillips maintains, no internal relation between one's level of philosophical understanding of a particular moral or religious outlook, on the one hand, and one's own moral or religious reactions, on the other. Thus, for example, there would be no inconsistency in developing a deep understanding of a religious ritual that involves animal sacrifice while at the same time being appalled by such rituals and wanting to bring them to an end (Phillips 2007a: 44). The point of philosophizing, according to this conception, is to elucidate the variety of perspectives, both religious and nonreligious, that human beings adopt in relation to the world, without trying to arbitrate between them in the name of some purportedly neutral and universally applicable standard of rationality (Phillips 2004b: 55; see also Winch 1996). It is the recognition and understanding of diversity that is prioritized, as opposed to the changing of one's interlocutors' views or attitudes. There is not a sharp distinction here, for bringing one's readers or interlocutors to see the sense in a perspective that they had previously failed to see, or had seen only in a partial or distorted manner, will inevitably effect some change on their part. The important point, however, is that seeing the sense in a perspective ought not to be conflated with adopting that perspective oneself: as Phillips was keen to emphasize, 'Conceptual clarification is wider than personal appropriation [or indeed personal repudiation]' (1999: 163).[5]

Accepting Phillips' contemplative conception as a genuine philosophical option has significant implications for the question of whether works of narrative fiction can themselves philosophize. Important among these implications is the fact that in order to arrive at an affirmative answer to the question, not only will it not be necessary to show that narrative fiction supplies the kinds of arguments to which someone such as O'Neill considers philosophy to be methodologically committed, but neither will it be necessary to show, as Diamond and Mulhall seek to do, that narrative fiction can engender moral transformation in its audiences. Instead, it will be necessary only to show that narrative fiction is capable of elucidating possibilities of sense – possibilities of moral, religious and nonreligious meaning – in ways that enable audiences to find that sense, or discover a richness of sense, where it had previously been opaque or entirely obscure to them. If narrative fiction can do that much, then it can profitably contribute to efforts in philosophy of religion more generally by making available to philosophers working in that field detailed embodiments of diverse perspectives – perspectives that might otherwise easily be neglected or conflated in the rush to pin down sharply definable 'positions' that are amenable to critical evaluation in terms of rationality and truth. Once again,

---

[5] See also, inter alia, Phillips (1970: 166): 'I have distinguished throughout between an elucidation of religious beliefs and an advocacy of them.'

there is no need to reject such evaluative approaches entirely in order to appreciate the kind of challenging and problematizing of hasty assumptions and homogenizing definitions that attention to particulars can afford.

Although Phillips himself is not concerned with explicitly pushing the contention that works of narrative fiction can or do philosophize, it is easy to see from the roles that narrative fiction plays in his work that no extravagant moves would be required to extend his claims on behalf of narrative fiction to embrace that contention. Like Mulhall, Phillips acknowledges that literature can offer more than mere examples that illustrate points derived from elsewhere. Instead, it constitutes a resource 'from which philosophy can benefit in wrestling with issues concerning the firm or slackening hold of various perspectives in human life' (Phillips 1982: 1), reminding us 'of the heterogeneity of values in human life, the variety of moral perspectives' (3). While some philosophers share O'Neill's view that literature's focus on specific characters and situations vitiates its capacity to inform the sorts of universalizable claims that are the proper outcomes of philosophical theorizing, Phillips maintains that it is precisely by attending to 'the detail and particularity displayed in literature' that the 'obscuring generality' typical of many 'philosophical theories about morality' might be avoided (4). As Phillips would freely acknowledge, these proposals apply as strongly to discussions of religious thought and life as they do to morality (see, e.g., Phillips 2006).

It is in the context of elaborating his notion of '[c]ontemplative attention to radical plurality' and the kind of disinterestedness that such contemplation requires that Phillips adduces his analogy with theatrical art. 'Comparisons have been made', he writes,

> between the philosopher's interest and that of a dramatist staging a play involving characters in conflict with each other, a conflict which may end in tragic irreconcilability. The dramatist is not interested in resolving that conflict (the familiar weakness of didactic literature), but in showing it to us, so that we may understand it. The dramatist's interest is in giving a faithful account of that segment of human life. Similarly, though inspired by the different questions of their subject, contemplative philosophers are engaged in the enormously difficult task of being conceptually faithful to the world. One's own values, which may be held very strongly, may well get in the way of seeing points of view which are other than one's own. One's own values may get in the way of the moral demands of philosophical enquiry.
>
> Phillips 2007b: 207–8

By 'the moral demands of philosophical enquiry', it is clear that Phillips means precisely the demands of suspending one's moral evaluations for the sake of achieving a more detached and disinterested perspective on the phenomena at issue. This, he suggests, is comparable to the disinterestedness of a playwright who, placing competing voices in juxtaposition to one another in order to accentuate the divergences between them, does not presume that they can ultimately be harmonized or reconciled. Needless to say, the analogy would not work in relation to every dramatist, for we ought not to assume that plays are never intended to portray the reconciliation of ostensibly incongruent positions. There are, as Phillips notes, didactic works of literature. The paradigm of a non-didactic dramatist that Phillips probably has most prominently in mind is William Shakespeare, who is frequently acclaimed by commentators and critics for his ability, especially in his later plays, to personify multiple perspectives in his characters without allowing his own authorial voice to interfere.[6] Phillips himself praises Shakespeare indirectly by observing that he was regarded by Wittgenstein 'with awe' for his ability simply to place a world before us and invite us to inspect it – in something resembling the manner in which, by presenting to us a 'city with no main road', Wittgenstein seeks 'to do justice to different ways of speaking and thinking' (Phillips 1999: 166).[7]

A central claim of mine in this chapter is that the analogy can be turned around: just as the contemplative philosopher brings out the radical plurality of human ways of looking at the world, so, when works of literary drama and other genres of narrative fiction serve to bring out that plurality, they too can be seen as engaging in contemplative philosophizing – a philosophizing that redirects attention from abstract generalities to concrete particularities. Whether this is really feasible cannot, however, be determined in the absence of specific examples of such literary contemplative philosophy. Before coming to my principal example, I want in the next section to develop the theme of narrative fiction as a form of philosophy of religion by discussing work not by Phillips but by another Wittgenstein-influenced philosopher, Stewart Sutherland.

---

[6] See, e.g., Bellette's (1978: 65) assessment that, in Shakespeare's late plays, 'Each person speaks in the way which is most directly expressive of his or her nature. Language never draws attention to itself: at its most densely involute and at its most rustically plain it has the same function, to embody a specific perception of the world which to the speaker is truth.'

[7] In fact, Wittgenstein's opinion of Shakespeare was ambivalent and complex, but this is not the place to get embroiled in that discussion; see, e.g., Huemer (2013) and Perloff (2014).

Narrative fiction as philosophy of religion

Although, arguably, the philosophical potential of works of narrative fiction has been underappreciated and poorly utilized in the philosophy of religion, there are some exceptions to the general rule. Stories from the Bible, for example, have been expounded and analysed in a major study of the problem of suffering by Eleonore Stump (2010). While biblical narratives are likely to be held by many believers to be better categorized as scripture or revelation rather than as fiction, Stump's work demonstrates one way in which narrative material can be treated as participating in philosophical activity in the study of religion – a way that looks to religious stories for articulations of how, often despite surface appearances, suffering may contribute towards the instantiation of redemptive meaning in a person's life.[8] Meanwhile, in the neighbouring discipline of theology, in which some engagement with scriptural sources is essential, certain authors have sought to inspire fresh approaches to scripture by looking to discussions in philosophy of how narrative fiction can philosophize. John Barton in particular has been prominent in drawing heavily upon work by Martha Nussbaum for this purpose (Barton 1996; 2000; 2003: 15–36; see also Chun 2014). Closer to the spirit of Phillips' contemplative conception of philosophy of religion, however, is Stewart Sutherland's (1977) work on Dostoevsky's *The Brothers Karamazov*, which Sutherland interprets as comprising not merely one of the profoundest challenges to Christian faith but also the exemplification of a possible response, constituted by the literary depiction of a form of religious life that persists in the face of the challenge in question. Examining Sutherland's discussion will, I propose, help to deepen our appreciation of how narrative fiction can participate in a specifically contemplative philosophical approach to religion.

Sutherland's aim is twofold. First, he wants to undermine the lazy assumption, albeit one that remains prevalent in contemporary philosophy of religion, that the difference between belief in God and atheism consists in a simple opposition of attitudes towards the proposition 'God exists' – an opposition in which the believer (or, as it is commonly put, 'theist') holds the proposition to be true or at least to be well supported by the available

---

[8] Stump's project has in turn spawned a fruitful critical debate concerning the project's strengths and weaknesses. Contributions include Efird and Worsley (2015), Fales (2013) and Morriston (2017).

evidence, whereas the atheist holds the proposition to be false or, at any rate, to be highly improbable in the light of the available evidence. Sutherland considers this to be a gross oversimplification of the nature and variety of the respective doxastic positions themselves and hence also of the complex relationship between them. To undermine this simplistic picture and replace it with a more nuanced one, Sutherland analyses the form of atheism exhibited by Ivan Karamazov (cf. Fig. 3.1) in Dostoevsky's famous last novel. Ivan's atheism consists not in an unequivocal denial of God's existence; rather, while admitting that he 'accepts God', Ivan maintains that he does not accept the world that God has created, for it is a world riddled with insufferable horrors, epitomized by the torture of children (Dostoevsky 1912 [1880]: 241, 251; Sutherland 1977: 28). While some commentators remain unconvinced that Ivan's stance can rightly be described as atheism at all (e.g. Battersby 1978), Sutherland argues that Ivan's use of phrases such as 'I accept God' are deliberate *misuses*, which are parasitic upon the primary uses deployed when those who believe in God confess their faith with due

Figure 3.1 Russian actor Vasily Kachalov as Ivan in *The Brothers Karamazov* [stage version], *c.* 1910 (b/w photo), Russian photographer. Private Collection / Look and Learn / Elgar Collection / Bridgeman Images.

emotional resonance. By uttering such phrases either without expressing the emotions that inform their primary usage or in order to express entirely contrary emotions, Ivan, on Sutherland's analysis, is rejecting, not affirming, belief in God (Sutherland 1977, esp. 55–6).

Having argued, then, that Ivan Karamazov, as portrayed by Dostoevsky, does indeed embody a form of atheism, Sutherland embarks upon the second main component of his project, which is to expound the response to Ivan's atheism that Dostoevsky offers in Book Six of the novel. Dostoevsky himself characterized his response as 'an artistic picture, so to speak' – one that does not directly address every point raised by Ivan, but addresses them 'only by implication'.[9] Sutherland argues that Dostoevsky's strategy can usefully be described by invoking Wittgenstein's notion of a form of life. What Dostoevsky presents us with is a detailed literary exposition of the form of life characteristic of a type of belief in God, namely the type exhibited by the monk Zossima and his disciple, the youngest of the Karamazov brothers, Alyosha. By doing so, Sutherland maintains, Dostoevsky shows us how the forms of religious language that are mocked in Ivan's deliberately vulgar appropriations have a vivacity, richness and coherence in the lives of genuine believers, which could hardly fail to be absent from the disingenuous tones of an atheist.

Central to Sutherland's argument is the idea that, by enabling the reader to imagine the form of life in question – indeed, by vividly displaying that form of life – a work of literature can disclose intelligibility in modes of language and action that readers may previously have struggled to discern. In developing this contention, Sutherland draws upon certain of Wittgenstein's remarks in which questions are being raised about what it means to discover that a sentence does or does not make sense and what it means to assert that one means something by one's words (Sutherland 1977: 86). In these remarks, Wittgenstein links the search for intelligibility with, first, the investigation of a sentence's application within a broader context or language-game and, second, the attempt to 'imagine something in connection with it', noting that '[a]n image often leads to a further application' (Wittgenstein 1981: §247). These associations between intelligibility and imaginability, combined with Wittgenstein's assertion elsewhere that 'to imagine a language means to imagine a form of life' (1958: §19), encourage Sutherland to argue for the merit of Dostoevsky's strategy, which consists in the construction of 'an

---

[9] Fyodor Dostoevsky, letter to Constantine Petrovich Pobedonostev, 24 August / 5 September 1879, in Coulson (1962: 224); also quoted in Sutherland (1977: 83).

artistic picture' displaying the intelligibility and depth of the modes of belief, action and discourse that Ivan's passionate diatribe has placed in doubt (Sutherland 1977: Ch. 6).

Assessing whether Book Six of *The Brothers Karamazov* is ultimately successful as a response to Ivan's challenge is no straightforward matter. There is a sense in which the question of success in a case such as this is not one that can be answered definitively or wholly objectively, a principal reason for this being precisely the even-handedness with which the author, Dostoevsky, delineates the perspectives in the novel. Just as Ivan's atheism has rhetorical force and psychological complexity, so also do the Christian lives of Alyosha and Father Zossima. Far from didactically insisting that the Christian life is the more authentic or genuine, a consequence of Dostoevsky's strategy is that the novel leaves open the possibility that readers' strongest sympathies will lie with Ivan's protest. This openness is implicitly evinced by the many theologians and philosophers of religion who cite Ivan's outrage at the suffering of children as an eloquent encapsulation of the darkest tragedy that believers or would-be believers in God must somehow confront.[10] It is the evocative strength of Ivan's animated interlocution with Alyosha that has resulted in its occasional inclusion in the 'problem of evil' sections of philosophy of religion anthologies (e.g. Rowe and Wainwright 1973: 197–205; Pojman and Rea 2012: 291–7).

One reason why the success of Dostoevsky's literary riposte to Ivan's challenge cannot be determined in strictly objective terms is that the success or failure of the depiction of a form of life – and hence whether that form of life, along with the varieties of behaviour and discourse that constitute it, is at all attractive or even intelligible – is not amenable to the sorts of criteria of evaluation that might be deployed in, for example, evaluating the logical validity of a deductive argument. The kind of coherence exhibited by a form of life consists as much in the lateral connections between its constituent features as it does in the patterns of inference that obtain within it. In other words, its coherence is liable to be more a matter of its various components 'hanging together' in relations of complementarity and mutual support than in linear paths of inferential reasoning.[11] And even in cases where drawing

---

[10] Such theologians and philosophers of religion include, in recent decades, Surin (1986: 96–105), Bauckham (1987), Trakakis (2008: 18–24) and Gleeson (2012: 1–6 *et passim*). See also Alexander Gibson's assertion that Dostoevsky 'changed the face of theology.... Henceforward, no justification of evil, by its outcome or its context, has been possible; Ivan Karamazov has seen to that' (1973: 176).
[11] Similar things are said by Mulhall in connection with his readings of certain films, readings whose aim is 'to show how various elements within [the films] have a significance that depends on the way they hang together with other elements to make a coherent whole' (2016: 91).

logical inferences from premises does play a constitutive role in a form of life, the coherence of the entire form of life cannot reasonably be determined in relation to isolated strands of argument; for coherence may be lacking in one or more constituents without its necessarily being lacking in the whole.

Moreover, even if Dostoevsky's depiction of a Christian form of life through his characterization of Zossima and Alyosha is deemed to be coherent, this will not secure its convincingness in the sense of leading the reader inexorably to the conviction that Ivan's rebellion is misguided or that the Christian message is true; for whether the response is convincing in that sense will depend on any number of psychological and biographical features of the reader in question. But whether the novel is successful in presenting to us a *possibility* of religious sense – a possible way of making religious sense of the world – does not require that it convince anyone of its truth. Sutherland follows Mikhail Bakhtin in regarding *The Brothers Karamazov* as a 'polyphonic' novel: a novel in which no single character constitutes a mouthpiece of the author and no viewpoint represents a reconciliation of contrary impulses. Rather, '*A plurality of independent and unmerged voices and consciousnesses, a genuine polyphony of fully valid voices* ... combine but are not merged in the unity of the event' (Bakhtin 1984a [1963]: 6, original emphasis) – in the unity, that is, of the shared world in which the characters in the novel coexist, for 'No single vision could encompass all that Dostoevsky refused to omit' (Sutherland 1977: 140).

This interpretation of Dostoevsky's literary production as an ongoing exchange of contrary voices, which effectively brings those voices into sharper relief by means of their juxtaposition, locates Dostoevsky's enterprise firmly within the sphere of what Phillips describes as the disinterested task of the writer, namely the task of presenting a faithful picture of divergent perspectives on human life without privileging one or other of them as preeminent. Notwithstanding his own personal religious commitments, Dostoevsky refuses to paint a watered-down version of anti-religious protest; he gives us what he considers to be an 'irresistible' case for the 'absurdity' of human life and history: 'the senselessness of the suffering of children'.[12] But then, in the dignified faith of Father Zossima, he goes on to try to refute that

---

[12] Dostoevsky, letter to N. A. Lyubimov, 10 May 1879, in Coulson (1962: 220). Cf. Barnhart (2005: ix): 'As an artist, Dostoevsky did not cheat his major characters. Whereas a lesser writer might have diluted Ivan Karamazov's moral protest against the horrors within creation, Dostoevsky, knowing that Ivan's "rebellion" would send arrows deep into Christian theodicy, let him release them with full force.'

case. The result is the vivid exposition of contrasting perspectives on the world, each of which is in its own way resolutely sincere.

Having seen, then, one example of how a great work of narrative fiction can plausibly be regarded as elucidating and thereby 'doing conceptual justice to' conflicting points of view, and having seen also how in the light of a contemplative conception of philosophy this very activity of elucidation can be construed as a mode of philosophizing, let us now turn to a further example: an example that contributes to the liberation of philosophy of religion from the confines of narrow Western-centric understandings of religious possibilities.

Wole Soyinka's *Death and the King's Horseman*

Wole Soyinka (b. 1934) has been a provocative and invigorating presence on the African – and the global – literary scene since the late 1950s. *Death and the King's Horseman*, published in 1975 and first performed at the University of Ife in December 1976, was his seventeenth play and was among the works cited by the Swedish Academy of Literature when Soyinka became the first African to be awarded the Nobel Prize for Literature in 1986 (Gibbs 1993: 58; Gikandi 2003: vii). Resonating far beyond its Nigerian context, the play has, according to more than one commentator, acquired a canonical status in the area of 'modern drama in general and African culture in particular' (Gikandi 2003: xix).[13] Its plot is based on events that began during late 1944 and culminated on 4 January 1945 in the Nigerian city of Oyo (Msiska 2007: 57), though Soyinka's own prefatory note to the published edition mistakenly ascribes the events to 1946 (Soyinka 1975: 6; cf. Gibbs 1986: 118).

The events in question revolved around the figure of the Elesin (Chief Horseman) of the Alafin (King) of the Yorùbá people of Oyo. When the Alafin died in December 1944 it was expected that, in accordance with a longstanding custom, not only would his favourite dog and horse be ritually killed, but the Elesin would himself perform ritual suicide on the night of the Alafin's burial in order to guide these animals 'through the transitional passage to the world of the ancestors' (Gates 1981: 167). To enact this self-

---

[13] See also Williams (1993: 72): 'Within Soyinka's corpus, *Death and The King's Horseman* has achieved the status of a classic.'

sacrifice was considered by the community not merely a matter of family honour on the Elesin's part but a necessity for maintaining both the social and the cosmic order (Ojaide 1992–93: 212); it was to be the defining moment of the Elesin's life. Before he could fulfil it, however, the Elesin was apprehended by the British colonial authorities specifically to prevent the 'savage' deed from being carried out. Hearing of this, the Elesin's youngest son killed himself in place of his father (Gates 1981: 167; Msiska 2007: 57–8).

Having long been fascinated by this poignant and tragic episode, Soyinka moulded its principal components into his dramatic retelling during his time as a visiting fellow at the University of Cambridge in 1973–74.[14] In Soyinka's rendition of the narrative, the Elesin (Fig. 3.2) is a flamboyant character who himself embodies a deeply rooted conflict between competing impulses. On the one hand, he is inexorably drawn into the ritual that surrounds him, the hypnotic drum rhythms calling to him like an evocative

Figure 3.2 Nonso Anozie as Elesin, with artists of the company, in the National Theatre's production of Wole Soyinka's *Death and the King's Horseman*, directed by Rufus Norris at the National Theatre in London, April 2009. Photograph by Robbie Jack.

---

[14] Soyinka was not the first to adapt the incident into a play. He was preceded by Duro Ladipo, whose *Ọba Waja* ('The King is Dead') encapsulates the events in five highly condensed acts comprising just nineteen pages in its original publication (Ladipo 1964: 54–72).

communication from Orun, the world of the ancestors. On the other hand, he feels comfortably embedded in the sensuality of his present world, enjoying the pleasures of food, fine clothes and sexual intimacy. This tension within the personality of the Elesin is among the factors that prevent Soyinka's play from becoming a simplistic portrayal of a binary opposition between two incompatible worldviews – the mythopoetic spirituality of the Yorùbá versus the hyper-rationalism of the British colonialists. It is precisely such a glib 'clash of cultures' interpretation that Soyinka warns his readers against in his prefatory note (Soyinka 1975: 6). The conflict at the heart of the play is undoubtedly culturally inflected, but it is made more nuanced by the fact that none of the central characters is a mere caricature: each harbours internal complexities that evolve to greater or lesser degrees as the play progresses. I shall here summarize the play before, in the next section, analysing its significance as an instantiation of contemplative, and radically pluralist, philosophy of religion in the form of narrative fiction.

Comprising five scenes, *Death and the King's Horseman* begins in the hustle and bustle of the marketplace. The Elesin, accompanied by drummers and praise-singers, converses rumbustiously with the market women, inviting them to clothe him in their finest garments. Spotting a young woman with whom he wishes to make love, the Elesin insists that she become his bride that very day, before he departs from the earth. The second scene takes us into the residence of the colonial District Officer, Simon Pilkings, and his wife Jane. Their musical accompaniment is a tango played on a hand-cranked gramophone, though the drumming that presages the Elesin's imminent death is audible from afar. The gramophone is turned off when Simon and Jane are interrupted by a local police sergeant, Amusa, who has come to inform them of the impending sacrifice and to request instructions on what to do about it. The Pilkingses, who are preparing to attend a fancy dress ball, are garbed in *egúngún*, ancestral costumes that have been confiscated from Yorùbá ritual participants (cf. Fig. 3.3). Despite being a Muslim, Amusa is shocked by this desecration of traditional sacred apparel. It is to a fourth character in the scene – a young Nigerian houseboy named Joseph who has been converted to Christianity by British missionaries – that Simon Pilkings turns for an interpretation of the distant drumming.

In Scene 3 we return to the marketplace, where Amusa and two constables are attempting to find the Elesin. They are obstructed by the market women, who taunt them mercilessly both with insinuations about their lack of virility and for being lackeys of the colonial regime. When the police officers have

Figure 3.3 An *egúngún* dancer, representing a Yorùbá ancestral spirit, in Ouidah, Benin, 10 January 2012. Photograph by Dan Kitwood / Getty Images.

fled, the Elesin emerges. Having consummated his marriage to his new young bride, he is apparently ready to complete the night's ritual by performing a final dance of death. The location of Scene 4 is the masked ball at the British colonial Residency, where the guest of honour is the Prince of Wales, who has stopped off as part of a tour of British colonies during this time of war. The Pilkingses' enjoyment of the party is curtailed by a messenger's bringing a note from Amusa declaring that the market women are 'rioting'. Shortly after Amusa's own arrival the chimes of midnight strike, this being the time at which the Elesin is due to die, prompting Simon Pilkings to hurry to the market himself with the constables. After this departure, the Elesin's son, Olunde, turns up at the Residency looking for Simon. Having been in England studying for a medical degree, Olunde has come back precisely to perform the burial that should follow his father's death. A long exchange with Jane Pilkings ensues in which he shares his misgivings about the culture he has encountered in England. Then Simon

Pilkings reappears along with a handcuffed Elesin. Olunde is appalled that his father has failed to execute his ritual duty. The Elesin is mortally ashamed.

Finally, Scene 5 witnesses the Elesin chained in a prison cell, despondent. He is visited by Iyaloja, leader of the market women, who castigates him for having 'betrayed' the King and the community. Other women then bring the body of Olunde, who, offstage, has killed himself in place of his father. The Elesin, overcome with despair, then ends his own life by swiftly pulling his prison chain taught around his own neck. The play ends with Iyaloja turning to the Elesin's young wife, who has been there all along, and recommending that she 'Now forget the dead, forget even the living' and (on the assumption that she has conceived a child with the Elesin) 'Turn your mind only to the unborn' (Scene 5, Soyinka 1975: 76).

Although this brief summary that I have provided hardly begins to do justice to the rich emotional and imaginative intensity of Soyinka's drama, it is essential background for our consideration of how *Death and the King's Horseman* might be regarded as a work of narrative fiction in the condition of philosophy of religion.

Death and the King's Horseman as philosophy of religion

As we have seen, D. Z. Phillips compares the task of the contemplative philosopher to that of the dramatist who seeks not to reconcile the divergent viewpoints of a play's characters, but to display the divergences so that the audience may better understand them. Having already considered one example – Dostoevsky's *The Brothers Karamazov* – of a work of narrative fiction that can be regarded as elucidating possibilities of religious and of nonreligious sense in a way comparable to that of Phillips' contemplative conception of philosophy of religion, let us now turn the spotlight on the specifically theatrical example of *Death and the King's Horseman*. To begin with, we might note that Soyinka's play immerses its audience in a cultural milieu characterized not merely by conflicting human voices but by an aesthetically rich melange of colour and sound. '*Death and the King's Horseman* can be fully realised', Soyinka writes, 'only through an evocation of music from the abyss of transition' (Soyinka 1975: 7), the 'abyss' being the space between life and the world of the ancestors, a space depicted in rhythm and dance, which generate 'an air of mystery and wonder' (Gates 1981: 168).[15] The play itself can be viewed as an instance of ritual, the borderline between drama and ritual being especially porous in certain African contexts (cf. Ojaide 1992–93: 211).[16] Indeed, Soyinka (1982: 241) has characterized modern drama as 'a contraction' of more traditional forms of communal activity that weave dramatic elements into festivals and ceremonies. By incorporating ritual motifs, *Death and the King's Horseman* becomes more than simply a play about the disruption of a ritual: it is in part the re-enactment of the very ritual that is disrupted.

Notwithstanding Soyinka's insistence that to conceive of the play as portraying a 'clash of cultures' would be overly simplistic, the range of conflicts exhibited in the play does include the opposition between the stuffy superficiality of the British colonials on the one hand, and the culturally and spiritually rich sagacity of the Yorùbá people on the other. This opposition is embodied in the architecture and atmosphere of what Soyinka describes in his stage directions as the 'tawdry decadence' of the masked ball at the colonial Residency (1975: 45), which stands in contrast to the colour and vibrancy of the Oyo marketplace. So, too, is the opposition manifested through the poetic resonances of the Yorùbá speech patterns, replete with idiomatic phrases and proverbial allusions, which give voice to modes of perception that elude the weary and cynical secularism of the colonial officials.

How the play avoids being reducible to this binary opposition between 'Europe' and 'Africa', or between the 'secular' and the 'spiritual', is by evincing internal complexity within both the colonial and the indigenous communities and also by illustrating the possibility of transcultural values and mutual understanding. In some instances the complexities are played out in the life and psyche of a single character, the Elesin himself being the principal exemplar. Entrusted by tradition with the responsibility of mediating the King's passage from this world to the world of the ancestors, the Elesin is ostensibly resolute in his enthusiasm to embrace this role: 'My soul is eager. I shall not turn aside' – 'I like this farewell that the world designed' (Scene 1, Soyinka 1975: 14, 18). But, at the same time, he is ineluctably drawn to the sensual enjoyments of his present environment: the aroma of the market women, 'their sweat, the smell

---

[15] Cf. Soyinka (1978: 145): 'Tragic music is an echo from that void; the celebrant speaks, sings and dances in authentic archetypal images from within the abyss.'
[16] 'Tragic theatre is a literal development of ritual' (Wole Soyinka, quoted in Gates 1981: 173).

of indigo on their cloth, this is the last air I wish to breathe as I go to meet my great forebears' (10). Although the colonial officials' intervention is patently momentous in vitiating the fulfilment of his destiny, it is the Elesin's own inner conflicts – between sensuality and mortification, between accepting and forestalling death – that establish him as, more than a passive victim of colonial power, a tragic protagonist, encapsulating the tensions that plague a culture torn between tradition and modernity.

Meanwhile, suggestions of transcultural values and potential cross-cultural understanding emerge through the dialogue at various moments, most notably in the fourth scene's extended colloquy between Jane Pilkings and the Elesin's son, Olunde. The latter's experience as a medical student in London has brought him into contact with war-injured soldiers, whose bravery he admires. His interlocutor, Jane, having remarked that the expat community to which she belongs has been somewhat remote from the war, mentions one exception – a 'bit of excitement' when a British ship in the harbour 'had to be blown up because it had become dangerous to the other ships, even to the city itself' (Scene 4, Soyinka 1975: 51). Recounting that the captain of the ship had remained on board in order to light the fuse, thereby sacrificing his life for the safety of others, Jane apologizes for welcoming Olunde 'with such morbid news' (ibid.). Olunde, by contrast, views the event not as morbid but as 'an affirmative commentary on life' (ibid.) – an instance of someone's acting out of a sense of responsibility for the surrounding populace rather than out of petty self-interest. There are, of course, pronounced differences between the sacrificial act of the ship's captain and the ritual self-sacrifice that Olunde's father is due to execute and which Olunde himself ends up making. As one commentator has put it, 'the sacrifice of the captain is entirely secular and practical. He dies to preserve the physical rather than the metaphysical safety of his community', whereas '[t]he sacrifice of Olunde which it foreshadows is ... essentially religious' (Booth 1993: 133). But insofar as both acts display an overcoming of attachment to one's individual existence on Earth, they represent at least a starting point for an exploration of common values.

Jane Pilkings is initially resistant to the idea that there could be anything valuable, anything worthwhile, in a rite of the sort that the Elesin is expected to perform. She can conceive of the act of self-killing only as something from which the Elesin must be protected. What Olunde tries to make clear to her, and what Soyinka elucidates through the character of Olunde, is that an alternative conception of protection is available, according to which being protected is not a matter of one's mere physical survival being safeguarded; rather, it is a matter of living in accordance with the cultural norms and customs that give meaning and significance to one's life, even when – or especially when – those norms and customs demand that one's this-worldly life be ended. 'What can you offer him', Olunde asks, 'in place of his peace of mind, in place of the honour and veneration of his own people?' (Scene 4, Soyinka 1975: 53). Although Jane's resistance to seeing anything other than barbarism and outdated feudalism in the Elesin's act persists for a while, there comes a moment – the moment in which Olunde is first confronted with the reality that his father's death has been prevented – when, in Soyinka's stage directions, we are informed that Jane finally understands (p. 60). Although we are not told exactly what she now understands, she displays in her gesture of gently trying to move Olunde, who has become frozen in horror at the calamitous truncation of the ritual, a recognition of what the ritual and the Yorùbá worldview of which it is an integral part mean both to Olunde and, by extension, to the indigenous inhabitants of Oyo more generally. In that moment, the audience sees realized the possibility of understanding across what had appeared an unbridgeable cultural divide.

The subtlety of Soyinka's dramatic characterization is evident, then, not only in the tragic figure of the Elesin, but also in other characters, including Jane Pilkings and Olunde. Having received medical training in London and adopted certain trappings of Western culture such as the wearing of a suit, Olunde exhibits 'the possibility of a *transgressive hybridity*' (Msiska 2007: 57), a dynamic confluence of European and Yorùbá elements that he personifies and articulates through his life and demeanour. And in the act of substituting his own ritual death for that of his father, he epitomizes the possibility of retaining a deep connection with one's religious and cultural heritage in the face of sustained colonial encroachment. Jane Pilkings, meanwhile, instantiates a widening of cultural horizons in her trajectory from perplexity to comprehension. 'I've always found you somewhat more understanding than your husband', says Olunde (Scene 4, Soyinka 1975: 52), and Jane does indeed 'feel a need to understand all [she] can' (p. 56). The understanding dawns gradually, through listening to Olunde and witnessing what the death ritual and all with which it is connected mean to him. In this respect, Jane Pilkings also reflects the insight gained by the play's audience as we are enabled to glimpse the sense of the Yorùbá worldview, not through reading *about* it but by experiencing its materialization in the staged performance. This glimpsing of a possibility of sense is itself a type of philosophical comprehension: an enrichment of one's appreciation of the possibilities of human life – a recognition that 'human life can be like that' (Phillips 2007b: 205).[17]

Among the characters that embody further perspectives on life, and not least upon the varieties of religious life, are Amusa, Joseph, Iyaloja and Simon Pilkings. Amusa's stiff posture and evident discomfort both in the presence of his colonial employers and when confronted by the local women, who deride him in the marketplace for being an 'eater of white left-overs' (Scene 3, Soyinka 1975: 39), contrasts starkly with Olunde's confident eloquence. The agitation exhibited by Amusa at the Pilkingses' contemptuous misappropriation of the sacred *egúngún* costumes discloses the fact that, as Olakunle George has observed, 'his conceptual universe remains deeply tied to traditional Yoruba culture even though the secular demand of his job requires him not only to repudiate that culture but also to subject it to the discipline of colonial modernity' (1999: 76). It is in large part in the earnestness of Amusa's reaction that we see the *egúngún*'s symbolic depth. While Simon and Jane Pilkings can see only superstition in Amusa's refusal to look at the *egúngún*, there is in this refusal also an unwillingness to treat death lightly. Despite having been among the police officers who confiscated the costumes from men whom Jane Pilkings describes as 'creating trouble in town', Amusa did not touch the *egúngún* itself: 'I treat *egungun* with respect' (Scene 2, Soyinka 1975: 25). One might say that Amusa recognizes in the costumes an acknowledgment of 'the majesty of death',[18] which need not preclude there also being a hint of superstition in his conviction that 'This dress get power of dead' (Scene 4, Soyinka 1975: 49).

In the character of Joseph, the young Nigerian boy who has been converted by missionaries, we descry an earnest Christian religiosity that contrasts with the flippancy and irreverence of the colonial officials typified by Simon Pilkings. While Joseph takes seriously the religious doctrines and customs into which he has recently been initiated, Pilkings is able to show respect neither for traditional Yorùbá cultural artefacts nor for the very Christian heritage that, within this colonial setting, is partially constitutive of his European identity (cf. George 1999: 75).[19]

---

[17] See also Phillips (2000: 42): '[T]he aim of [philosophical] discussion is not truth or correctness . . . but a contemplation of possibilities which leads to an understanding that life can be like that.'
[18] Cf. Wittgenstein, who, in his notes on James Frazer's account of the ritual killing of the King of the Wood at Nemi, invites us to 'Put that account . . . together with the phrase "the majesty of death"' and to see that 'The life of the priest-king shows what is meant by that phrase' (1979: 3e). The phrase also occurs, of course, in Emily Dickinson's poem, *Wait till the Majesty of Death* (1998, vol. I: 205).
[19] See, e.g., Pilkings' derogatory remarks about 'all that holy water nonsense' in Scene 2 (Soyinka 1975: 30).

Finally in this overview of alternative religious perspectives embodied in the play, let me again mention Iyaloja, who, as leader and 'mother' of the market women, personifies the voice and guardian of Yorùbá tradition. Initially shown as displaying reverence for the Elesin – 'Father of us all, tell us where we went astray' (Scene 1, Soyinka 1975: 16) – and urging her fellow stall holders to 'robe him richly' in 'cloth of honour' (p. 17), Iyaloja gradually comes to discern the flaws in the Elesin's temperament. When the Elesin, in metaphorical language, alludes to his wishing to take as his bride on the night of his self-sacrifice a young woman who, unbeknown to him, is already betrothed to Iyaloja's son, Iyaloja says she 'dare not understand' what he is suggesting, but neither dare she refuse (p. 21). While conceding to his demand, she begins to see how tied the Elesin is to the pleasures of this world; she urges him not to make a mess of things here before he departs for the hereafter. Later, in the final scene, Iyaloja becomes the voice of rebuke, condemning the Elesin not merely for failing in his ritual duty, but for impregnating his new wife with a child whose very life will be an accursed reminder of its father's betrayal: 'Who are you to bring this abomination on us!' (Scene 5, Soyinka 1975: 68). Once the Elesin, upon being shown the lifeless body of his son Olunde, has throttled himself with his prison chain, Iyaloja turns her ire upon Pilkings, who, while meddling with the lives of those whom he does not understand – even appropriating 'the vestments of our dead' – nevertheless presumes to be free from 'the stain of death' (76).

We thus witness in the character of Iyaloja a movement from deference to suspicion, and finally to a recognition that the Elesin, whom she had assumed to manifest the will of the community, is unworthy of his title. Far from giving up on the Yorùbá tradition, Iyaloja speaks with the confidence of a faith in its veracity. It is from the strength of that faith that the force and poetry of her admonitions derive.

Concluding remarks

Although cultural differences and conflicts between sets of values are at the heart of *Death and the King's Horseman*, it would, as Soyinka insists, be a travesty of the complexities of these differences to reduce them to a simple bifurcation between two mutually incompatible cultures. Instead of a binary opposition, Soyinka's subtle characterization enables us to see tensions internal to both the British colonial and the indigenous Yorùbá communities. Indeed, in some cases he even shows us how tensions can obtain within the life and psyche of a single character (most notably the Elesin) or how someone (such as Jane Pilkings) can undergo a shift in understanding, from ignorance about a cultural or religious perspective to seeing how the perspective in question can infuse a life with meaning. This shift of understanding on the part of a character foreshadows the dawning of understanding that may occur among members of the audience. What I have been arguing is that by facilitating such understanding on the audience's part, a work of drama or of narrative fiction more generally, of the quality of Soyinka's play, fulfils a philosophical purpose. That purpose consists in the kind of elucidation of possible perspectives on the world that D. Z. Phillips has termed a contemplative conception of philosophy or a hermeneutics of contemplation. For this to be the case it does not matter in the least that, at the end of the play, the audience do not feel compelled to adopt in their own lives one particular religious or cultural viewpoint rather than another; for a contemplative approach to philosophy of religion sets out not to convert but simply to make intelligible – to indicate how a way of looking at the world has the sense that it does within a given sociocultural milieu.

Many philosophers of religion will not be satisfied with a contemplative approach. They will insist that philosophy's foremost task is to critically evaluate the phenomena it investigates, and in the case of religious and moral perspectives this evaluation consists in determining which perspective should be adopted, either because it is true or because it is valuable in some non-epistemic way – perhaps because it will improve one's own or others' well-being. The proper task of philosophy remains an ongoing question for philosophy itself. In the early portions of this chapter I have highlighted how responses to that question have been played out in debates over the philosophical significance of works of narrative fiction, whether these be filmic or literary works. I have not tried to argue in favour of one conception of philosophy or another but merely to affirm that there are indeed different conceptions and that a contemplative conception has a legitimate place among them. What is gained from a contemplative approach is what Phillips terms a 'kind of philosophical attention which seeks to do justice to the world' (2001b: 33), by which he means 'doing conceptual justice to the world in all its variety' (2003: 182). By switching the focus away from building an argument in support of one particular viewpoint and against others, and endeavouring instead to maintain a disinterested stance, the philosopher is at least in principle less open to the temptation to distort the phenomena under investigation or to privilege certain aspects over others for the sake of making an optimally convincing case.

The examples I have discussed offer fertile resources for further contemplation. With regard to *Death and the King's Horseman* in particular, a more thorough treatment would need to consider whether Soyinka really does maintain a disinterested stance in relation to his characters or whether, instead, the play is implicitly arguing for a specific point of view. At least one commentator has claimed, for instance, that the character Olunde 'is the ideological spokesman for the playwright, who is obviously in profound sympathy with the young man's aspirations' (Williams 1993: 74).[20] This commentator views Olunde's self-sacrifice as Soyinka's means of asserting that, 'if suicide is the ultimate option available to Africa's revolutionary intelligentsia in the struggle for a cultural revalidation of the continent, it must be embraced without flinching' (75). It would of course be naïve to suppose that there are no ideological motivations behind Soyinka's literary works. So too would it be naïve to presume that merely bringing out the intelligibility of certain perspectives – such as the perspectives present among a colonized people vis-à-vis those of their colonizing antagonists – does not in itself have ideological, political and religious ramifications. But a work of narrative fiction can wear its ideological affiliations more or less lightly. As both Diamond (1982: 30) and Phillips (2007b: 207), among many others, readily acknowledge, there are such things as didactic works of literature, and when didacticism is present it frequently detracts from the artwork's overall quality. However we interpret the ideological implications of a work such as *Death and the King's Horseman*, an injustice would be done to the work's sophistication were we to suggest that these implications lie close to the surface.[21] On the contrary, Soyinka's play, like almost any great work of art, is amenable to multiple interpretations. That is one of the factors constitutive of its greatness.[22]

My purpose in discussing Soyinka's *Death and the King's Horseman* and also Stewart Sutherland's treatment of Dostoevsky's *The Brothers Karamazov* has not been to provide thoroughgoing – still less definitive – interpretations of these works, but simply to illustrate my contention that some works of

---

[20] See also George (1999: 87): 'Olunde is the one figure who not only takes it upon himself to initiate some kind of redress but also has the wherewithal to do so. In this sense he is the playwright's alter ego, and the play is the idiom of redress.'

[21] Soyinka is well known for rejecting reductive ideological readings of his works; see, e.g., Soyinka (1988).

[22] As Hugh Curtler remarks, a great literary work 'does not have "a point"; it has many', a consequence of which is that 'it yields multiple interpretations and invites repeated reading' (1997: 131).

narrative fiction can usefully be regarded as doing philosophy of religion in a contemplative vein. Even if one wishes to quibble with the description of these works as doing philosophy, it will, I hope, be evident that the contemplative philosopher, along with philosophers of religion more generally, has much to gain from engaging with narrative fiction. The methodological lesson to be learnt from my discussion is, as I noted earlier, not that philosophers of religion should write plays or novels instead of academic books and essays – though there have of course been great philosophers who have also been literary virtuosos[23] – but rather that works of narrative fiction should be taken seriously as more than mere 'illustrations for truths philosophy already knows' (as Cavell so perceptively remarks). Beyond this, such works can be, as it were, dialogue partners who disclose ways of deepening reflection on the multiplex phenomenon of religion, not by giving us a clear-cut definition with which to demarcate the religious from the nonreligious, but precisely, at least in many cases, by exposing through richly textured modes of thick description its complex and unstable conceptual boundaries, serving to inform rather than settle debates over the category of religion.

Both ethnographic studies of the religious forms of life of diverse communities and works of narrative fiction that juxtapose the viewpoints of diverse characters bring to our notice a 'hubbub of voices', assisting the philosopher as well as other scholars of religion to avoid what Wittgenstein terms the 'craving for generality' (1969: 17–18), which seeks a unified account of phenomena at the expense of attention to particular cases. It is attention of the latter kind, combined with an eye for resemblances and broader implications where they obtain, that is among the factors that will enable the horizons of philosophy of religion to expand well beyond the limited sphere of an abstract and largely decontextualized 'theism', thereby permitting conceptual justice to be done to the radically pluralistic nature of religious, nonreligious and religiously ambivalent perspectives in the contemporary world.

Subsequent chapters, constituting Part Two of this book, will continue and deepen this exploration of diversity, beginning in Chapter 4 with an examination of the diversity within Buddhist traditions in particular – traditions that offer multiple perspectives on the variegated concept of compassion.

---

[23] Obvious examples include Voltaire, Rousseau, Sartre, de Beauvoir and Camus, though we might also view certain composers of philosophical dialogues, from Plato to Berkeley and from Cicero to Hume, as imbuing their work with a degree of literary theatricality.

Part Two

Exemplifying a Radical Pluralist Approach

4

'Compassion beyond Our Imagination': Radical Plurality in Buddhist Ethics

The phrase 'compassion beyond our imagination' derives from an essay by Tenzin Dorjee (2012), the then Executive Director of Students for a Free Tibet, a campaigning organization that 'works in solidarity with the Tibetan people in their struggle for freedom and independence' (Students for a Free Tibet 2019). Dorjee's essay, published on the *CNN Belief Blog*, is itself a response to an opinion piece published there six days earlier by Stephen Prothero (2012), Professor of Religion at Boston University. Prothero, referring to a wave of self-immolations carried out in Tibet by protestors against the Chinese occupation, was critical of the public stance taken by the Dalai Lama, who had declined to either support or condemn these normally fatal acts of self-burning. 'I know it is impolitic to criticize the Dalai Lama', Prothero writes, 'But he deserves criticism in this case.' In Prothero's view, the

Dalai Lama's reluctance 'to speak out unequivocally against these deaths' leaves him with 'blood ... on his hands.' While recognizing 'that there is a tradition of self-immolation in Buddhism dating back at least to the fourth century', Prothero observes that 'there is also a strong ethic of compassion. So where is the compassion here?'

In his riposte, Dorjee accuses Prothero of disingenuously blaming the Dalai Lama for actions for which the Chinese leadership is ultimately responsible, for it is the latter that has forced the Tibetan people into a corner, from which burning oneself to death is one of few acts of defiance left open to them. 'By demanding that the Dalai Lama condemn these individuals who have shown compassion beyond our imagination', Dorjee writes, 'Prothero has betrayed a colossal indifference to the courage and circumstances of those fighting for the same democratic freedoms and human rights that he himself enjoys' (2012).

My primary purpose in citing this exchange between Prothero and Dorjee is to highlight the clash of conceptions of compassion it exemplifies. On the one side is the view that self-immolation and the Dalai Lama's ambivalent attitude to it are contrary to compassion. On the other side is the view that, insofar as they are motivated by the altruistic impulse to affirm the freedom of the Tibetan people as a whole, these acts of self-immolation themselves embody compassion of a profound sort – 'compassion beyond our imagination'. From Dorjee's perspective, if the Dalai Lama were to call for an end to the self-immolations he would in effect be doing an injustice to the sacrifices of those who have already died; he would be failing to honour the selfless courage they have displayed through surrendering their lives in an agonizing way out of compassion for their fellow Tibetans. Whether or not we share Dorjee's view of the matter, by voicing an understanding of the acts as compassionate he shows us a possible conception of compassion. And Prothero shows us another.

Compassion is among the virtues that are often picked out as epitomizing the very heart not only of Buddhism in particular but of a religious or spiritual life more generally – an essence that runs through and unifies multiple religions. As James Gilman puts it, it is compassion, as opposed to 'some common core of belief or practice', that 'constitutes the shared territory and public space between religions', inspiring their adherents to play 'a vital role in promoting and preserving civility' (2007: 13). Similarly, the historian of religion Karen Armstrong affirms that 'All the great world religions agree that compassion is the chief religious virtue, and far more important than ideological or sexual orthodoxy' (2008: 21). And, as we have seen in

Chapter 1, John Hick, famous for contending that 'the great world religions' are diverse 'human responses to the one divine Reality, embodying different perceptions which have been formed in different historical and cultural circumstances' (1980: 6), maintained that central to these religions is 'the moral ideal of generous goodwill, love, compassion epitomised in the Golden Rule' (2004: 316).

A danger of these characterizations of compassion as a common thread connecting all religions – or at any rate all 'the great world religions' – is that they obscure from view the genuine diversity not only between religions but also within them. The characterizations in question do this in a twofold homogenizing manoeuvre: first by assuming that a concept such as that of compassion has a stable and internally cohesive meaning or use; and second, by assuming that this supposedly unified concept of compassion can be unproblematically deployed in describing multiple systems of religious ethics. As we have already seen, the concept of compassion can be invoked in strikingly contrasting ways. In certain instances what may appear to one person as a contravention of compassion may appear to someone else as its quintessential expression.

In keeping with the critically descriptive function of a radical pluralist approach to philosophy of religion, my aim in this chapter is to disrupt facile assumptions concerning the supposed universality of compassion in religions. I do not intend to show that 'compassion', 'love' and similar terms are not routinely used to identify desirable virtues or attitudes within religious contexts, but rather to cast doubt on the assumption that we know perfectly well what such invocations amount to in advance of careful attention to the contexts themselves. Since surveying even a small proportion of the religions of the world on this matter would require a book-length study in itself, my method will be to focus on Buddhist traditions in particular. If it can be shown that there are multiple understandings of compassion even within this cluster of closely related traditions, then a case will have been made for being at least cautious about assuming that the term 'compassion' applies univocally across religions in general. Contrary to Hick's style of religious pluralism, which affirms the unity of religions on the basis of an artificially homogenized ethical criterion, I shall be taking the approach, expounded in Chapters 2 and 3, of devoting '[c]ontemplative attention to radical plurality' (Phillips 2007b: 207). While not disregarding commonalities and resemblances where they exist, this approach involves looking out for nuances and particularities that add complexity to the overall picture without immediately trying to fit them into a preconceived theory.

The next section opens the discussion with an acknowledgement of the plurality of perspectives among Buddhist traditions and of the way in which certain Mahāyāna authors in particular have lauded their own elevated conception of compassion as typifying the ethical superiority of Mahāyāna over other forms of Buddhism. Further sections then examine and illustrate different orientations that have been adopted vis-à-vis compassion in Buddhist traditions. These include, respectively: familial relationships as a model for compassion; bodily sacrifice, a version of which is the kind of self-immolation that has already been mentioned; and the transgressive compassion that is linked with the doctrine of skilful means (*upāya kauśalya*). Rather than presenting these as an exhaustive and strictly demarcated typology, my purpose is merely to highlight the range of ways in which what is designated as compassion manifests in Buddhist scriptural, narrative and lived traditions. While none of this refutes, or is intended to refute, the contention that compassion is central to Buddhist ethics, it does suggest that an ethic of compassion can manifest in an apparently indefinite variety of ways. Hence any claim to the effect that compassion constitutes Buddhism's essence or core cannot be more than provisional, and is liable to be misleading unless accompanied by explicit recognition of the diverse meanings of 'compassion' (and of its equivalents and near equivalents in indigenous languages) across multiple Buddhist contexts. *A fortiori* we ought to be sceptical that anything very informative has been said when it is asserted that compassion lies at the heart of all (the 'great') religions.

Varieties of Buddhism and the rhetoric of compassion

Before turning specifically to the notion of compassion, it is important to register the diversity that obtains among the religious and cultural phenomena typically identified by the term 'Buddhism'. In view of this diversity, it is becoming increasingly common for scholars, when referring to these phenomena, to use plural nouns such as 'Buddhist religions', 'Buddhist traditions' or 'Buddhisms' (e.g. Ling 1993; Strong 2015), thereby mitigating the impression that what is being discussed constitutes a monolithic category. As the authors of a popular introductory textbook put it, if we are to retain the singular term 'Buddhism' at all, it is advisable to regard it 'as describing a family of religions, each with its own integrity, much as *monotheism* covers a family of religions' (Robinson, Johnson and Thanissaro 2005: xxi).[1] While this may indeed be a helpful starting point, we should also remain alert to the possibility that, in at least some cases, the apparent 'integrity' of these more or less distinguishable Buddhist religions itself masks a high degree of hybridity, fluidity and internal variegation.

There are, of course, threads of continuity and resemblance between the multiple Buddhist schools and traditions, and an emphasis on compassion is one such thread. Relevant non-English terms that are commonly translated as 'compassion' include *karuṇā* (and also *anukampā*) in Pāli and Sanskrit, *hi* in Chinese and Japanese (Ives 1992: 28) and *nying je* (also transliterated *snying rje*) in Tibetan (Kalu Rinpoche 1986: 47). As we shall see, however, the manifestations of this virtue across the various traditions and textual genres take many forms. A conventional assumption among scholars of Buddhism has been that one of the principal differences between the earliest forms of Buddhism, on the one hand, and the various strands of Mahāyāna Buddhism, on the other, consists in a divergence concerning how compassion is understood. It has been assumed that early Buddhist teachings, which have to some extent been preserved in the Theravāda traditions prevalent in Burma (Myanmar), Cambodia, Laos, Thailand and Sri Lanka, give to compassion a lesser degree of importance than it acquired in the Mahāyāna Buddhisms that, having emerged in India from around the first century BCE, then spread to several countries to the north and east, including China, Korea, Japan, Tibet and Vietnam.[2] In the words of one commentator writing in the mid-twentieth century, 'The concept appears in both earlier and later Buddhism, but while present from the beginning, the idea of compassion achieves its greatest importance in the Mahāyāna, or Great Vehicle, branch of the religion' (Hamilton 1950: 145). Although this way of putting it is not necessarily false, we should be cautious not to base our assessment of the relative importance of compassion in different Buddhist traditions exclusively on the polemical asseverations of Mahāyāna proponents themselves.

Distinctions commonly affirmed in Mahāyāna sources include the twofold division between the Hīnayāna and the Mahāyāna and the threefold

---

[1] Indicative of increasing sensitivity to plurality is the fact that the title of the fifth edition of the book by Robinson, Johnson and Thanissaro is *Buddhist Religions* (plural), whereas the four previous editions had been called *The Buddhist Religion* (singular).

[2] The date of Mahāyāna Buddhism's emergence remains disputed. Those who favour the first century BCE as its likely period of origin include Akira (1990: 252). Others have referred to this as a period during which 'proto-Mahāyāna sūtras began to be written down' (Skilling 2013: 104).

division between the Śrāvakayāna, Pratyekabuddhayāna and Bodhisattvayāna (Bielefeldt 2009: 66). *Hīnayāna* (literally 'low vehicle' or 'inferior vehicle') is generally agreed by scholars to be a pejorative designation that plays the rhetorical role of classifying the 'other' from which votaries of the Mahāyāna ('great vehicle') wish to be dissociated (Nattier 2003: 172–4; Skilling 2013: 75–9). *Śrāvakayāna* ('vehicle of listeners' or 'vehicle of disciples') and *Pratyekabuddhayāna* ('vehicle of solitary buddhas'), though not straightforwardly pejorative, are also terms in Mahāyāna texts to designate those Buddhist paths that are held to fall short of the Bodhisattvayāna, the latter being the vehicle (*yāna*) of those who are dedicated not only to becoming buddhas themselves but also to liberating all living beings from the suffering and dissatisfaction that pervade the ongoing flow of life, death and rebirth (Harrison 1987). The renowned Tibetan Buddhist philosopher Tsong kha pa (1357–1419) writes, for instance, that although those who follow the Śrāvaka or the Pratyekabuddha path no doubt possess 'the immeasurable love and compassion' that consists in wishing all beings could be happy and relieved of suffering, they lack the tenacity exhibited by adherents of the Mahāyāna, who vow to actively work to secure those universal ends (Tsong kha pa 2004: 32–3). The distinction to which Tsong kha pa is alluding is between, on the one hand, those practitioners who strive to achieve nirvāṇa for themselves without vowing to continue assisting others thereafter and, on the other hand, those who commit themselves to stay within the cycle of rebirth for as long as it takes to enable all beings to achieve that goal (cf. Conze 1975: 58; Williams 2009: 56).

The proclivity of Mahāyāna advocates to valorize their own compassionate resolve by contrasting it with the purportedly self-serving aspirations of other practitioners ought not to blinker us to the expressions of altruistic generosity present in pre-Mahāyāna sources, which remain vital to the living Theravāda tradition. In the pre-Mahāyāna Pāli Canon, for example, the Buddha's own decision to disseminate the wisdom he had accessed through his spiritual awakening is represented as being motivated by 'compassion [*anukampā*] for the world, for the good, welfare, and happiness of gods and humans' (*Bhayabherava Sutta* 21, trans. Ñāṇamoli and Bodhi 2009: 104); in response to the god Brahmā's request that he should share with everyone what he has learnt, the Buddha looks upon the world 'out of compassion [*karuṇā*]' for all the beings who live there (*Ariyapariyesanā Sutta* 21, trans. Ñāṇamoli and Bodhi 2009: 261). In discourses such as the *Tevijja Sutta* (Walshe 1995: 187–95) the rhetorical strategy is to juxtapose the pre-existing Brahmanical aspiration for 'union with Brahmā' with the Buddha's own injunction to suffuse the world with 'loving-kindness' (*mettā*), 'compassion' (*karuṇā*), 'sympathetic joy' (*muditā*) and 'equanimity' (*upekkhā*), qualities that were subsequently to be characterized as the four *brahma-vihāra*s – the 'sublime states' (Nyanaponika 1958) or 'divine abidings' (Shaw 2006: Ch. 10). As Richard Gombrich has pointed out, there is thus a sense in which the notion of a cosmic or pervasive consciousness, typified in Brahmanical texts such as the *Bṛhadāraṇyaka Upaniṣad*, is replaced in the Buddhist sources by the idea of a specifically 'ethicised consciousness' that expands to encompass all things: 'to be totally benevolent is to be liberated' (Gombrich 2006: 61–2).

It is evident, then, that the salvific importance of cultivating a universal and apparently unconditional compassionate sensibility is far from exclusive to the Mahāyāna traditions; though this importance has no doubt acquired novel modes of articulation there, it has also continued to do so in the traditions of Theravāda. Questions remain, however, about what the compassionate sensibility practically consists in. The remainder of this chapter assembles examples from several scriptural, narrative and lived contexts to illustrate the variety that characterizes Buddhist traditions across the board.

Images of familial love and abandonment

Prominent among the images deployed in Buddhist traditions to encapsulate the spirit of loving-kindness and compassion is that of the bond between members of a family, especially between mother and child. For example, the *Karaṇīyamettā Sutta* ('Discourse on Loving-Kindness'), which is regularly utilized in Theravādin meditative and liturgical practice, enjoins the practitioner to embrace 'with a boundless heart ... all living beings', 'as a mother protects with her life ... her only child' (trans. Amaravati Sangha 2013).[3] This image takes on new resonances when the simile of a mother's love for her child is synthesized with the doctrine of rebirth; for in the light of the thought that every living being has undergone a beginningless series of lifetimes, it becomes possible to declare that all beings have, at some time in the past, stood in every conceivable relationship to one another, including

---

[3] For exposition of the *Karaṇīyamettā Sutta*'s application in Buddhist practice, see Gombrich (2000: 183–4; 2009: 327–9).

the relationships of mother, father, brother, sister, son, daughter and so on. Initially put forward without explicit ethical intent in the *Anamatagga Saṃyutta* of the Pāli collection known as the *Saṃyutta Nikāya* (Bodhi 2000: 659), this idea of recognizing one's familial connections with all living beings becomes fully ethically suffused in certain Mahāyāna teachings.

Instead of cultivating the thought that all living beings should be regarded as though they were one's only child, as in the *Karaṇīyamettā Sutta*, a well-known Mahāyāna meditation seeks to foster a sense of benevolent gratitude by remembering that all living beings have been one's mother in innumerable former lives. As elaborated by Tsong kha pa, the practice consists in first enhancing an appreciation of the kindness of one's mother by recognizing that she has protected and nurtured one not only in this life but 'an incalculable number of times throughout beginningless cyclic existence' (2004: 38). One then progressively extends this appreciation to others by looking upon them, too, as having been a mother to oneself in previous existences, extending the attitude initially to other relatives and to one's friends, then to people to whom one is normally indifferent and then, further, to one's enemies. Eventually, by coming to see 'that all beings in the ten directions are your mothers', one aims to engender 'a remembrance of their kindness' and a wish to repay it through compassionate service (39).

To indicate the heterogeneity of imagery in Buddhist sources, we should acknowledge that aside from constituting a model of the benevolent disposition towards others that ought to be promoted, familial relationships are sometimes cited for very different purposes. Notably, they can be emblematic of precisely the sort of emotional attachments that the Buddhist practitioner is encouraged to relinquish. Thus, in some places, the ethical message, far from recommending that everyone be cared for as though they were one's mother or one's only child, is more readily understood to mean that one's ties to others, including immediate family, should be loosened to the point where one is capable of abandoning those relationships with ease. Typifying this emphasis on detachment are many of the stories recounted in the Jātakas – the 'birth stories' depicting incidents from the Buddha's previous lives, multiple versions of which are popular throughout both Theravāda and Mahāyāna traditions.[4] The following section will mention a selection of these stories that involve forgoing attachment to one's own body. Of

---

[4] 'No book finds, even to the present day, so much favour as the Jātaka with the peoples who follow Buddhism' (Winternitz 1983 [1912]: 148).

particular interest here, meanwhile, is the widely esteemed *Vessantara Jātaka*, in which Prince Vessantara, who is customarily regarded as the final human incarnation of the buddha-to-be prior to his life as Siddhattha Gotama himself,[5] is depicted as the epitome of generous giving.

In view of the simile of parental love that we have seen in the *Karaṇīyamettā Sutta*, it is ironic that Vessantara's boundless generosity is represented by his giving away not only his kingdom and material possessions but ultimately his children and then his wife. Having handed his children over to a brahmin who treats them as slaves (Fig. 4.1), Vessantara resists the impulse to take them back by reminding himself that 'It is not fitting to be regretful after giving a gift' (trans. Appleton and Shaw 2015: 604). Without simplistically inviting its readers to follow Vessantara in being willing to abandon their

Figure 4.1 Jūjaka [a brahmin beggar] requests Vessantara to give him his children as servants and then leads them away. Scene from the Thai version of the *Vessantara Jātaka*, British Library, London, UK. © British Library Board. All Rights Reserved. Bridgeman Images.

---

[5] One must say final *human* incarnation because immediately after his life as Vessantara, and before being reborn as Gotama, the buddha-to-be underwent a life 'in heaven' (*Vessantara Jātaka* verse 786, trans. Appleton and Shaw 2015: 639).

families, the Jātaka nevertheless exhibits such abandonment as an ethical and soteriological possibility, which is in principle not merely compatible with generosity and goodwill but a genuine mark thereof. While his loving-kindness (*mettā*) for living beings in general is said to radiate for miles around (ibid.: 575), any compassion that Vessantara displays for his wife and children is represented as a weakness to be overcome. Charged with emotional complexity, the story vividly portrays the tension between familial attachment and the spirit of renunciation. It may thus be characterized, especially when acted out in public performance, as incorporating 'elements of both tragedy and melodrama' (Collins 1998: 46). It also prefigures the classic hagiographic narratives of the Buddha's life as Prince Siddhattha, who, at the age of 29, leaves his wife and newborn son in order to pursue the spiritual life – a prefiguring accentuated by the long-established identification of Vessantara's wife Maddī with Yasodharā, the wife of Siddhattha Gotama (Obeyesekere 2009: 22).

Bodily sacrifice as heroic virtue

While Prince Vessantara is depicted as giving away his worldly possessions and his family out of a motive of selfless generosity, other Buddhist sources extol the voluntary sacrifice of one's own body, in whole or in part, as displaying what several commentators have termed 'heroic compassion' (Grieve 2012: 253; cf. Smart 1973: 124). Among the Jātakas, such compassion is typified in the stories of King Śibi, who saves the life of a dove by offering his own flesh to be consumed by a hawk in its stead (Ohnuma 2007: 5–6), and Prince Mahāsattva, who allows a starving tigress to lick his blood and then eat his body to prevent her needing to devour her own cubs (Frye 2006: 15–16). The theme of bodily sacrifice is also present in tales concerning other former lives of the Buddha. These include: King Candraprabha, who grants permission for his head to be cut off by a brahmin in order to complete 'the perfection of giving' (ibid.: 117); the ascetic Kṣāntivādin, who endures with patience (*kṣānti*) the hacking off of his limbs by a jealous king (Warder 1990: 252); and Emperor Kaśapala, who consents for his body to be 'pierced with a thousand shafts and burnt with torches' in exchange for receiving instruction in the true teachings (*dharma*) (Frye 2006: 2). In all these cases the heroism of the buddha-to-be is symbolized by his detached attitude towards bodily life – the privileging of virtue above his own physical well-being. Even if, as Reiko Ohnuma has stressed, the Buddhist practitioner is expected not to 'foolishly try to imitate a literal gift of the body' but rather to cultivate 'the nonattachment and spirit of self-sacrifice that underlie the bodhisattva's deed' (2000: 66), Jātaka tales of the sort just outlined nevertheless provide a narrative backdrop against which bodily sacrifice gains a sense that it would otherwise have lacked. Borrowing a phrase from Charles Goodman, we might describe the resultant disposition as comprising 'both the noble altruism and the frightening extremism of Buddhist ethics' (2009: 52).

The motif of bodily sacrifice is prevalent, too, in non-narrative Buddhist teachings. The eighth-century Mahāyāna philosopher and monk Śāntideva, in expounding the way of life demanded of a bodhisattva, declares himself ready (and thereby enjoins others who wish to pursue the path to spiritual awakening) to 'give up everything' to alleviate the suffering of living beings (Śāntideva, *Bodhicaryāvatāra* 3.10 (1995: 21)). Perhaps alluding to the example of Prince Mahāsattva, who gave his body to the hungry tigress, Śāntideva vows to 'become both drink and food in the intermediate aeons of famine' (3.8). Although this latter affirmation lends itself to metaphorical interpretation as a commitment to assist those in need of nourishment, either physical or spiritual, Śāntideva remains vehement in his derogation of the body: 'I make over [my own] body to all embodied beings to do with as they please. Let them continually beat it, insult it, and splatter it with filth' (3.12). What they do with it, Śāntideva insists, is no concern of his (3.13).

The act of 'abandoning the body' has often taken a dramatically ritualized form: an extravagant gesture of self-renunciation described as an act of homage either to the Buddha or to some other personification of spiritual awakening. The practice of such abandonment specifically through burning oneself to death – referred to in modern literature as self-immolation or, less frequently, as auto-cremation[6] – receives its foremost narrative articulation in the *Lotus Sūtra* (c. first century BCE to third century CE), which has been described as perhaps 'the most influential book in all of premodern Asia' (Kieschnick 1997: 42). The *Lotus Sūtra's* twenty-third chapter tells of a former life not of the Buddha himself but of the Medicine King (*Bhaiṣajyarāja*); it ends with the King's anointing his body with aromatic oils, wrapping it in a jewelled garment and then setting himself alight as 'a

---

[6] It has been claimed that the term 'auto-cremation' is more precise than 'self-immolation' because the latter has often been used to denote a category that includes other methods of killing oneself in addition to death by fire (see Benn 2007, esp. 8; Plank 2016: 175). Early occurrences of the term 'auto-cremation' (or its French equivalent, *auto-crémation*) include Grady (1898: 231) and Lamotte (1965: 163; 1987: 113).

true Dharma-offering' to a buddha named 'Pure and Bright Excellence of Sun and Moon' (Hurvitz 1976: 295). This narrated performance on the part of the Medicine King, whose name in the life in question is 'Seen with Joy by All Living Beings', was subsequently invoked by numerous Buddhist monks, nuns and laypeople in China and other parts of East Asia who, through comparable acts of self-burning, sought to demonstrate their reverence for those who have achieved buddhahood (Benn 2007: 59). Traditional sources frequently declare that in addition to the auspicious rebirths or spiritual awakenings gained by the self-immolators, the sites of the burnings become loci for miraculous events such as healings, the spontaneous blossoming of flowers and the animation of statues (ibid.: 73).

Although Buddhist history since around the fourth century CE abounds with accounts of partial or complete self-burning, it was a specific series of incidents in the 1960s that brought to world attention the phenomenon of Buddhist voluntary death by fire and indelibly linked this practice with the term 'self-immolation' (Biggs 2006: 174). On 11 June 1963 a 66-year-old Buddhist monk named Thích Quảng Đức sat calmly in the middle of a Saigon road junction and set himself ablaze (Fig. 4.2), ostensibly as a response to repressive actions taken by the Vietnamese government against Buddhists in general and against pro-Buddhist campaigners in particular.[7] With American reporters and photographers amid the gathered crowd, a fellow monk proclaimed over a loudhailer in both Vietnamese and English, 'A Buddhist priest burns himself to death. A Buddhist priest becomes a martyr' (Halberstam 2008: 128–9). In haunting film footage now readily accessible via the internet (e.g. An Viên Television 2014), Quảng Đức's body is seen blackening and falling backwards as another monk kneels and bows before him in an attitude of veneration. The highly publicized nature of this incident constituted self-immolation's spectacular entry into 'the global vocabulary of politics and protest' (Shakya 2012b), inspiring either directly or indirectly many further deployments of the method – or iterations of its 'vocabulary' – over subsequent weeks, years and decades in diverse milieus.[8] It has also been widely interpreted, both by fellow Buddhists and by others, in terms of compassion. 'When you are motivated by love and the willingness

---

[7] Some commentators (e.g. Jones 2003: 268) assume Quảng Đức's age to have been 73, but it is fairly well attested that he was born in 1897 (Corfield 2013: 289).

[8] As Nora Alter (1995: 11) observes, 'Thich Quang Duc's dramatic (some said ultimate) form of protest was repeated at various times during the following years: a total of eight Americans immolated themselves between 1965 and 1970 [and we] may never know how many Vietnamese were to follow Quang Duc into the flames.'

Figure 4.2 Buddhist monk Thích Quảng Đức (1897–1963) committing self-immolation at an intersection in Saigon, South Vietnam, in protest against the anti-Buddhist measures of President Ngô Đình Diệm and his treatment of protestors, 11 June 1963. Photograph by Malcolm Browne. Granger / Bridgeman Images.

to help others attain understanding', wrote the well-known Vietnamese monk and peace campaigner Thích Nhất Hạnh, 'even self-immolation can be a compassionate act' (Nhat Hanh 1995: 81). Notwithstanding contrarian voices such as that of Stephen Prothero, whom I cited in the introduction to this chapter, the construal of self-immolation as compassionate sacrifice has been prevalent also in the Tibetan context, to which we now turn.

'Lamps of their precious bodies'

In response to the spate of self-immolations by Tibetan monks and nuns over the course of 2011,[9] the Tibetan musician Tashi Tsering composed a

---

[9] There were twelve self-immolation attempts in Tibet during 2011, ten of which were carried out by monks or former monks and two by nuns. Eight of the attempts are known to have resulted in death. The total number of self-immolation attempts in Tibetan areas from February 2009 to December 2018 stands at 155, the majority of which were carried out by laypeople. A further ten have been performed by Tibetans living in exile. For details, see International Campaign for Tibet (ICT) (2018).

song in which he praises 'Our heroes and heroines' who, 'by upholding Tibetans' heartfelt pride, offered lamps of their precious bodies' (quoted in Makley 2015: 463).[10] This same motif of making of one's body a lamp for others features in a tape-recorded message produced by Lama Sobha, the highest-ranking Buddhist monastic to have participated in the self-burnings thus far. Before drinking and dowsing his clothing with kerosene and setting himself alight on the morning of 8 January 2012 in the Chinese-controlled Golog Tibetan Autonomous Prefecture, Lama Sobha recorded the message in which he speaks of giving away his body 'as an offering of light to chase away the darkness, to free all beings from suffering, and to lead them – each of whom has been our mother in the past . . . – to the Amitabha, the Buddha of infinite light' (quoted in ICT 2012). Echoing Śāntideva's vow to 'be a light for those in need of light . . . a servant for those in need of service, for all embodied beings' (*Bodhicaryāvatāra* 3.18 (1995: 21)), Lama Sobha's words poignantly connect the phenomenon of Tibetan self-immolation with the bodhisattva ideal of altruistic self-renunciation.[11] Referring also to the Jātaka tale of Mahāsattva, which I mentioned briefly in the previous section, Lama Sobha's message declares his action to be one of bodily sacrifice 'with the firm conviction and a pure heart just as the Buddha bravely gave his body to a hungry tigress' (quoted in ICT 2012).[12]

Verbal and visual representations of the acts of self-burning carried out by Tibetans (e.g. Fig. 4.3) have themselves become embroiled in an interpretive battleground. When the Chinese authorities blocked occurrences of the term 'self-immolation' on the internet, young Tibetans adopted 'lamp offering' as a term to denote those who have committed the act in question: the phrase 'a lamp has been lit' was used 'to give voice to the religious meaning of these acts of self-sacrifice and offering' (Woeser 2016: 87). When outright suppression of information is not feasible, Chinese authorities have promoted media coverage that represents the self-immolators as lone criminals, sufferers from mental illness or impressionable young people

---

[10] The slightly different translation of these lines in Tsering (2011) reads: 'Our fearless martyrs / By upholding Tibetan's [*sic*] pride to heart / Offered lamps of their precious lives.'

[11] See also Woeser (2016: 27): 'Self-immolators are bodhisattvas sacrificing the self for others. . . .'

[12] With regard to the significance of the *Mahāsattva Jātaka* for Tibetan Buddhist ethics, John Whalen-Bridge remarks that 'in three decades of reading books by Tibetan Buddhist teachers and hearing talks, I do not remember the hungry tigress coming up once' (2015: 84). Against this, we might note the prominence of an artistic depiction of the Jātaka on the west wall of Pewar Buddhist monastery in Kham, eastern Tibet (Logan 2002: 87), and the popularity 'throughout Central and East Asia' (Cohen 2001: 149 n. 12) of the collection of Jātakas known as the *Sūtra of the Wise and the Foolish*, which includes the story of Mahāsattva.

Figure 4.3 'Burning Tibet', bronze sculpture by Chinese artist Chen Weiming, 2014; a memorial to Tibetans who have died in self-immolations in protest at the Chinese occupation of Tibet. Located at the H. H. Dalai Lama Main Temple, Dharamsala, India. Photograph by Paul Kennedy / Alamy Stock Photo.

manipulated by the 'Dalai clique' (China Tibet Online 2012; Associated Press 2012) – the term 'Dalai clique' being a dysphemism for the Central Tibetan Administration (or 'Tibetan government-in-exile') based at Dharamsala in northern India. Tibetans who sympathize with the actions, by contrast, routinely refer to those who carry them out as *pawo* (*dpa' bo*, masc.) or *pamo* (*dpa' mo*, fem.). These terms translate as 'hero' and 'heroine' respectively (Buswell and Lopez 2014: 209, 979; Diemberger 2005: 128), though Tibetans who speak English often render them provocatively as 'martyr' (Buffetrille 2012: 10–11). In the light of terminological and ideological issues such as these, John Whalen-Bridge (2015) speaks of the 'rhetoric of self-immolation'. By this he means not to denigrate or trivialize the acts or the debate surrounding them but rather to emphasize the sense in which designating an act as one of self-immolation – as opposed to, say, 'political self-murder' – is integral to a rhetorical strategy on the part of Tibetan campaigners aiming to build group solidarity as well as to elicit support from outsiders (see esp. Whalen-Bridge 2015: 6–7).

We might connect the latter point to the observation that many concepts are 'thick' in Bernard Williams' sense of this term, to which I referred briefly in Chapter 2 (p. 64 *ante*); this is to say that their use typically carries evaluative as well as descriptive weight (see Williams 1985). The concepts of honesty, bravery and heroism are cases in point, and so may be the concepts of self-immolation and self-sacrifice, which have often been treated as having connotations different from those of the concept of suicide. Thích Nhất Hạnh was well aware of these connotations when, in an open letter to Martin Luther King Jr, first published in 1965, he distinguished between suicide and the 'self-burning of Vietnamese Buddhist monks' that had taken place a couple of years earlier. The former, he proposes, 'is an act of self-destruction' precipitated by loss of hope and an inability to contend with life's difficulties, whereas the latter consists in suffering and dying 'for the sake of one's people' (Nhat Hanh 1967: 106–7).

Since talk of compassion, too, is a mode of discourse charged with political as well as ethical and religious ramifications, we might again usefully invoke the idea of the 'rhetoric of compassion'. Ṭhānissaro Bhikkhu (2010: 27) has applied this phrase to the words of the Buddha himself, remarking that the Buddha's style of teaching can be described in these terms because he deployed his words judiciously, 'skillfully', to engender a certain movement of thought and attitude in his audience. Beyond this usage, however, what I have in mind is the sense in which describing acts as motivated by compassion is itself a rhetorical manoeuvre. In this sense, Ṭhānissaro's own description of the Buddha's pedagogical methods as compassionate is an instance of the rhetoric of compassion, for the description is designed to persuade readers to view those methods in a favourable light. Likewise, to affirm, as Tenzin Dorjee does, that those Tibetans who have immolated themselves 'have shown compassion beyond our imagination' is to utilize the concept of compassion in a strategic manner, as a polemical move in a conflict over how the acts should be conceptualized. Prothero, as we have seen, resists the description of the acts as compassionate. By asking 'where is the compassion here?', he both questions the purportedly compassionate nature of the acts themselves and implies that the Dalai Lama has fallen short of Buddhism's compassionate ethic by failing to condemn them. Meanwhile, some Tibetans have also espoused alternative articulations of the acts: not because they wish to express criticism, but rather because they feel that the emphasis on compassion downplays the extent to which these acts, fuelled by a 'sense of marginalisation' among the Tibetan people, are best viewed 'as a demonstration of collective disaffection and rage at their conditions' (Shakya 2012a: 38).

Whether the self-immolations are motivated by compassion or by rage is considered by some to be a matter of deep importance for the question of whether they can be construed as genuinely Buddhist acts. In April 1998, Thubten Ngodrup, a 60-year-old former monk and former soldier living in exile in Delhi, became the first Tibetan to set himself on fire as a form of protest. He did so as Indian police were breaking up a hunger strike organized by the Tibetan Youth Congress.[13] The following day, as Ngodrup lay dying in a Delhi hospital, he was visited by the Dalai Lama, who said to him: 'Do not pass over with hatred for the Chinese in your heart. You are brave and you made your statement, but let not your motive be hatred' (quoted in Bartholet 2012). Elsewhere the Dalai Lama has reiterated the point, remarking that if an act of burning oneself to death is motivated by 'too much anger, hatred, then [it is] negative', whereas 'if the motivation [is] more compassionate' and the act is performed with a 'calm mind', then it may be 'positive' (Times Now 2013). This, of course, is precisely the kind of ambivalence that those who share Prothero's view are apt to regard as evasive equivocation. While the Dalai Lama's insistence on the crucial role of motivation in determining an action's moral valence is consistent with a mainstream view of Buddhist ethics (see Keown 1992: 178–9), the issue of whether self-killing can ever be justified by reference to Buddhist principles remains fiercely disputed.[14]

There is much else that could be discussed in connection with the Tibetan self-immolations, not least the way in which their profoundly unsettling nature – eliciting what one observer has identified as the disturbing combination of '[f]ascination and disgust' (Warner 2012) – disrupts attempts to do justice to these acts in an academic register at all. Also of vital importance is the socio-political and historical context in which the acts are occurring; for, notwithstanding the efforts of the Communist Party of China to paint a different picture, there is no doubt that the self-immolations are responses to the sustained repression of the Tibetan people, which has frequently been described in terms of cultural genocide (Tsering 1997;

---

[13] For thorough discussion of the incident, including the context of the hunger strike and its relation to issues of nonviolent protest more generally, see Ardley (2002: Ch. 3). For harrowing video footage of the event, see TA (2012).

[14] See, e.g., the debate in the *Journal of Law and Religion* involving Keown (1998–99), Harvey (1998–99) and Florida (1998–99).

Novic 2016: 1). Here, however, my principal purpose, as in this chapter as a whole, has been to emphasize the complexity of Buddhist conceptions of compassion. Although the importance of a compassionate motivation or intention (*cetanā*) assuredly has a central place across multiple formulations of Buddhist ethics, how that motivation or intention may legitimately manifest is a contested matter. Acts involving the agent's own death are one especially contentious area; another is the broader issue of whether, under certain circumstances, basic Buddhist principles such as the prohibition on lying and on committing violence against others may be reinterpreted and transformed in the light of the doctrine of 'skilful means'. I shall turn to that issue in the next section.

Transgressive compassion and skilful means

Translations of the Sanskrit term *upāya kauśalya* (which is sometimes abbreviated as simply *upāya*) include, among others, 'skilful means' (Pye 2003), 'skill in means' (Tatz 1994), 'tactful methods' (Katō et al. 1975) and 'expedient devices' (Hurvitz 1976).[15] Although not exclusively a Mahāyāna concept,[16] the idea or doctrine of skilful means has received extensive elaboration in various Mahāyāna texts and traditions. The overarching feature of this doctrine is the principle that, provided a practitioner has attained a sufficiently high degree of wisdom, he or she may, out of compassion for others, perform actions that are ostensibly in breach of standard Buddhist ethical precepts. Thus, for example, an accomplished teacher of the dharma, and hence *a fortiori* the Buddha himself, may adapt the teachings in accordance with the level of understanding possessed by the audience, even if this involves offering a rendition that is merely partial, provisional or, ultimately, false (Ziporyn 2000: 153). The locus classicus of this contention is the *Lotus Sūtra*, in which the apparent falsity of an assertion is said to be cancelled out if the motive is good, such as when a father entices his children out of a burning house by telling them that their favourite

---

[15] The Pāli is *upāya kosalla*; equivalents in Chinese include *fang pien*, in Japanese *hōben* and in Tibetan *thabs la mkhas pa* (Powers 2000: 231).
[16] For discussion of relevant pre-Mahāyāna examples from the Pāli Canon, see Pye (2003: Ch. 7) and McFarlane (2006: 157–8).

playthings are waiting for them outside when in fact they are not (at least initially); under such circumstances the father would not be guilty of deception because his intention is to expedite the children's escape (Hurvitz 1976: 64). More controversial than this are the examples of skilful means that involve violence or killing in the name of compassion.

A widely cited story illustrative of the complexities of compassionate killing occurs in the *Upāyakauśalya Sūtra* (*c.* first century BCE; Tatz 1994: 1, 8). It tells of a bodhisattva named Mahākāruṇika ('Great Compassionate') – held to be the Buddha in one of his former lives – who, when captaining a ship carrying five hundred merchants, learns by means of a divinely inspired dream that there is a thief on board who is planning to rob and kill all five hundred passengers (Tatz 1994: 73). The Captain considers informing the merchants, but dismisses this option because he fears they would kill the would-be thief out of anger and thereby condemn themselves to hell. After much deliberation, he decides that he himself should kill the thief. By doing so, he prevents both the thief and the merchants having to suffer the torments of hell and takes on that suffering himself (74). As it turns out, the Captain is not reborn in a hell realm; the only apparent ill effect of killing the thief is that in his life as the Buddha he steps on an acacia thorn, which pierces his foot. In a further twist to the story, however, the *Upāyakauśalya Sūtra* declares that even this incident is not really a consequence of the Buddha's having killed the thief in a past life; it is yet another instance of skilful means: the Buddha presents his stepping on the thorn as though it were a result of the previous action, but does so solely in order to teach the law of retributive karma. By performatively demonstrating the karmic law in this way, he opens the eyes of thousands of creatures to the dharma and persuades twenty potential murderers in his assembled audience to forego their murderous ambitions (76–7). As Stephen Jenkins has pointed out (2011: 317), the story of the ship's captain is thus misinterpreted if it is viewed as showing that the act of killing has generated, as Peter Harvey puts it, 'various bad karmic consequences, though not as bad as if it had not been done with such a compassionate motivation' (Harvey 2000: 136). On the contrary, the compassionate motivation completely transforms what would otherwise have been a karmicly disastrous action into a thoroughly benevolent one with favourable outcomes for all concerned, both 'victim' and 'perpetrator'.

Other narrative sources, especially some of those depicting the lives of great Tantric yogins or siddhas ('perfected ones'), contain examples of compassionate violence that are more extreme than that of the ship's captain. As Paul Williams observes, 'The *siddha*'s actions may shock, may be antinomian; he or she is a person of power operating for the benefit of beings from the position of a Buddha, behind and beyond all laws' (2009: 188). For instance, in a hagiography of Padmasambhava (Fig. 4.4), who is revered among Tibetan Buddhists for having converted Tibet 'into a realm of Dharma' in the late eighth century (Lin 2003: 150), we find tales of his conversion methods that appear to revel in subverting expectations of how a Buddhist adept should behave. In one particular episode, Padmasambhava, referred to in the story as 'the prince' (*rgyal sras*), has been living in a charnel ground, practising yogic techniques, clothing himself in the flayed skin of human corpses and eating their flesh for food (Tsogyal 1993: 39). Learning of a despotic king named Śakrarāja whose tyrannical reign is forcing his subjects to act in ways that doom them to rebirth in 'the lower realms', the prince determines that the only way to convert them is by means of subjugation and 'wrathful activity' (ibid.). The text then recounts how Padmasambhava embarks on a mission that involves slaughtering every male that he meets, devouring their flesh and drinking their blood, and 'unit[ing] with all the females', thereby bringing everyone under his control and gaining the title Rākṣasa Demon (ibid.). While we should not overlook the possibility of more or less elaborate allegorical interpretations of a story

Figure 4.4 Padmasambhava. 135 ft tall statue on Samdruptse Hill, Namchi, Sikkim, Northeast India. Dinodia Photos / Alamy Stock Photo.

such as this,[17] the fact that on the face of it Padmasambhava, who is considered by the Nyingma school of Tibetan Buddhism to be 'an embodiment of the compassion of all the buddhas of the ten directions' (Rangdröl 1993: 16), is portrayed as enacting his compassion by means of rape, cannibalism and massacres should alert us, once again, to the complexity of conceptions of compassion in Buddhist traditions.

Concluding remarks

Although the episode from a life-story of Padmasambhava summarized in the last section is an extreme case, the principle of transgressive compassion, according to which spiritually accomplished individuals may transgress standard Buddhist moral precepts whenever they deem it appropriate, is a prevalent doctrine in Mahāyāna Buddhism. As Śāntideva puts it, 'Even what is proscribed is permitted for a compassionate person who sees it will be of benefit' (*Bodhicaryāvatāra* 5.84 (1995: 41)) – the compassionate person being, of course, the bodhisattva who, as the earlier philosopher and ethicist Asaṅga (fourth century CE) asserts, acts with 'superior wisdom and skillful means' (2003: 86).[18] The doctrine of skilful means has undoubtedly been pivotal in opening up the possibility of construing virtually any action as potentially compassionate insofar as it could conceivably be done with compassionate intent. Questions might be raised here about whether it *is* genuinely conceivable that an act of rape or murder be motivated by compassion, or whether we lose our grip on what 'compassion' could mean in such circumstances. Were we to pursue that line of questioning further, we should also need to inquire more deeply into what purposes are served by the kinds of narratives involving the extreme antinomian antics of yogins and siddhas – an inquiry that would require more than a single chapter to prosecute.

As I have emphasized, my own principal purpose has been, by assembling illustrative examples, to demonstrate the heterogeneity of Buddhist conceptions of compassion, a heterogeneity that casts doubt upon facile

---

[17] 'There is a systematic tendency in the Tantric tradition for scholarly monastic exegetes to try to reinterpret the outrageously antinomian features of Tantric texts as metaphors for internal meditative processes' (Goodman 2009: 229 n. 22).
[18] Other highly regarded Mahāyāna philosophers who endorse this point include Vasubandhu, Āryadeva, Bhāviveka and Candrakīrti (see Jenkins 2011: 309–10).

claims to the effect that compassion constitutes the essence or core of Buddhist ethics. It calls such claims into question not by showing them to be false, but rather by destabilizing the assumption that we know what 'compassion' and its non-English equivalents (or near-equivalents) signify across multiple Buddhist contexts. Even if we admit that Buddhist traditions almost universally accentuate the importance of a compassionate motive or intention, this admission does not take us very far towards comprehending what such a motive or intention consists in. Developing that comprehension would require looking to particular texts and traditions to see what 'acting from a compassionate motive' comes to in those specific places. And by acknowledging that attention to particulars is necessary, we recognize that talk of compassion as Buddhism's 'heart' or 'essence' can, at most, be only a starting point, a spur to investigating the plurality that confronts us.

So too, then, is it unhelpful to assume that we know very well what is being said when it is claimed that compassion constitutes the 'shared territory' or 'chief religious virtue' or 'moral ideal' of all religions or 'all the great traditions'. Again, at best such claims are a point of departure, and probably a misleading one at that. For those whose principal goal is to promote a normative agenda according to which all religions, and perhaps all people whether religious or not, share some basic set of values, talking in sweeping terms about essences and common ideals may be pragmatically astute. But if our aim is to deepen and enrich our understanding of religion in all its messy variety rather than of merely one aspect of it, then keeping an eye out for the differences as well as for the similarities is a crucial part of the task.

In this chapter we have drawn upon multiple Buddhist sources to consider the complex concept of compassion. The next chapter turns primarily to ethnographic studies of an indigenous community in western Brazil to illustrate how attitudes of compassion and respect may be seen in forms of action that many are liable to regard as surprising, even shocking – notably, the eating of human corpses.

5

'Ways of Being Human': Cannibalism and Respecting the Dead

Like the many priests, missionaries, colonial officers, and others who considered cannibalism antithetical to what it means to be human, scholars who insist that all accounts of cannibalism must be false seem to assume that cannibalism is by definition a terrible act – so terrible, in fact, that it could only have been invented by those with damaging ulterior motives. They appear blind to the possibility that people different from themselves might have other ways of being human, other understandings of the body, or other ways of coping with death that might make cannibalism seem a good thing to do.

(Conklin 2001: 6)

In an ethnographic study of the Wari' people of western Brazil, Beth Conklin argues against the tendency among certain scholars to infer that because allegations of cannibalism have sometimes served political interests, all attributions of cannibalism must therefore be sheer inventions – products of the colonial imagination used to derogate the indigenous inhabitants of regions targeted for imperialist exploitation. Notwithstanding the well-meaning ideological motivations of scholars who maintain that cannibalism is a mere myth, anthropologists such as Conklin have shown that this attitude of denial is itself based on fantasy. The fact is that cannibalism – the eating of human bodies in whole or in part by other human beings – has occurred in a variety of forms among numerous communities throughout history and across the world. Sometimes it has been forced upon people when other forms of sustenance are unavailable; in a small number of instances, which have gained considerable notoriety, it has been carried out to satisfy a sadistic sexual craving on the part of the killer; but in the vast majority of cases it has been an integral component of a culture, one feature of a form of life – a way of being human.

The subject of cannibalism affords a poignant focus for exploring what Peter Winch, in a well-known essay first published in 1964, encourages not only anthropologists but also philosophers to explore, namely the diverse ways of 'making sense of human life' (Winch 1964: 321). 'What we may learn by studying other cultures', Winch writes, 'are not merely possibilities of different ways of doing things, other techniques.' Beyond this, he continues, 'we may learn different possibilities of making sense of human life, different ideas about the possible importance that the carrying out of certain activities may take on', not least for someone 'trying to contemplate the sense of his life as a whole' (ibid.). For many philosophers, it will not be obvious why exploring diverse conceptions of human life should be an activity in which philosophers ought to engage. Mere exploration, or observation and description, of forms and conceptions of human life are, they might think, tasks for sociologists and anthropologists, whereas philosophy is concerned with issues of truth and evaluation – determining which conception is the correct one. The proper task of philosophy remains, however, an open question. As I acknowledged in Chapter 2, many philosophers do indeed consider matters of truth and evaluation to be their main interest, yet there are alternative visions of philosophy that accentuate the elucidation of possibilities of sense, which include, precisely, possible ways of making sense of human life. By investigating these possibilities, we enlarge our appreciation of what it is to be a human being, and hence of what it is to be the kind of beings we are. Such investigations do not, of course, preclude the asking of questions about rightness or correctness, about which of the many possible and indeed actual 'ways of being human' is to be preferred, whether for epistemic or ethical or pragmatic reasons. But they do serve to refocus attention in such a way that it becomes the sheer variety – what I am calling in this book the radical plurality – of forms and conceptions of human life that takes priority. Instead of rushing to arbitrate between them in the name of some supposedly universal standard of rationality or truth, one abides with the phenomena themselves, noticing their particularities without hastily subsuming them under a general theory: pausing to wonder at the differences rather than always seeking the common essence. This is integral to a contemplative conception of philosophy in general and to a radical pluralist approach to the philosophy of religion in particular.

My task in this chapter is to contemplate the heterogeneous nature of human life through an examination of the variegated phenomenon of cannibalism. If we wish to test the limits of a contemplative approach to philosophy, then cannibalism is an apt topic to select, as the eating of people has routinely been characterized as a paradigmatically aberrant (not to mention abhorrent) form of human behaviour: something that, epitomizing the depths of depravity, is beyond the pale of imaginative empathy and moral comprehension. If we can come to see that cannibalism is not all one kind of thing – that it is in fact many kinds of thing – then we shall have enriched our understanding of a surprisingly prevalent aspect of human life. And if, in this process, we come to see a possible sense in (some forms of) cannibalism – a way in which cannibalism makes, or has made, sense for some people at some times – then, I suggest, we shall have enlarged our conception of what it is to be human.

Our point of departure will be a discussion by Cora Diamond of why, she thinks, it is essential in moral debates surrounding the treatment of animals to recognize that the very concept of a human being, unlike the concept of a nonhuman animal, includes the notion that such a being 'is not something to eat' (1978: 468). From there I proceed to examine the idea of cannibalism, with a view to explicating a range of ways of understanding human beings in which the possibility of a person's being something to eat is not excluded. The most sustained part of my discussion draws upon the example of the Wari', whom Conklin in particular has investigated so insightfully and sensitively. I propose that examples such as this, in addition to expanding our conception of the heterogeneity of human life and of human religious practices, also demonstrate how much scope there is for productive mutual engagement between philosophy and anthropology in engendering that expanded conception.

Eating animals but not eating people?

In one of her best-known essays on the ethical treatment of animals, 'Eating Meat and Eating People', Cora Diamond argues that if one's aim is to convince people that eating animals is morally wrong, it is misguided to try to argue that this is because animals share certain purely physiological or cognitive properties with human beings, such as the ability to suffer pain and distress. This is misguided, Diamond maintains, because it ignores something essential about the very concept of a human being, which is that human beings are conceptualized, in large part, in contrast to animals. Crucially, a central way in which humans are distinguished from animals is that unlike animals – or, at any rate, unlike many of them – human beings are not something to be eaten by us. Hence one of the ways in which '[w]e learn what a human being is' is by sitting down to meals at which we are the eaters and animals are among the items to be eaten: 'We are around the table and they are on it' (Diamond 1978: 470). In view of this fact, Diamond contends, the force of any argumentative strategy that relies on highlighting certain physiological or cognitive capacities possessed by animals will be extremely limited, since it is, as it were, built into the very meanings of the terms 'animal' and 'human being' that the former may be eaten and the latter may not.

Diamond's alternative proposal is to look to literature, especially poetry, for exemplifications of how certain specifically moral concepts might be extended to embrace animals within their ambit. Thus, for example, by exhibiting how a bird might be seen as 'happy company' and a 'tiny son of life', Walter de la Mare's poem 'Titmouse' (1941: 124) facilitates the extension of concepts such as those of friendship and kinship beyond the human sphere – an extension that is prefigured in other places, such as Robert Burns's 'To a Mouse', in which the poem's narrator describes himself as the mouse's 'poor, earth-born companion' and 'fellow-mortal' (Burns 1947: 71; see Diamond 1978: 473–4). What Diamond's discussion endeavours to foster is the recognition that moral values and attitudes are unlikely to be transformed by appeals to concepts that are not themselves already morally resonant. It is precisely because the literary works she cites are operating with distinctively moral concepts, as opposed to concepts of biological or cognitive science, that, on Diamond's account, they are capable of nurturing what she elsewhere calls an enlargement of 'the reader's moral and emotional sensibilities' (1982: 30).

Whatever one thinks of the general account of moral transformation that informs Diamond's argument, one might have concerns about the way in which she characterizes the concept of a human being. Indeed, one might have concerns about the very idea that there is a single unified concept of a human being at all, supposing instead that what it is to be human and to live a human life amounts to many different things across diverse times and places. In short, one might suspect that treating as homogeneous the concept of the human is a temptation to be resisted,[1] and this suspicion is liable to be accentuated when one considers the decidedly moral weight that Diamond attributes to the concept and the role that she accords to it in considerations of what is and what is not to be eaten. Even if, as Diamond sometimes does, one were to use phrases such as 'our concept' or 'our notion' in place of '*the* concept', this would be unlikely to ameliorate the impression of undue homogenizing, especially when the scope of 'our' is left unspecified.

There are in fact resources within Diamond's own discussion for encouraging the recognition of conceptual complexity and thereby problematizing the suggestion of a homogeneous concept of the human. When talking about human dietary behaviour, for instance, Diamond notes that 'a lot of different cases' are covered by the basic idea of eating animals (1978: 471). Among the cases it covers are those of people who raise and look after the well-being of animals prior to killing them for food, as well as those of people who merely purchase prewrapped pieces of meat from the supermarket. On the thinnest description, these two cohorts of people both eat animals, but the contexts diverge dramatically. A comparable acknowledgement of plurality might be applied to the concept (or concepts) of a human being and, moreover, to the concept of eating people. These also cover 'a lot of different cases' – too many for it to be more than a parochial observation that our not eating them is among the factors that signally contribute to an understanding of what human beings are. To elaborate this point, let us consider the notion of cannibalism and some of the various forms that eating people, or parts of their bodies, has taken.

---

[1] This point is emphasized in Phillips (1992), which is itself in large part a response to ideas expressed in Diamond (1988).

Varieties of cannibalism

The first occurrence of the Spanish word *canibales* is generally attributed to an entry in Christopher Columbus's diary dated 23 November 1492, the surviving evidence for which is an abridged copy written in the 1530s by the historian and Dominican friar Bartolomé de las Casas (Dunn and Kelley 1989: 4). The abridged entry reports Columbus's being told by certain Arawak Indians whom he had picked up on his travels that the inhabitants of an island named Bohío included some 'called cannibals [*canibales*]', who eat people and are 'very well armed' (Las Casas 1989 [1530]: 167). It appears that Columbus did not simply take his Indian informants' claim for granted, for the entry proceeds to suggest that the accusation of people-eating may have resulted from some of the Arawak merely having been captured by the island's inhabitants: since those who had been captured had not returned to their homelands, their fellows 'would say that [the cannibals] ate them' (ibid.).[2]

Although the most direct verbal source of 'cannibals' appears to be the Arawak term *caniba* (itself a version of *cariba*, the self-designation of certain people of the Lesser Antilles), it has been speculated that Columbus conflated this with the Latin term for 'dog' (*canis*), a conflation encouraged by his Arawak informants' having described their purportedly people-eating enemies as being endowed with 'snouts of dogs' (*hoçicos de perros*) (Las Casas 1989: 132, 133).[3] Adding to the etymological intricacy is the fact that Columbus identifies the Caniba with 'the people of the Grand Khan' (*la gente del Gran Can*) (Las Casas 1989: 217), this being an appellation borrowed from Marco Polo, who had used it to denote the people of the Mongol Empire. Believing that his voyage had, as was intended, brought him to the eastern coastline of Asia, Columbus was under the impression that the region over which Kublai Khan had ruled in the thirteenth century was nearby (see Tokumitsu 2015: 99; Gužauskytė 2014: 73). Notwithstanding these confused origins, over the course of the sixteenth century 'cannibal' gradually supplanted older terms such as 'anthropophagi' and 'androphagi' ('human-eaters'), the latter of which had been used by Herodotus (fifth century BCE) to designate a nomadic group with 'manners ... more savage than those of any other race' who reside somewhere to the north of Greece,

---

[2] For further discussion, see Hulme (1986, esp. Ch. 1).
[3] For discussion, see Lestringant (1997: 15–22).

on the far side of the Black Sea (*Historiae* 4.106 (1859: 94)).[4] The term 'cannibal' has remained in common usage to this day, and in modern anthropology the category of cannibalism has come to be subdivided into several varieties, the most salient of which I shall outline below.[5]

An initial distinction can be made between, on the one hand, normative or institutionalized cannibalism, which is part of a cultural system or way of life, and on the other hand, non-normative forms that are out of step with the standard values of the culture in which they occur. In the latter category belongs the survival cannibalism or hunger cannibalism that is resorted to under conditions of extreme food scarcity by people who would normally reject the eating of human flesh, a well-documented case being that of the survivors of Uruguayan Air Force Flight 571, which crashed in the Andes mountains in October 1972 (see Read 1974). A second variety of non-normative cannibalism is that pursued by lone individuals who prey on vulnerable people, kidnapping and murdering them before consuming parts of their bodies, typically to satisfy a desire for power or sexual gratification. The widespread public fascination with such individuals, catered to by lurid books and films documenting their troubled lives (e.g. Brottman 2001), is a remarkable phenomenon in itself, though it is not among my main concerns in this chapter.

The principal category in which social or cultural anthropology has been interested is what I above termed normative or institutionalized cannibalism, which itself is commonly divided into *exocannibalism* and *endocannibalism*, a distinction apparently originated by Rudolf Steinmetz (1896). Exocannibalism is the consumption of the bodies or body parts of people from outside one's own society and is normally associated with intergroup rivalry and conflict. In a study of the Baktaman people of New Guinea, for example, Fredrik Barth documents how 'cannibalism is an escalation of the war against the enemy, and is done in anger and lust for revenge' (1975: 152). Endocannibalism, meanwhile, is the consumption of

---

[4] Cf. Motohashi (1999: 87). See also Pliny the Elder's *Natural History* (77–79 CE), in which 'certain tribes of the Scythians, and, indeed, many other nations' are referred to as eaters of human flesh or 'Anthropophagi' (*Naturalis Historia* 7.2 (1855–57), vol. II: 122, 122 n. 29; see also 4.26 (vol. I: 335) and 6.20 (vol. II: 36)).

[5] The anthropologist Carlos Fausto has proposed a distinction between cannibalism and anthropophagy: 'cannibalism' denotes the eating (literally *or* symbolically) of persons who are regarded as agents with intentionality and subjectivity, whereas 'anthropophagy' denotes the eating of human bodies that are regarded as desubjectivized objects or 'merely food' (see Fausto 2007, esp. 504, 508). Although this conceptual distinction is significant, Fausto's particular terminological stipulation has not been widely adopted and I shall not be utilizing it here.

the bodies or body parts of people from within one's society, often from one's own kinship group in the context of a funerary or mortuary practice (Goldman 1999: 14). A third category that is sometimes added is *autocannibalism*, the phenomenon of someone, normally under extreme duress, eating part of his or her own body. Gertrude Dole, who appears to have coined the term (1962: 567), cites an article by Ales Hrdlička in which it is stated that certain Amerindians of Canada and New York would torture their prisoners by forcing them to eat pieces of their own flesh (see Hrdlička 1907: 201).

Both exo- and endocannibalism (but not autocannibalism) occurred until the 1960s among the Wari' studied by Conklin and others, and hence I shall elaborate these forms in my discussion of the Wari' in the next section. Before coming to that discussion, though, one further type of cannibalism that ought to be mentioned, however briefly, is what has been termed *medicinal cannibalism*, which involves consuming products made from human bodies for medicinal or pharmacological purposes. One reason why this practice is especially noteworthy is that it was widespread in Europe from the sixteenth to eighteenth centuries and, as several researchers have pointed out, 'was not limited to fringe groups of society, but was practiced in the most respectable circles' (Gordon-Grube 1988: 406; see also Himmelman 1997). Although it will not be my main focus here, the prevalence of this 'corpse pharmacology'[6] in the early modern West goes a long way towards undermining certain stereotypes about cannibalism, such as the conception of it as an exclusively non-Western or premodern phenomenon – an exotic curiosity typifying the otherness of supposedly 'primitive' or 'uncivilized' peoples. In fact, cannibalism, at least in this medicinal form, has had a notable presence in Western culture.

Wari' ways of respecting the dead

To introduce the theme of alternative forms that respect for the dead can take, let me begin with an observation from Wittgenstein. In some of his notes on James Frazer's *The Golden Bough*, Wittgenstein muses upon the variegated nature of human ritual actions. At one place, to illustrate the point, he invites his imagined reader to recall that following Franz Schubert's

---

[6] For the term 'corpse pharmacology', see Noble (2004; 2011: 2 *et passim*).

death, some of his scores were cut up by one of Schubert's brothers, who then gave pieces comprising a few bars each to Schubert's favourite pupils. Wittgenstein, regarding this as an act of piety on the brother's part, then adds that the act is no less comprehensible to us than would be an alternative such as preserving the scores in a pristine and inaccessible condition. Moreover, 'if Schubert's brother had burned the scores, that too would be understandable as a sign of piety' (Wittgenstein 1993: 127). Regardless of how much truth there is in the anecdote itself – and, as it happens, it seems that there is some truth in it[7] – Wittgenstein's point is to draw attention not only to the variety of forms that an act of pious respect for the dead might take, but also to the variety of acts in which we may readily recognize such piety. Wittgenstein maintains that, at least in many cases, it is a mistake to go searching for a rationale to explain why such acts are performed, for it is likely that they originate from a source so deep in human nature that it makes more sense to think of that source as an instinctive reaction than as an intellectual rationale. Any putative rationale that is given, even by the agent himself or herself, may be viewed as something accompanying the ritual or indeed as part of the ritual, but to view it as the underlying reason why the ritual is performed would be to over-intellectualize what is going on. As Wittgenstein puts it at one point: 'the characteristic feature of ritualistic action is not at all a view, an opinion, whether true or false, although an opinion – a belief – can itself be ritualistic or part of a rite' (1993: 129).

My reason for beginning this section with the above ideas of Wittgenstein's is that the orientation of Wittgenstein's thinking helps to free us from the assumption that for something to count as a way of respecting the dead, it must take a certain form. Just as various ways of treating a dead composer's manuscripts may all be signs of respect, so too can respect be shown through various ways of disposing of the body of the deceased. The mistake would be to take the narrow selection with which one is already familiar – such as, perhaps, cremating the corpse or placing it in a coffin and burying it in the ground – as not merely typifying but veritably exhausting the range of possibilities. Importantly, it should also be recognized that what counts for one group of people as an expression of respect may look to another like an affront to decency. Thus someone might at first assume that cutting up a dead composer's manuscripts or burning them must be a means of expressing disdain for the composer, whereas locking the manuscripts away where no

---

[7] The brother in question was Schubert's half-brother Pater Hermann Schubert (see Smallshaw 2015).

one can access them must constitute a gesture of respect. But which, if any, of these acts is the expression of disdain and which is the gesture of respect will depend on the surroundings. That is, it will depend on what goes along with the act and on what precedes and follows it: the context that imbues the action with the meaning that it has and thereby makes it the action it is. What I wish to add to Wittgenstein's point is that, in the case of practices that occur in societies very different from one's own, becoming sufficiently familiar with the surroundings is apt to require, if not spending time in the society oneself, then at least giving careful attention to available ethnographic accounts of the people concerned.

Now let us turn to the Wari'. They are a people, numbering a little over two thousand, who live primarily in the north-western Brazilian state of Rondônia, which is just to the northeast of Bolivia. Commonly known to outsiders as the Pakaa Nova – a term derived from Pacaás Novos, the Portuguese name for one of Rondônia's many rivers – this group of people are now referred to in anthropological literature by their own indigenous term *Wari'* (pronounced wah-*REE*), which is their first-person plural inclusive emphatic pronoun, equivalent to 'We!' and implying 'human beings' or 'people' (Everett and Kern 1997: ix, 295; Conklin 2001: xv; Vilaça 2010: 99). Prior to the mid-1950s they had violently resisted any involvement with people of European descent, but this began to change from 1956 onwards when they sought outside assistance to help reconstruct their society (Vilaça 2010: 2, 5–6). Unfortunately, the closer interaction with outsiders introduced new contagious diseases into the Wari' community that resulted in massive epidemics. It also led to significant cultural changes, including changes to mortuary customs.

Until the early 1960s, cannibalism had been common in Wari' society, and it had taken two very distinct forms. On the one hand was Wari' warfare cannibalism, a form of exocannibalism perpetrated against enemy groups in acts of aggression and revenge. Having been killed and procured through combat, the enemies' bodies would be dismembered and brought back to the Wari' village to be eaten by other members of the community as a deliberate expression of supremacy over the vanquished adversaries (Conklin 2001: 32–3; Vilaça 2000, esp. 90–2). On the other hand was Wari' funerary or mortuary cannibalism, a form of endocannibalism that is described by the Wari' elders who remember it as enacting respect, affection and compassion for the dead (Conklin 2001, esp. 81, 97). It is mainly upon this latter form of cannibalism that I shall focus in the remainder of this chapter.

Wari' funerals would typically be carried out some days after the death of the person, and hence the corpse would already be starting to fester. Eating the body, or substantial parts of it, was perceived as an act of compassionate duty rather than as a pleasure – a duty performed by the affines (in-laws) of the deceased both for the deceased person and for his or her consanguines (blood relatives) as a means of easing their sorrow (ibid.: xviii, 94). The cutting of the body was accompanied by vocal effusions of grief, which has sometimes been 'explained' by the Wari' themselves as helping to deter the deceased's ghost from remaining near at hand. The whole practice of consuming the body is couched by the Wari' in terms of facilitating a more thorough relinquishment of emotional attachments to the deceased by ritually eliminating the bodily object of mourning. To the same end, the practice was complemented by the burning of the deceased's possessions, including his or her house (ibid.: xxi–xxii, 84).

In stark contrast to the types of burial practices characteristic of many other cultures, including that of the Protestant missionaries who laboured to prohibit mortuary cannibalism both among the Wari' and among other South American indigenous peoples, it was regarded by the Wari' as important that no part of the corpse be allowed to enter or even touch the earth, for the earth was associated with dirt and pollution – a cold and damp place to which neither the body nor even any of its substances should be abandoned (ibid.: 57–8).[8] To prevent its fluids flowing onto the ground as the corpse was dismembered, a close relative would sometimes lie prone beneath it with the corpse resting on his back (Conklin 2001: 79). In cases where the deceased happened to be a child, as its body was being roasted over a fire its parents or grandparents would prevent the melting fat from falling into the fire by catching it in a clay pot, from which, 'as an expression of love', they would 'smear the child's fat over their own heads, hair, and bodies as they cried' (81).

Unlike animal meat, which the Wari' would hold with their hands, the human flesh eaten at funerals was held on thin splinters of wood. The blood relatives of the deceased would separate the flesh from the bones, sometimes placing it into a pot cradled in the lap, 'in the loving position in which Wari' support relatives' heads in illness or when grooming or comforting someone' (83). The flesh would be distributed to the affines, who would eat it unhurriedly and reverentially along with corn bread, interspersing the eating

---

[8] Compare Clements Markham on the Cocama people of the Peruvian Amazon: 'In 1681 [as reported by Jesuit missionaries] they were still in the habit of eating their dead relations.... They said it was better to be inside a friend than to be swallowed up by the cold earth' (Markham 1910: 95).

with moments of sobbing, and wiping any grease that dripped onto their hands on the heads and bodies of the deceased's close kin (ibid.).

Missionaries who tried to bring an end to Wari' mortuary cannibalism, and eventually succeeded in doing so, insisted that 'People are not animals; people are not meat to be eaten' (see ibid.: 57, 204). They thereby, in effect, pre-echoed Cora Diamond's contention that it is internal to understanding what a human being is that one differentiate between humans and animals, and that an essential component of that differentiation is the recognition that it is the animals – and only the animals – that may find themselves on the table for humans to consume. Articulating the Wari' worldview (in contrast to the one advocated by the missionaries), Conklin remarks that 'the magic and power of human existence derive from the commonality of human and animal identities, from the movements between the worlds of people and animals created through participation in both sides of the dynamic of eating and being eaten' (2001: 204). The fluidity between humans and animals to which Conklin alludes is exemplified by Wari' talk of human spirits going to the same realm as animal spirits after death, from where they sometimes return to be reborn as white-lipped peccaries (xxi). As for the theme of people being on both sides of the divide between eaters and eaten, this obviously comes through most vividly in the practices of cannibalism, though also pertinent is the Wari' conception of a close affinity between themselves and jaguars: both Wari' and jaguars are hunters, and each can be the prey of the other (Vilaça 2016; Conklin 2001: 186–8).

It would be going too far to suggest that the Wari' do not draw a distinction between humans and animals. It is just that the distinction is not made in terms of those who are and those who are not to be eaten, for in traditional Wari' customs, and still today embedded in Wari' folktales and recent memory, is the idea that humans as well as animals may be eaten, albeit in particular circumstances and typically not for appetitive or gastronomic purposes. When cannibalism was practised by the Wari', one way in which the distinction between humans and animals would manifest was in the forms that these different acts of eating took. The eating of human bodies generally had for the Wari', as it does for most other peoples who have engaged in cannibalism, a potent symbolic dimension. In the case of warfare cannibalism, the bodies of slaughtered enemies would in fact be treated with *less* respect than those of animals that had been killed for food. While animals would be consumed in their entirety, it being considered disrespectful to their spirits to allow any of the meat to go to waste, much of the bodies of enemies would be left behind, with only the head and limbs being taken back to the village (Conklin 2001: 92–3). Even though there is an obvious sense in which human flesh is being treated as food in these instances of exocannibalism, there is also a sense in which the very treating of them as food serves the symbolic purpose of denigrating and humiliating the victims. In other words, the very unceremoniousness of the consumption fulfils, as it were, the ceremonial function of epitomizing superiority and scorn.

In mortuary cannibalism, meanwhile, something patently different, though at least equally symbolic, is going on. The consuming of the body was interfused with highly ritualized performances signifying the deep mutual dependencies between different members of the community. The affines present at the funeral would be expected throughout the ceremony to assist the deceased's blood relatives, who included the spouse of the dead person (since the mixing of bodily fluids in sexual intercourse is considered tantamount to a sharing of blood), and the blood relatives would depend on the affines to actualize the disposal of the corpse through ingestion. The blood relatives' abstention from consuming the corpse themselves has sometimes been articulated in terms of a taboo against autocannibalism: so intimate is the connection between consanguines held to be that to eat a blood relative was conceptualized as equivalent to eating oneself, a mode of suicide (Conklin 1995: 80–1; 2001: 122).

The cannibalistic act was preceded by a ritualized display of reluctance on the affines' part. The deceased's blood relatives' initial requests having ostensibly been declined, the affines would acquiesce only after persistent imploring. As Conklin notes, in view of the putrid condition that the body was typically in by the time of the funeral, the hesitancy may have been more than a merely formal gesture on the affines' part (2001: 82). But still, the performance of supplication followed by refusal and then eventual consent was one of the ways in which the consumption of human flesh, in the context of a funeral, was dramatically demarcated from the routine activity of eating the flesh of animals as food.

What we see in Wari' mortuary cannibalism is thus not a complete subversion of the contention typified by Diamond, that there are significant differences between the concept of a human being and the concept of a nonhuman animal and that these differences have an ethical dimension that shows itself in particular attitudes and forms of action. What we see, rather, are ways of signalling those conceptual differences that do not involve erecting a firm dividing line between the edible and the not-to-be-eaten and placing animals on one side of the line and humans on the other. One way of characterizing the situation would thus be to say that the Wari' have a different concept or 'notion' of a human being from the one to which Diamond is referring when she affirms that its being the case that we do not eat one another is among the factors that 'go to build our notion' of what human beings are (Diamond 1978: 469–70). But this could be a misleading way of putting it if it were understood to imply that the concept at issue is readily identifiable independently of an enormously complex network of other concepts and understandings of the world.

There is something right about the Wittgensteinian pronouncement that 'to imagine a language means to imagine a form of life' (1958: §19) and that learning a concept is not something one can do in isolation from other components of the language (and hence of the form of life) that are intimately interwoven with it. As forms of life change, so do concepts; and what can be seen in Wari' society since the 1960s is a palpable change in concepts integral to a certain traditional form of life that is itself changing radically under the influence of religious and cultural forces from outside. Burying the dead is now universally practised by the Wari'. As Conklin reports, 'the younger generation thinks of cannibalism as a curious custom that their grandparents tell about from the old days "when we used to live in the forest."' Having 'grown up with other ways of living and dying', she continues, 'the practice of cannibalism has no part in their images of themselves' (2001: xix).

It was not as a consequence of rational argumentation that the Wari' came to replace cannibalism with burial as a means of disposing of the dead. Dramatic cultural changes rarely, if ever, happen in that way. Nor should we assume that the Wari' have been passive victims in the process of cultural transformation they have undergone (see Vilaça 2010). The full story would be too long and complicated to be broached in this chapter. The important point for our purposes is that there is nothing obviously rationally superior about burial, or about cremation, over the kind of mortuary cannibalism that used to be practised by the Wari'. What we see in this range of practices are different ways of expressing respect for the dead, ways that are intimately bound up with, to borrow Winch's phrase again, 'different possibilities of making sense of human life'.

Concluding remarks

The eating of human beings is often assumed to be something in which only barbarians could indulge – something terrible, horrific, even evil. For some commentators with a postcolonial sensibility who wish to critically interrogate the representations of non-Western peoples that pervade not only early travellers' tales, missionary reports and colonialist tracts but also much anthropological literature, it has thus been viewed as imperative to deny the prevalence, and sometimes even the existence, of cannibalism among human societies throughout history and across the world. It has occasionally been argued that cannibalism is a myth created by those who define their own condition of 'civilization' in contrast to the 'primitive' ways of others. This binary opposition has been sustained, it is proposed, by assertions to the effect that cannibalism is what *they* – and never what *we* – do (see Arens 1979, esp. 184–5). But the very contention that normative or institutionalized cannibalism is a mere myth for which there is no reliable evidence not only ignores the wealth of evidence that exists (cf. Sahlins 1979, Rivière 1980); it also relies on an unduly constrained conception of what cannibalism consists in, for it presupposes that cannibalism could only be something odious. Overlooking the variety of forms that the eating of human beings can take is one means of neglecting the heterogeneity of ways of being human.

As long as one fixates on the image of cannibalism as an intrinsically violent expression of contempt – perhaps maximal contempt – towards those who are eaten, one is liable to view the accusation of cannibalism as itself something that expresses disdain for the accused on the part of the accuser. Undoubtedly, cannibalism has often been part of a violent display of superiority over the victims, intended, it would seem, to inflict the ultimate humiliation upon one's enemies. But the eating of human beings, or parts of human bodies, need be neither violent nor contemptuous. As certain forms of mortuary cannibalism illustrate, there need be no disrespect involved. On the contrary, consuming pieces of the corpse may be integral to particular modes of mourning and of paying homage to the deceased. There are many ways in which respect and piety can manifest, and cannibalism is one of them. If one is unable to see this initially, it is through reading and reflecting upon detailed ethnographic studies that its possibility may become intelligible, whereas if we assume that a prohibition on eating people is internal to any concept of a person, then that intelligibility may continue to elude us.

The broader lessons for philosophy from this kind of inquiry could be articulated in terms of ethnocentrism and its overcoming. Western philosophy is beginning to break out of its introverted predicament, as an increasing number of Western philosophers make efforts to explore philosophical and religious traditions that obtain in other parts of the world – and also as philosophers from non-Western traditions become more conspicuous and more vocal. There remains, however, a danger of being limited to the perspectives of highly literate peoples, since philosophers are accustomed to working primarily with texts. Engagement with ethnography, and with anthropological sources more generally, opens a window onto other cultural vistas and forms of life, including those that themselves have little in the way of a literary heritage. Nor need the direction of illumination be all one way: anthropology and ethnography can learn as much from philosophical modes of thinking as can philosophy from anthropology and ethnography, and the intellectual traffic between the disciplines has long been stimulating and fruitful.[9] This is hardly an original observation on my part, but it bears repeating.

What I have argued in this chapter is that insofar as one considers the task, or *a* task, of philosophy to be that of contemplating the many possible ways in which sense might be made of human life, it behoves the philosopher to resist the temptation of assuming too quickly that certain activities are simply out of bounds, whether morally or religiously or perhaps even conceptually. In this particular case, if we were to assume that cannibalism – eating the bodies of dead human beings – could have no part to play in coping with death and bereavement, we would thereby have risked closing our minds to one of the many remarkable, and remarkably prevalent, ways of being human – of being the kind of beings we are.

In Chapter 6 we shall further extend the inquiry into ritual activities that have received little, if any, sustained attention from philosophers of religion. There, the principal focus will be on rituals involving divine possession and the sacrifice of animals.

---

[9] For a historical treatment, see Adams (1998). For a recent collection exhibiting mutual engagement between philosophy and anthropology, see Giri and Clammer (2014). See also Burley (forthcoming).

6

'Awe at the Terrible':
Divine Possession,
Blood Sacrifice and
the Grotesque Body

Preamble: studying ritual philosophically

It has been observed, notably by Kevin Schilbrack (2004a: 1), that philosophers, including philosophers of religion, have rarely shown much interest in the study of rituals. Schilbrack considers this lack of interest to stem from the assumption that rituals are 'thoughtless' or 'unthinking' in the sense that they are viewed 'as mechanical and instinctual' rather than as 'activities that involve thinking and learning' (ibid.; see also Schilbrack 2014b: 35). He seeks to counter the assumption by treating rituals as 'cognitive activities' that provide occasions for practitioners 'to inquire into self, other, and world' (Schilbrack 2014b: 32, 45). The assumption identified by Schilbrack could well be part of the reason for the paucity of discussion of ritual in the philosophy of religion. But Schilbrack's response raises the further question of whether, to be deserving of philosophical attention, rituals must be deemed to instantiate cognition and inquiry in the ways that he proposes. To treat rituals in these terms may be appropriate in some instances. Indeed, just as, in Chapter 3, I have concurred with those who argue that certain works of narrative fiction can profitably be regarded as doing philosophy, so this thought could be extended to encompass particular forms of ritual activity. Rituals can embody modes of thinking and conceptualizing, and some of these modes may qualify as philosophical or, at any rate, as harbouring philosophical ideas.

But to assume that the principal means, let alone the only means, of vindicating philosophical attention to ritual practices is to foreground these cognitive potentialities runs the risk of distorting the phenomena. While some rituals may furnish their participants with 'opportunities for inquiry' (Schilbrack 2014b: 44), there is no reason to assume that all rituals are well described in these terms. Moreover, there are likely to be rituals for which a description in terms of processes that are 'mechanical and instinctual' is far more apt. In developing a philosophical investigation of rituals, therefore, the important thing is not to set out with the aim of demonstrating whether rituals are or are not 'cognitive'. The important thing is to be open to the phenomena and willing to recognize radical plurality wherever it obtains, without rushing to squeeze all rituals into a preconceived and overgeneralizing theory. Although Schilbrack does not succumb to the temptation to overgeneralize, his emphasis on cognition, thinking, inquiry and so on comes close to bolstering rather than countering the very intellectualist bias in the philosophy of religion that, as we observed in Chapter 2, he claims to want to move beyond.

As an alternative to over-intellectualized approaches to ritual, one option is to turn to ideas deriving from Wittgenstein. In response to reading Frazer's *The Golden Bough*, Wittgenstein commented on the 'deep and sinister' character of sacrificial – and of mock sacrificial – rituals (Wittgenstein 1979: 16e; 1993, esp. 147). Following Wittgenstein, others have expressed similar thoughts in terms of a sense of wonder at that which is a source of destruction and terror: the possibility of treating it 'as a sacrament' precisely because of its disturbing character and not merely because one hopes that, by registering its devastating potential, one stands a higher chance of evading whatever it is one fears (Rhees 1994: 578). In drawing a contrast between his own radical pluralist approach and the sort of 'theological pluralism' typified by John Hick, D. Z. Phillips cites rituals involving human sacrifice as an example of a topic that is unlikely to receive much attention from proponents of the latter style of reflection upon religion. If such rituals are mentioned at all, they are liable to be denigrated by these proponents 'as primitive, superstitious practices; as understandable, but mistaken attempts to appease supernatural powers, in an effort to ward off the terrible in human life' (Phillips 2007b: 205). By contrast, a radical pluralist approach, while not denying 'the possibility of rituals which fit this description', would resist 'the general thesis that this is all human sacrifice *can* amount to'; for among the possibilities that a general thesis of this sort ignores is 'that what gives rise to such terrible rituals is precisely that – awe at the terrible' (ibid.). Although my purpose in this chapter is not to dwell on human sacrifice in particular, my discussion will encompass practices that could readily be described as exhibiting, among other things, a sense of awe and wonder at the terrible. These practices include, most notably, the performance of divine possession and the sacrifice of animals.

The phenomenon that social and cultural anthropologists most often call 'possession' or 'spirit possession' has been a prevalent feature of popular religion in many parts of the world. As several scholars have observed, possession is not 'a unitary phenomenon' (Ram 2013: 273), 'not just one thing' (Smith 2006: 10), but more like 'a complex series of patterns of thinking and behaviour' (Cohen 2008: 105). We should therefore be cautious before attempting any general description. What is legitimate to say, however, is that the complex patterns of thinking often involve talk of a person's being 'entered' or 'taken over' by someone or something else[1] – by a demon or spirit or deity – and the complex patterns of behaviour often include exuberant, sometimes wild and chaotic, bodily movements. Indeed, energetic dancing to the accompaniment of loud and repetitive rhythmic percussion is a widespread feature of possession episodes, not least in South Asian contexts (Alter 2008, Basu 2008).

---

[1] See, among many other sources, Flood (2006: 87), Alexander (2003: 313), Sumegi (2008: 77), Winzeler (2008: 202).

This chapter focuses especially on aspects of possession in relation to a specific festival celebrated annually in Assam in Northeast India. The festival, which takes place over three days from the seventeenth to the nineteenth of August, is referred to by various names. One name for it is *Manasā Pūjā* (or Assamese equivalents such as *Mārai Pūjā, Māre Barat*, etc.[2]), meaning the worship (*pūjā*) of Manasā, she being a goddess who is especially popular in parts of Northeast India, West Bengal and among the Hindus of Bangladesh.[3] Other common names for the festival, which emphasize a particular aspect of it, include *Deodhanī Nāc, Deodhanī Nṛtya, Deodhanī Utsav*, etc. The precise meaning of the term *deodhanī* is disputed, but one purported derivation is from the Sanskrit *devadhvani*, meaning 'sound or echo of the deity' (Smith 2006: 140–1).[4] *Nāc* (from Sanskrit *nāṭya*) means 'dance' in Assamese and certain other North Indian languages, and *nṛtya*, borrowed from Sanskrit, has the same meaning; *utsav* (from Sanskrit *utsava*) can be rendered simply as 'festival'. Those who do the dancing are called *deodhās*, the meaning of which term is again commonly said to be 'echo of the deity' (Mahanta 1997: 311; 2008: 275) or 'echoes or voices of the gods' (Dold 2011: 53). Although dances referred to as *Deodhanī Nāc* in certain parts of Assam are performed by women (Sarma 1988: 44), the festival as it occurs at the major temple of Kāmākhyā to the northwest of the city of Guwahati is one in which the dancers are exclusively men. It is claimed of these dancers that they are possessed by deities, the majority of whom are goddesses, including among them the most notoriously ferocious female deities of the Hindu pantheon. The festival incorporates animal sacrifice, which is a regular occurrence at the Kāmākhyā temple, the principal sacrificial victims being pigeons and young male goats. At certain times during the festival the deodhās, in keeping with the macabre personas of the deities they are said to embody, ritually drink the blood of these animals.

Compared with many other strands of South Asian – and in this case broadly Hindu – religion, the traditions and practices of India's most north-

---

[2] 'The Manasā-pūjā is also known as *māre-pūjā, mārai-pūjā, māre-barat* or simply *māre*, and the goddess is associated with death, particularly with unnatural death' (Sarma 1992: 115). See also Sarma (1988: 49).

[3] For comprehensive discussion of the goddess Manasā, see Maity (1966; 1989: 71–81) and Haq (2015).

[4] In Assamese script, the word is normally spelt দেওধনী, but at the Kāmākhyā temple the official spelling is দেৱধ্বনী, which could be transliterated (somewhat awkwardly) as *dewadhbani* or (more pronouncably) as *dewadhvani*. Besides *Deodhanī* (which I shall continue to use in this chapter), other variant transliterations include '*deodhānī*' (Mishra 2004), 'Debadhanī' (Dold 2013: 124), '*debaddhani*' (Smith 2006: 141) and 'Devadhani' (Goswami 2000: 67).

eastern states remain underexplored. With a few notable exceptions, studies of divine possession and goddess worship in India, and of the Kāmākhyā temple complex in particular, have said relatively little specifically about the Deodhanī or Manasā festival.[5] The present chapter contributes towards filling that lacuna by drawing upon both textual research and first-hand observations of the festival that I made during a visit to Assam in August 2017. The result is a contextualized analysis of the festival that focuses especially on the themes of blood, divine possession and the transgression of widely accepted norms of social and religious behaviour. Finding points of connection with existing debates in philosophy of religion, however, is far from easy. Topics such as divine possession, shamanistic dancing and blood sacrifice are hardly ever mentioned in the philosophical literature. But this difficulty is itself telling, as it makes all the more apparent the narrow range of issues with which philosophy of religion has typically been preoccupied. For this reason, merely by describing the festival and situating it in relation to its broader religious and cultural setting, one opens up the possibility of a cultural critique of philosophy of religion, in the sense of critical reflection upon its predominant enthusiasms and its relative neglect of forms of religiosity that are in fact remarkably prevalent in many societies across the world.

This critically descriptive task itself raises questions about the appropriate places to look for conceptual resources and an adequate descriptive vocabulary with which to do justice to the activities and forms of life under consideration. In this chapter, in addition to Indological and ethnographic sources on Tantric Hinduism, spirit possession and the worship of female deities, I also draw upon certain motifs from theories of art and literature. I invoke in particular the notions of the *grotesque* and the *grotesque body* that have been delineated by the Russian philosopher and literary theorist Mikhail Bakhtin (1895–1975) in his study of the writings and cultural milieu of the sixteenth-century French author François Rabelais (Bakhtin 1984b). Distinguishing between, on the one hand, a medieval and Renaissance conception of the grotesque – typified by Rabelais – and, on the other hand, a conception of the grotesque that emerged in the European Romantic movement of the nineteenth century, Bakhtin characterizes the latter as displaying a sombreness that he considers to be absent from the more

---

[5] As Frederick Smith noted in 2006, divine possession in Assam 'has been almost entirely unresearched' (2006: 139). Since then, the studies that have become available include a documentary film by Cartosio and Majo Garigliano (2013), a PhD thesis by Majo Garigliano (2015, esp. 95–100, 202–6) and a recent article by Urban (2018).

flamboyantly 'carnivalesque' atmosphere of the earlier period (e.g. Bakhtin 1984b: 47). Setting aside the question of whether Bakhtin's model of transition from one conception of the grotesque to another would hold up in the face of robust historical scrutiny, it is my contention that the conceptual framework that informs the study of the grotesque, to which Bakhtin made a seminal contribution, can profitably be utilized in thickly describing the kinds of ritualized performances of possession exhibited in the Deodhanī festival. Before turning, in subsequent sections, to the subject of spirit possession and then to that of the temple of Kāmākhyā and the dance of the deodhās itself, I therefore begin by explicating some pertinent aspects of the notion of the grotesque.

The grotesque

The term 'grotesque' derives from the Italian *grottesche*, which itself means 'of or pertaining to underground caves [*grotta*]' (Harpham 2006: 31). It originated in late fifteenth-century Italy, where excavations of the Domus Aurea, an unfinished palace built for Nero after 64 CE, revealed cavern-like (or grotto-esque) rooms and corridors that had sunk deep into the ground. Upon the columns, walls and ceilings of these rooms and corridors were murals depicting creatures that combine human, animal and plant motifs. It was to these that the neologism *grottesche* was first applied (Remshardt 2004: 4–5). Aesthetic and philosophical reflection upon the concept of the grotesque has been pursued since the mid-eighteenth century.[6] Amid the multiple interpretations of the concept, a common way of understanding the grotesque has been as encapsulating what Dieter Meindl calls 'a tense combination of attractive and repulsive elements, of comic and tragic aspects, of ludicrous and horrifying features'; while, in any given context, either its lighter or its darker dimensions may be accentuated, 'a certain collision or complicity between playfulness and seriousness, fun and dread', is constitutive of the grotesque (Meindl 1996: 14).

Bakhtin was therefore far from being the first thinker to ruminate upon the grotesque, but his study of Rabelais, first published in Russian in 1965, gave fresh impetus to discussions of the topic and has become an important reference point for subsequent investigations. The grotesque is, for Bakhtin,

---

[6] See, e.g., Möser (1766), first published in German in 1761.

characteristic of certain forms of literary and artistic production but also of the wider culture out of which those forms emerge. Thus, for example, Bakhtin views the ancient satyric dramas and comedies of Attica as originating in the Dionysian festivals, and the medieval and Renaissance grotesque as being associated with 'the culture of folk humor', especially as it manifests in carnivals (1984b: 46, 47). Bakhtin describes the carnival as a subversive countercultural arena in which normal rules of social etiquette and divisions of hierarchy are temporarily suspended. Rather than being a spectacular performance watched by a relatively passive audience, the carnival, as Bakhtin envisages it, is a celebration of equality in which everyone participates. Its spirit is one of jocularity and antiauthoritarianism and its targets of ridicule include symbols both of political and of religious authority, notably the king and God. This spirit, Bakhtin maintains, was not restricted to specific historical occasions, but is an enduring principle that, despite its erosion in the post-Renaissance era, 'continues to fertilize various areas of life and culture' (1984b: 33–4).

The grotesque could, then, be described as an aesthetic sensibility that, according to Bakhtin, originates in the atmosphere of the carnival. It is the sensibility that takes pleasure in portraying life and the world, and especially the human body, in ways that emphasize, typically by means of exaggeration, their earthy, indelicate and sometimes downright obscene aspects. It is his attention to the 'grotesque body' in particular that has occasionally been cited as Bakhtin's most distinctive contribution to discussions of the grotesque (see, e.g., Meindl 1996: 17; Czachesz 2012). Central to his account is the observation that depictions of the grotesque body accentuate its most conspicuous points of contact with its environment, especially its orifices and protrusions that facilitate the exchange of substances between the body and the rest of the world. Thus, 'the open mouth, the genital organs, the breasts, the phallus, the potbelly, the nose' are played up, along with the activities of 'copulation, pregnancy, childbirth, the throes of death, eating, drinking, or defecation' (1984b: 26). These are, on Bakhtin's reckoning, precisely the features and functions that most incontrovertibly disclose the body's condition as being both 'ever unfinished' and 'ever creating' – a constantly changing entity in porous and fluid intercourse with the world around it (ibid.). Of particular significance for a theme that will emerge in my discussion of the Deodhanī festival is Bakhtin's highlighting of the imagery of devouring in Rabelais's *Gargantua and Pantagruel*. Having registered the pervasiveness of references to food and drink in this literary work, Bakhtin remarks that the grotesque body's mode of engagement with the world is 'most fully and concretely

Figure 6.1 Illustration for the works of Rabelais (engraving), Gustave Doré (1832–83) (after). Private Collection. © Look and Learn / Bridgeman Images.

revealed in the act of eating'; it is in this act that, by transgressing its own limits, the body, and hence the human being, 'triumphs over the world, devours it without being devoured himself' (281): 'The victorious body receives the defeated world and is renewed' (283). Emblematic of this devouring body is the focality of the mouth in the grotesque face (Fig. 6.1). Such a face 'is actually reduced to the gaping mouth; the other features are only a frame encasing this wide-open bodily abyss' (317).

Bakhtin's periodization of formulations of the grotesque presents the Renaissance grotesque, epitomized in Rabelais' writings, as the paradigm in relation to which the Romantic and modernist formulations amount to a regression. While the euphoric spirit of the carnival had been integral to the Rabelaisian grotesque, Bakhtin contends that this spirit retains only a residual presence in later forms, with an air of 'gloom' having entered into the Romantic conception (1984b: 47). Rather than revelling in victory over that which is 'dark and terrifying' by transforming it into something risible, the Romantic grotesque unites the comic with the terrible in an ambivalent hybrid image. Typifying this combination is Victor Hugo's description of the grotesque as creating both 'the formless and the horrible' on the one hand,

and 'the comic and the buffoon-like' on the other (Hugo n.d. [1827]: 10).[7] Similarly, John Ruskin characterizes it as, 'in almost all cases, composed of two elements, one ludicrous, the other fearful'; these elements, he adds, can hardly be separated, for 'there are few grotesques so utterly playful as to be overcast with no shade of fearfulness, and few so fearful as absolutely to exclude all ideas of jest' (Ruskin 1881: 126).

Ruskin presumes his characterization to apply as much to the Renaissance as to later versions of the grotesque, and he is far from alone in taking that view.[8] We should thus be cautious about taking for granted Bakhtin's assertion that 'the medieval and Renaissance grotesque, filled with the spirit of carnival ... takes away all fears and is therefore completely gay and bright' (1984b: 47). But neither should we infer that Bakhtin has simply overlooked a sinister dimension that is really present in Renaissance works such as Rabelais's *Gargantua and Pantagruel.* The issue is complicated by the fact that judgements about what is straightforwardly hilarious in contrast to what is darkly humorous may differ over time and between cultures. As Gregory de Rocher has observed, certain episodes involving mass death that Rabelais depicts in highly unrealistic terms will strike modern readers as laughable, whereas episodes that are less fancifully represented are liable to evoke more mixed responses, including feelings of dismay and alienation (Rocher 1979: 67, 63).

This is not the place to enter into detailed exposition of the examples that Rocher adduces from Rabelais's oeuvre.[9] An important reminder to take from his contention, however, is that in coming to comprehend a given episode, whether in a work of narrative fiction or in a religious ritual, there is inevitably an interplay between the phenomena constitutive of the episode, on the one hand, and the personal and cultural perspective of the observer, on the other. It is in part for reasons such as this that, in the context of the study of religion, it is advisable to follow D. Z. Phillips in treating the hermeneuticist's role as one of elucidating *possibilities* of sense, the purpose being to prevent oneself and one's readers from prematurely foreclosing certain interpretive possibilities as a consequence of unwarranted assumptions or prejudices about what the object of interpretation 'must' consist in. This is a very different

---

[7] Hugo's remark is quoted in Bakhtin (1984b: 43). Here I have slightly amended the translation in that text.

[8] The view that the grotesque, in general, combines horror with humour, fear with laughter, has been dubbed the 'fusion thesis' and attributed to several authors, including Kayser (1963) and Thomson (1972); see Cassuto (1995: 126 n. 2).

[9] For further discussion, see not only Rocher's own treatment but also that in Bergman (2003: 186–8).

emphasis from that of a study which claims to be providing the one correct interpretation.

For my purposes in this chapter, it is not necessary to resolve disputes over whether Bakhtin has accurately characterized changes in the grotesque between the Renaissance and Romantic periods. It is important to recognize two main points: first, that within the capacious conceptual field of the grotesque as a whole, the presence of a curious and dynamic amalgam of horrific and comedic elements is a prominent characteristic; and second, that Bakhtin's conception of the grotesque body, and especially of the grotesque face, poignantly captures certain features that, once brought to our attention, we may see emphasized in rituals of possession. The philosopher of religion is thus afforded a richer conceptual palette with which to develop an account of ritual practices that is more phenomenologically and hermeneutically illuminating than it would otherwise be. With these points in mind, let us turn to the topic of spirit possession. In the next section, I consider in particular both how the ambivalence or equivocation between the horrific and the comedic manifests in cases of spirit possession and how, in such contexts, heavy rhythmic sound serves to create a conducive and potent ritual environment.

'Horrific comedy' and the formation of a ritual sound-world

Without explicitly invoking the concept of the grotesque, anthropologists sometimes describe episodes of spirit possession in terms that combine elements of comedy with something more serious or even terrifying. Michael Lambek, for example, remarks of possession that it is often 'a kind of serious parody of orthodox religion, social convention, or the accepted language of power relations' (1989: 54). In this respect, we might add, it exhibits features of both the grotesque and the carnivalesque as expounded by Bakhtin. Paul Stoller, meanwhile, coins the phrase 'horrific comedy' to capture something of the nature of spirit possession as it occurs among the Songhay of southern Niger (Stoller 1984; 1995: 7). Of several families of spirits or deities that are held to take temporary possession of people in this community, one is known as the Hauka – a term meaning 'craziness' or 'unruliness' in the Hausa language (see Miles 1994: 335). A notable characteristic of Hauka possessions is that dancing and ostensibly aggressive movements and gestures are interspersed with burlesque mockery of European colonialists. Although the French granted independence to the Republic of Niger in 1960, the colonial influence and European presence remains a target of resistance, prompting continued ridicule and parodic derision (Stoller 1984: 184).

In an especially vivid description, Stoller recounts his 'first exposure' to the horrific comedy of the Hauka that occurred in 1969. Near the compound of a Songhay possession-cult priest, a crowd had gathered around a trio of musicians comprising two calabash drummers and a player of the *godji* (monochord violin). As the musicians played, a young man in the crowd suddenly 'vomited up a black liquid' and proceeded to roll on the ground throwing sand over himself and shoving it into his mouth. Upon standing up, he stared at the audience and spat sand at Stoller. With eyes bulging and a mouth frothing with saliva, he flailed around as though trying to lash out at onlookers. Subsequently, the young man participated in a terse verbal exchange with Stoller, during which he evoked scornful mirth from the audience by issuing lewd remarks about Stoller's parents (Stoller 1984: 166). In this incident as a whole we see the grotesque motifs of the contorted body and a mouth that ingurgitates dirt and also salivates, vomits, spits and spews obscenities.

The strange mixture of the horrific and the comedic is likely to be among the factors that have deterred close attention to the phenomenon of possession in much scholarship on South Asian religion in particular. As Frederick Smith has observed, neither Western academics nor educated orthodox Hindus have known what to make of this phenomenon, which is perceived as falling 'outside the realm of both reason and social accountability' (2006: 3). As a consequence, despite their ancient roots and historical continuities, practices of possession have tended to be marginalized in mainstream scholarly, religious and nationalist discourses (Ram 2013: 226). Nevertheless, in the everyday contexts of lived religion, 'possession is the most common and ... most valued form of spiritual expression in India' (Smith 2006: xxv).

In discussing the Koṭai ('Offering') festival in the Nāñcil Nāṭu region of southernmost Tamil Nadu, Stuart Blackburn describes how each possessed dancer becomes a 'kinetic icon' – a fluidly moving embodiment of divinity that constitutes a site of adoration and a vehicle of communication between audience and deity (1988: 41). While verbal exchanges may take place between devotees and their objects of worship through the medium of the possessed body, it is the dance that establishes the credibility of the possessed individual as an authentic deific voice (ibid.). As the ethnomusicologist Andrew Alter has remarked, in the divine possession tradition of Garhwal in northern India, 'Gods possess humans if they are pleased, and this pleasure is usually expressed through dancing' (2008: 21). For this reason, the music that evokes the dance – often dominated by loud and prolonged rhythmic drumming – is itself the driving force of many possession performances, generating the 'charged' and 'exhilarating' atmosphere that 'summons the deities' to participate in the dance (Alter 2008: 133–4, 3).[10]

Garhwali musicians refer to their knowledge of the rhythmic performance as an 'ocean of drumming' (ḍhol sāgar) (Alter 2008: 9, 83), a phrase that could aptly be applied to the sound that results when a large number of drums are played in unison, as is the case at the Deodhanī festival in Assam. Over the three days of this festival, those who are present in and around the Kāmākhyā temple are immersed in an ocean of sound comprising the seemingly relentless pounding of drums and clashing of cymbals, at a volume that is not only raucously audible in the ears but also felt as a pulsating force that pummels and vibrates one's body. Edmund Burke, in his famous essay on the concepts of the sublime and the beautiful, observes that '[e]xcessive loudness' is among the phenomena capable of stirring 'a sublime passion' that 'is sufficient to overpower the soul, to suspend its action, and to fill it with terror' (1759: 150–1). Although it would be an exaggeration to suggest that the souls of the crowd at Kāmākhyā are filled with terror, the drumming nonetheless instils an aura of heightened tension. At times, the rhythm resembles an immense heartbeat, which might be imagined as the heartbeat of the goddess Kāmākhyā (Dold 2011: 55). At other times, it accelerates and intensifies, rising in a crescendo that elicits 'shrieking, howling and jumping' from the dancing deodhās (Maity 1966: 297) – a veritable enactment of horrific comedy.

These themes of the horrific and comedic grotesquery of the ritualized performance and the salience of drumming will recur in the descriptions of the Deodhanī festival that come shortly, after we have examined some background information about the festival venue: the temple of the goddess Kāmākhyā (Fig. 6.2).

---

[10] For examples from diverse South Asian regions, see Caldwell (1996), Walter (2001) and Sax (2011). For an African example, see Spencer (1990: Ch. 6).

Figure 6.2   Kāmākhyā temple, Assam, during the Deodhanī festival. Photograph by Mikel Burley, 19 August 2017.

Kāmākhyā, desire and the womb of the Goddess

The Kāmākhyā temple has been described as 'the most celebrated Shakti *pitha* in the *tantrik* world' (Jha 1991: 32). A *pīṭha* is, literally, a firm seat or bench, and *śakti* ('power', 'energy') is a term for the Goddess (Brown 1998: 239; Fuller 2004: 44). A Śakti *pīṭha* (or, more strictly, *śākta pīṭha*) is thus a 'seat of the Goddess' – a place where her power is centred. 'Tantric' (*tāntrika*) is harder to define concisely, since its semantic range is extensive. The meaning that is most relevant to the present context, as well as to the main themes I am covering in this chapter as a whole, is that which emphasizes the role of desire in spiritual practice. To paraphrase a much-cited definition of Tantra, or Tantrism, this is a tradition that seeks to utilize desire (*kāma*), 'in every sense of the word' (including sexual desire), for the purpose of gaining spiritual liberation (Padoux 1990: 40).[11] Tantric adepts are expected to

---

[11] Padoux himself cites Madeleine Biardeau without naming a specific text. Relevant, however, is Biardeau (1981: 161–70; 1989: 148–58).

cultivate a feeling of intimate congruity between themselves and the cosmos as a whole, a sense of 'integrat[ion] within an all-embracing system of micro-macrocosmic correlations'; rather than being suppressed, desire is accentuated and mobilized in a controlled fashion, to promote 'worldly and supernatural enjoyments' as well as special capacities and, ultimately, 'liberation in this life' (Padoux 1987: 273). The theme of desire is present in the very name of the goddess Kāmākhyā. Although the etymology of the name has been disputed,[12] it is commonly understood to denote the 'Goddess of Desire' (Biernacki 2007). The *Kālikā Purāṇa* (*c.* tenth century CE) elucidates the name by attributing to the god Śiva the declaration that the goddess is called Kāmākhyā because she is 'the giver or fulfiller of desire, desiring, desirable, beautiful' (*Kālikā Purāṇa* 62.2, quoted in Avalon 1964: 132), who 'has come to the great mountain Nīlakūṭa to have sexual enjoyment with me' (62.1, trans. Shastri 2008: 453).

This Nīlakūṭa ('blue peak') or Nīlācala ('blue hill'), on which the temple of Kāmākhyā stands, is located on the south bank of the Brahmaputra River, to the northwest of Assam's capital city, Guwahati. The temple is revered not merely as a seat of the Goddess but as the site where, in the myth of the goddess Satī, her vulva (*yoni*) fell to Earth. According to the myth, Satī immolated herself in protest at her father Dakṣa's refusal to invite Śiva, her husband, to a sacrificial ceremony. In the version of the story recounted in the *Kālikā Purāṇa*, Śiva's subsequent grief erupts in a torrent of caustic tears that threatens to 'burn the entire world' as he roams 'like a madman', carrying Satī's body over his shoulder (*Kālikā Purāṇa* 18.11–37, trans. Shastri 2008: 94–7). Apparently in an effort to ameliorate Śiva's anguish by removing its immediate object, the gods Brahmā, Viṣṇu and Śanaiścara[13] 'entered the corpse of Satī in order to tear it to pieces so that holy places could come up wherever these pieces fall' (18.40, quoted in Mishra 2004: 27). The feet, thighs, breasts, arms, neck and head were scattered in various directions; the *yoni* fell on Kāmagiri ('hill of desire') in the land of Kāmarūpa ('embodiment [or form] of desire'), and the navel fell on ground nearby (18.41–3).

Two inscriptions on the walls of its antechamber (*antarāla*) record that the Kāmākhyā temple was rebuilt upon existing foundations in 1565 CE

---

[12] Kakati (1948: 38) suspects that *Kāmā* in *Kāmākhyā* is not of Sanskrit derivation, but corresponds 'to Austric formations' such as '*Kanoi*, Demon; *Kamoit*, Devil; *Komin*, Grave; *Kamet*, Corpse (Khasi); *Kamru*, a god of the Santals'. See also Kakati (1941: 53–4) and Sircar (1973: 15 n. 1).

[13] Śanaiścara (lit. 'He who moves slowly'), also known as Śani, is a name for the planet Saturn and of the deity personifying that planet (Mevissen 2000). In Shastri's translation of the *Kalikā Purāṇa* (2008), Śanaiścara's name is consistently mistransliterated as 'Śanaiśvara'.

(Das 2007: 41). However, its sanctum sanctorum, known as the 'womb chamber' (*garbhagṛha*) or 'cave of desire' (*manobhava guhā*[14]) has been estimated 'to date back to around the seventh century' (Goswami 2015: 61). Entering this 'womb' of the Goddess, one descends a short flight of stone steps into a scarcely lit reverberant cavern, a grotto. There, in a sunken portion of the cavern below the level of the main floor, is a large black stone, kept smooth and moist by the trickling water of an underground spring. The stone, with a groove running along its centre, is venerated as the *yoni* of the Goddess. (Is the goddess in question Satī or Kāmākhyā? Their identities become fused in the aniconic emblem of the *yoni*.) After making an offering, and bowing to touch the stone and to scoop a handful of spring water into his or her mouth, the devotee receives from the officiating priest a smear of vermilion paste across the forehead, resembling a bloody wound.[15]

To the west of the part of the temple containing the *garbhagṛha* are three further chambers, the westernmost of which is the 'dancing hall' (*nāṭamandira*), which was constructed in the mid-eighteenth century (Mishra 2004: 165). This, in turn, is connected by a short roofed walkway to the 'sacrifice house' (*balighar*), in which animals are ritually beheaded. The majority of the victims are pigeons and young uncastrated male goats, but others include water buffaloes, sheep, ducks and fish. Certain vegetables are also offered, principally ash gourds (*komora* or 'winter melon') and sugarcane stalks; these are typically chopped in half with the same type of sword as that which is used to decapitate goats and the other smaller animals.[16] Unlike the worship of other goddesses, which centres on the sacred *yoni* in the *garbhagṛha*, the worship of Manasā is restricted to the dancing hall and treats an earthen 'auspicious pot' (*maṅgala ghaṭa*) as Manasā's symbolic embodiment, the pot being an object that itself has traditional associations with the womb.[17] These factors have led some scholars to speculate that the

---

[14] *Manobhava*, which literally means 'mind-born' or 'existing in the mind', is an epithet of Kāma, the god of desire. The epithet derives from the view that desire depends on the memory of previous experiences and hence 'is rooted in the mind' (Benton 2006: 43–4).

[15] I went into the *garbhagṛha* at Kāmākhyā temple on 15 August 2017. For other descriptions of it, see Shastri (1989: 123), Goswami (1998: 14) and Ramos (2017: 45–6).

[16] During my visit to Kāmākhyā in August 2017, I witnessed the sacrifice of pigeons, goats, a water buffalo, a gourd, a stem of sugarcane and what looked like a catfish. The sacrifice of a sheep and a duck at Kāmākhyā is reported in Choudhury (2002) and Dold (2004: 117). The sacrifice of numerous other species of animals, and also human beings, is enjoined in traditional texts such as the *Kālikā Purāṇa* (55.3–6; 67.3–19), *Yoginī Tantra* (2.9.158, 2.7.170) and others; see Urban (2010: 210 n. 49).

[17] 'The words, *ghata*, *kumbha*, or *garaga* are synonymous with the meanings of both "pot" and "womb." In other words, the pot represents the womb of the goddess holding life in its seed form' (Padma 2013: 85).

worship of this snake goddess was originally incorporated only 'grudgingly' into the temple's regular religious calendar (Mishra 2004: 54). Moreover, the dance of the deodhās that constitutes the centrepiece of Manasā Pūjā as it is celebrated at the Kāmākhyā temple, is thought to be strongly influenced by 'shamanistic dances' that have long been performed by indigenous inhabitants of the surrounding region, especially the Bodo-Kachari people (Sarma 1988: 52; Goswami 1960: 57). It is to a closer examination of the deodhās' dance that we now turn.

Deodhās and deities

A myth of origin of the Deodhanī festival declares that there was once a Mahārāja ('great king') who yearned to have a son. Praying to the goddess Bhairavī, the king promised that he would give her his own head as an oblation if a son were to be granted to him. Approving of this pledge, Bhairavī fulfilled the king's request. But in his delight, the king forgot to discharge his side of the bargain until the goddess reminded him of it in a vision. In response, the king decapitated himself with a golden knife, offering the head to Bhairavī. By this act the king attained a divine status and subsequently 'possessed a local male devotee, thus beginning the *debaddhani* [= *deodhanī*] tradition' (Smith 2006: 141). No explicit mention is made of Manasā in this story. Bhairavī is traditionally regarded as one of the ten Mahāvidyās ('great wisdom [goddesses]'), all of whom have a strong association with the Kāmākhyā temple complex (Dold 2004). In common with many other Indian goddesses, Bhairavī is considered to have both destructive and beneficent aspects. In the form of Kāmeśvarī, she is a goddess of desire and of its fulfilment, much like Kāmākhyā (Kinsley 1997: 172); as such, both of these goddesses are commonly prayed to as embodiments of fertility and givers of offspring.

Manasā, too, is a goddess of fertility (Fig. 6.3), though her association with snakes is symbolic of violence and destruction as well as regeneration (Dimock 1962: 317). She is the bringer of life, reproduction and relief from illness on the one hand and the bringer 'of death, decay and misfortune' on the other (Sen 1953: xxix). Exactly how her own festival of Manasā Pūjā became entwined with the Deodhanī dance at Kāmākhyā remains unclear, but the same ambivalences that characterize the imagery and mythology that surround her are vividly present in the activities of the deodhās. In practice, neither the direct participants in the dance nor the devotees who

Figure 6.3 Lithograph of the goddess Manasā (16.2 cm x 22.2 cm), *c.* 1895, from an album of popular prints, artist unknown. © The Trustees of the British Museum.

come to observe it, nor indeed the priests who officiate over the proceedings, appear to distinguish sharply between the multiple goddesses – or forms or embodiments of the one Goddess – that are being propitiated. The goddesses are all, ultimately, 'Mother' (*Mā* or *Mātā*), and hence there is no impropriety in someone such as Jadunath Sharma, a priest and administrator at the temple, sliding seamlessly from speaking of the Deodhanī festival as a reflection of 'the significance of Goddess Kāmākhyā' to describing the dance of the deodhās as 'a unique way of offering prayers to the Serpentine Goddess'. In turn, it is unsurprising that the presenter of the news report in which the interview with Jadunath Sharma is featured refers to 'the Serpent Goddess Kāmākhyā', thereby fully conflating the identities of Manasā and Kāmākhyā (Roving Report 2016).[18]

These conflations are consistent with the deodhās' self-presentation as 'temporary seats of the divine power' (Sarma 1988: 50), for although it is claimed of the deodhās that they become 'vehicles' for the deities they incarnate (Mahanta 2008: 275), the respective personae of these deities are hard to differentiate on the basis of the deodhās' appearance and behaviour. Ranging in number from sixteen to twenty-one,[19] all the deodhās wear simple cotton dhotis and receive garlands of flowers around their necks from devoted spectators. Most of them are besmeared with red vermilion paste, a prominent exception being the deodhā who embodies Kubera (king of the yakṣas [roughly, 'nature spirits'] and 'guardian deity of wealth and treasure'[20]), whose dhoti is dyed indigo and whose body is smeared with indigo paste. They all wield weapons of some sort over the course of the proceedings: in most cases these are slender batons but they also include tridents and swords, especially the long sword of the type used for decapitating water buffaloes.[21] The majority of the deodhās engage, at intervals, in wild and exuberant dancing, making triumphal gestures with their arms and hopping around on one leg with the opposite knee bent out sideways. Pulling exaggerated – grotesque – facial expressions, they roll their eyes, project their tongues and bear their teeth ghoulishly.

Visually identifying which deodhā is possessed by which deity is far from straightforward, and lists of the deities in question tend to be incomplete and mutually inconsistent. Nevertheless, there are several names that recur across otherwise partially divergent lists. Of these, the male deities comprise Mahādeva (Śiva), Mahārāja (the divinized king who donated his head to Bhairavī), Gaṇeśa (the elephant-headed god), Nārāyaṇa (Viṣṇu), Kubera (or Dhanakubera) and Jalakubera. The female deities by whom deodhās are said to be possessed are greater in number, comprising Bagalā, Bhairavī, Cāmuṇḍā, Chinnamastā, Kālī, Śmaśānakālī ('Kālī of the cremation ground'),

---

[18] A full transcript of the news report is contained in ANI (2016).

[19] 'Out of twenty-one *deodhās* representing various gods and goddesses, six are from the temple complex itself and the rest are from different parts of lower Assam' (Mishra 2004: 55).

[20] See Sutherland (1991: 61–3). On the etymology of the name Kubera (probably from the verbal root *kub* or *kumb*, 'to cover over'), see Hopkins (1913: 56–7).

[21] The sword is referred to in Assam as a *dākhar* (Sarma 1988: 52). Elsewhere, especially Nepal, it is known as a *rām dāo* (see, e.g., Cowper 1906: 148).

Tārā, Ugratārā ('Fierce Tārā'),[22] Bhuvaneśvarī, Calantā, Kāmākhyā (or Burhī Kāmākhyā, lit. 'Old Kāmākhyā'), Manasā and Śītalā.[23] Of these thirteen female deities, the iconography and mythology associated with the first eight normally depicts them as truculent, dangerous and destructive; and of the remaining five, Manasā (the snake goddess) and Śītalā (the goddess of smallpox) are ambivalent inasmuch as they are typically characterized as both the instigators and the removers of affliction.[24] This abundance of pugnacity and ambivalence in the characters of the deities contributes to the general air of untamed and volatile energy that pervades the Deodhanī festival. While there is rarely a sense that spectators are in real danger of physical harm,[25] the deodhās' movements tread an uneasy line between mock ferocity and actual aggression, enacting a form of 'horrific comedy' that, I want to suggest, may illuminatingly be described in terms of the exhibition of grotesque bodies.

Ritualized transgression and the performance of divine possession

In bringing out the grotesque dimensions of the Deodhanī festival, I shall focus primarily upon two major and interrelated themes, namely the ritualized transgression of traditional religious norms and the performance of divine possession. The term 'performance' here has the dual sense of, on the one hand, the mere carrying out of an activity (performing a task) and, on the other hand, the playing of a role for the purpose of entertaining or stimulating an audience.

---

[22] 'Ugratārā is a Hindu adaptation of the Buddhist Tantric Mahācīna(krama)tārā or Ugratārā, who was most likely originally a tribal goddess of the Himalayan region' (Bühnemann 2000: 97).

[23] The sources from which I have synthesized the foregoing lists of male and female deities are Sarma (1988: 50), Mishra (2004: 56–7), Goswami (2006: 137), Filippi (2008: 14 n. 13) and Dold (2011: 55–7). See also Urban (2018: 315).

[24] On the ambivalence of deities such as Manasā and Śītalā, see Kinsley (1986: 208–11). On Śītalā in particular, see Mukhopadhyay (1994).

[25] Over the three days of the festival in August 2017, I witnessed only one physical injury to a member of the crowd. Ironically, it was a police sergeant, who, while trying to keep spectators out of the way of the deodhās, received an inadvertent blow to the back of his head from a deodhā's elbow as the deodhā ran between the sacrifice house and the dancing hall. The injury was not serious, but, needless to say, the sergeant was less amused by the incident than were several members of the crowd who saw it.

Assam has been described as 'the tantric country par excellence' (Eliade 1969: 305), and, as I have noted, a salient motif of at least some Tantric traditions is the exploitation of desire to achieve both worldly and spiritual power. This emphasis on desire is integral to a more encompassing orientation, which seeks to overcome dualistic categories by deliberately subverting or inverting orthodox Brahmanical religious and social norms. Thus, contrary to a conception of desire as needing to be strictly regulated and, ultimately, suppressed or subordinated to soteriological aspirations, certain Tantric movements have reconceptualized desire as itself a means of spiritual empowerment. The motif of inversion is also vividly present in Tantric rituals that contravene Brahmanical conventions concerning purity and impurity. Tantric animal sacrifice, for example, is not only at variance with widespread Hindu opposition to the slaughter of animals in general, but normally utilizes a method of killing, namely decapitation, that emphatically violates the ancient Vedic requirement to suffocate sacrificial animals to avoid the shedding of blood as they are dispatched (Oldenberg 1988: 202). Being considered an inherently dangerous and impure substance, any blood that was used in Vedic rituals would be offered only to 'demons' (*rakṣas*) and 'not to the primary Vedic gods' (McClymond 2008: 180–1 n. 50). In the case of Tantric sacrifice, by contrast, blood is the staple offering to the primary deities. Moreover, the selection of animals for sacrifice again flouts Vedic purity norms, according to which the buffalo is classified among those that are 'unfit for sacrifice' (*Śatapatha Brāhmaṇa* 7.5.2.37, trans. Eggeling 1894: 412).[26] Indeed, the choice of water buffaloes for many ritual occasions (albeit not as part of the Deodhanī festival) is probably an inheritance from non-Brahmanical indigenous traditions (Urban 2010: 64).

Also exemplifying the principle of transgression is the practice among some Tantric groups of incorporating into ritual acts the production and oral consumption of substances deemed to be paradigms of impurity by orthodox Brahmanical standards. For example, a Tantric text known as the *Kaulajñāna Nirṇaya*, estimated to have originated in eleventh-century Assam, is among those that enjoin the preparation by ritual participants of various concoctions, including a blend of menstrual blood, semen, alcohol and clarified butter (*Kaulajñāna Nirṇaya* 18.7–9, in Bagchi 1986: 103). The drinking of liquor and eating of flesh is prescribed and so too, by implication,

---

[26] See also Urban (2010: 63): 'In Assam, Bangla, and parts of South India, the preferred victim is the buffalo – an animal that . . . is explicitly identified as wild, impure, and unfit by the *brāhmaṇic* texts'.

is the ingestion of the mixture comprising further bodily substances (18.19–23): 'Using all ritual accessories, and with due preparation, one becomes fit to attain the special powers (*siddhis*) by this method' (18.23).[27] As a rationale for consuming substances such as these, the esteemed exponent of Kashmir Śaivism, Abhinavagupta (*c*. 950–1020 CE[28]), declares that 'they dissolve the impurity that is plurality'; in other words, by freeing oneself from the contracted state of mind that feels 'doubt' or 'inhibition' (*śaṅkā*) in the face of such activities, 'one throws off the contamination imposed by the restrictions of the bound' (*Parātriṃśikā Vivaraṇa*, quoted in Sanderson 2013: 15–16).[29] Although the Deodhanī festival does not include sexual practices or the consumption of sexual fluids, the swallowing of the raw flesh and blood of animals by the deodhās constitutes a cynosure of the ritual activities; in these performances, the grotesque image of the devouring mouth becomes prominent. Two events within the festival are especially pertinent in this connection, each of which takes place initially on the second day of the festival and is repeated on the third. I shall describe each in turn.

The first of the events in question begins with the deodhās bringing into the temple courtyard two long sacrificial swords of the sort used for decapitating water buffaloes. As several deodhās gather round, two of them hold the swords horizontally alongside each other with the sharp edge of the blades turned upwards. In anticipation of what is to happen next, a section of the watching crowd closes in around the deodhās and the spectators on the stone steps beside the courtyard rise to their feet. After a few minutes of growing expectancy on the part of the audience, another of the deodhās comes running enthusiastically into the courtyard with a fist in the air like a celebrating athlete and the knot of spectators separates sufficiently widely to let him through. He bows down momentarily before a group of six or seven prepubescent girls, who represent the power of the Goddess in the form of virginal 'princesses' (*kumārīs*). Having received the Goddess's blessing from these girls, the deodhā then stands upon the blades of the swords, normally steadying himself with a hand on top of the head of one of the two deodhās who are holding them, and raising his other arm aloft in an exultant posture. Published non-academic accounts frequently describe the standing – or

---

[27] I have amended Michael Magee's translation in Bagchi (1986: 105). For discussion of this passage from the *Kaulajñāna Nirṇaya*, see Urban (2015: 74).

[28] Estimates of Abhinavagupta's dates vary. Here I have followed Rastogi (1979: 157).

[29] Or, in Jaideva Singh's translation: 'When that doubt is instantly dissolved, then the stain of the trouble of the psycho-physical limitations of the aspirant is cast out' (Abhinavagupta 1989: 222). Singh renders *śaṅkā* as 'doubt' whereas Sanderson renders it as 'inhibition'.

'dancing' – upon the swords as one of several 'miraculous physical feats' accomplished by the deodhās, other such feats including licking the sacrificial blade and dancing with it 'placed on the nape' (Goswami 1960: 53, quoted in Maity 1966: 297).[30]

As the drums continue to pound and the cymbals clash, the crowd whoop and cheer. Many of the women ululate: issuing a shrill cry while moving the tongue rapidly from side to side.[31] Live pigeons are raised in the air by some of the spectators or temple assistants and handed to the deodhā mounted on the swords. Seizing a pigeon in his hand, or in some instances taking its head directly into his mouth, the deodhā clamps his teeth down on the bird's neck and tugs its body away from him, snapping its head off. Some of the deodhās do this to two, three or four pigeons in quick succession, each time throwing the headless body into the crowd, often with its wings still flapping reflexively. Making an emphatic display of crunching up the head in his mouth, the deodhā's eyes widen into a maniacal glare (Fig. 6.4). He chews and swallows bone, flesh and feathers in hyperbolic motions, spitting out the residue.

Figure 6.4 A deodhā during the Deodhanī festival at Kāmākhyā. Photograph by Pinku Haloi, 19 August 2017.

---

[30] See also Devsharma (2014: 57), Smith (2006: 142).
[31] Cf. Dold (2013: 141 n. 78): '[T]hey ululate, with that piercing, reverberating cry that women achieve by rapidly striking the sides of their open lips with their tongue. The cry expresses intense emotion, sometimes joy, sometimes grief, often exultation.'

Bakhtin writes of the medieval carnival that it lacks any distinction between audience and actors: it 'is not a spectacle seen by the people; they live in it, and everyone participates because its very idea embraces all the people' (1984b: 7). Although, in the case of the Deodhanī dance, a demarcation between spectators and performers is retained, there is undoubtedly a high degree of audience participation, whereby this boundary becomes less pronounced. It is the incessant throbbing of the percussive instruments that instigates the highly charged atmosphere both within and around the temple. But the anticipatory eagerness of the onlookers thickens this atmosphere, reaching a peak of intensity with the thronging and vocalization surrounding the pigeon-biting incident. Moreover, throughout the festival it is members of the public who donate animals for sacrifice and drape garlands of flowers over the necks of the deodhās before bowing down to touch their feet in acts of homage. Such acts, while maintaining the distinction between devotees and objects of devotion, are nevertheless constitutive of the overall event.

A second instance of ritualized transgression occurs during one of the few intervals when the drumming temporarily pauses. At approximately 6.30 p.m. on the evenings of the second and third days of the festival, the deodhās, about sixteen in number, congregate on the ground next to the sacrifice house. Sitting in a roughly circular formation, they are handed the severed heads of freshly sacrificed goats from which to suck the blood and bite off pieces of flesh. On the second day, only a few of the deodhās drink from the heads. On the third day a dozen goats are consecutively sacrificed and each of the deodhās is invited to drink in turn. As the lifeless head of one goat is being handled by a deodhā, another goat bleats frantically in the sacrifice house. Its front legs are wrested behind its back by one of the sacrificer's assistants, who then holds the goat in the air by its now dislocated forelegs with one hand while, with his other hand, grabbing its hind legs, which had previously been kicking furiously. The goat, with legs now immobilized, screams out in pain and terror, extending its neck forwards – 'Waah! Waa-aa-aah!' The sound is eerily similar to the distressed cry of a human infant. Swinging the goat into position above the U-shaped block, the assistant jams the goat's neck down into the slot and pulls back on the legs, thereby forcing the base of the goat's skull against the block and maximally elongating the neck, at which point the goat is no longer able to make a sound. In some instances a second assistant holds the goat's head in place while the sacrificer (the *balikaṭā*: literally, the one by whom the offering – *bali* – is cut – *kaṭa*) brings the sword down and slices through its neck, but often the head is left to fall onto the floor before being picked up and passed to the deodhās.

Having dispatched the goats, the sacrificer comes out into the courtyard where the deodhās are sitting. Kneeling with a sword's hilt resting in his lap and the blade turned upwards, he cuts the heads off numerous pigeons, which have been readily donated by onlookers. In some instances, parents will first hand the pigeons to their child, who in turn gives them to the sacrificer. Once decollated, the pigeons' heads and bodies are distributed to the deodhās, again for them to drink the blood. Though not generating the same level of excitement as the episode in which pigeons' heads are actively bitten off, this macabre meal nonetheless constitutes an ostentatious display of ritualized transgression in which audience members participate through the donation of the animals whose blood is to be ingested.

Reflecting both upon the ritual biting off of pigeons' heads and upon the meaning of animal sacrifice at Kāmākhyā more generally, Patricia Dold considers whether these are manifestations of 'bloodlust'. She observes that when an animal is sacrificed, 'people watch it with serious solemnity and the moment of the animal's death is sacred and so priests do not allow it to be photographed' (Dold 2011: 55). If this was the case when Dold witnessed the festival in 2009, it seems that audience responses have changed somewhat in the interim. Solemnity is indeed sometimes observed, but this is intermingled with other emotions. These include both a sense of elation and glee as the heads of the pigeons are being bitten off and their headless bodies thrown into the crowd, and a curious mix of nonchalance and morbid fascination as the goats are being slaughtered and the deodhās are drinking their blood. Photography, while certainly forbidden within the temple building, is freely permitted in the surrounding courtyard. If any nominal prohibition exists, the priests make no effort to enforce it. So, in these days of the smartphone, not only are photographs and videos of animal beheadings taken without sanction, but some of the resulting material is subsequently uploaded to social media and video sharing websites.

Dold concludes that animal sacrifice (*bali*) 'is not a celebration of death or of the power to kill. Perhaps then, the crowd at Debaddhanī celebrates the living presence of goddesses as the Deodhas accept animal offerings' (2011: 55). But there is no reason to assume that these attitudes are mutually exclusive. When, for example, a deodhā who is standing on the swords receives a pigeon's head directly into his open maw and holds it there while the pigeon flaps in a desperate attempt to free itself, only to then be decapitated by the deodhā's crunching teeth, why should we not describe this as a celebration *both* of death and the power to kill, on the one hand, and of the living presence of goddesses, on the other? The goddesses that are being celebrated include those who are associated precisely with the power to kill as well as with the power to heal and to grant new life. The pigeon with its head in the mouth of the deodhā vividly represents the precarious contingency of life and death. There is a figurative sense in which we all have our heads in the mouth of powers that are beyond our control.

In the eleventh chapter of the *Bhagavad Gītā* (*c.* first century CE), upon seeing Lord Kṛṣṇa's true and terrifying form in a theophanic vision, the warrior-prince Arjuna declares of his fellow combatants on the battlefield that 'They quickly enter Your fearful mouths, / Which gape with many tusks; / Some are seen with crushed heads, / Clinging between Your teeth' (11.27, trans. Sargeant 2009: 479). Here, as Bakhtin says of the grotesque face, the most salient characteristic is 'the gaping mouth', which 'dominates all else', the other features becoming merely the 'frame encasing this wide-open abyss' (1984b: 317). Comparable images of voracious mouths populate the mythology and iconography of the aggressive female deities in the Hindu traditions. The mouth, with its 'long fangs' and 'lolling tongue', is the focal point of the 'horrific' goddess 'who lurks in battlefields and cremation grounds consuming human flesh' – 'an ambivalent fusion of death and sensuality, of terrifying violence and erotic power' (Urban 2003: 172) (Fig. 6.5).

THE GODDESS KALI.

Figure 6.5 The goddess Kālī (engraving), English School, 19th century. Private Collection. © Look and Learn / Bridgeman Images.

The dance of the deodhās is not erotic, but it is sensual in the broadest sense: in the sense, that is, that it is emphatically bodily and earthy, assaulting the sensory organs of both performers and spectators. The drumbeat resonates in the ears and chest. The dancing bodies, smeared both with vermilion paste and with animal blood, stamp the ground, running and leaping; they sweat and dribble and breathe and yell. It is an energetic performative portrayal of divine possession.

Concluding remarks

What we have seen in this chapter is a glimpse of one festival at one particular site in contemporary India. However, by my contextualizing of this festival both geographically, in relation to some of the history and mythology surrounding the Kāmākhyā temple, and conceptually, by noting connections with aspects of spirit possession more generally, a deeper understanding of the Deodhanī festival has been enabled than that which could have resulted from a more thematically restricted treatment. Also providing conceptual enrichment has been the motif of the grotesque body, which I have drawn from the work of Bakhtin and other commentators on literary and visual artistic forms. There are many conceptual lenses through which a phenomenon such as the dance of the deodhās could be viewed, but that of the grotesque offers especially fertile discursive resources with which to articulate the deep ambivalences of imagery and ambience that pervade this cultural and religious event. Furthermore, by exemplifying how the concept of the grotesque may be applied to this specific festival, opportunities are opened up for applications to other religious happenings of this and related concepts – for example, concepts such as those of 'dark comedy' (Styan 1968), the 'theatre of cruelty' (Bermel 1997) and the 'aesthetics of discomfort' (Aldama and Lindenberger 2016).

Some readers may wonder what the kind of material expounded in this chapter has to do with philosophy, or why more distinctively 'philosophical' questions have not been raised in relation to it. Such questions might include those concerning the metaphysics of 'possession'. For example: how can a deity take possession of a human being, and does the intelligibility of such an idea hinge upon the viability of a conception of persons as comprising ontologically separable minds and bodies? Other questions might concern the ethics of animal sacrifice: is it justified, and if so, on what grounds? In principle, there would be nothing wrong with raising questions of these sorts, but asking them in a meaningful way would require close attention to the phenomena at issue. In the absence of such attention, one is liable to mischaracterize what it is one is asking about. As in the case of D. Z. Phillips' reflections upon child sacrifice, which we saw in Chapter 1 (pp. 36–7), we might worry that, if we 'do not know what sacrifice means' for the people who perform it, then our judgement about what is going on is destined to be, at best, superficial. Similarly, if we do not situate the performance of divine possession within the broader ritual and mythic framework that gives it the sense that it has, we may miss its religious and cultural significance, failing to appreciate the kind of performance that it is. None of this need involve simply accepting as veridical the participants' view of things. But it does involve trying to understand what their view of things is, and thus what the activities they engage in are. It is this logically fundamental, yet persistently difficult, task – the task of thick description and contemplative hermeneutics – that this chapter has been concerned with in the case of the Deodhanī festival. In common with Norman Denzin's construal of thick description, the chapter has begun to articulate some of the constitutive features of the lifeworld in which the practices of animal sacrifice and divine possession have a place, and to thereby make 'a space for the reader to imagine his or her way into the life experience of another' (Denzin 2001: 99, quoted on page 63 *ante*).

The dearth of existing debates in the philosophy of religion that come even close to engaging with topics such as divine possession, shamanistic ritual and blood sacrifice creates the difficulty of finding points of connection between the material discussed in this chapter and what usually goes by the name of philosophy of religion. But this very difficulty is itself significant, for it accentuates the narrowness of the conception of religiosity with which philosophy of religion characteristically operates. With that narrow purview in sight, a sustained hermeneutical treatment of a religious event such as the Deodhanī festival facilitates a cultural critique of philosophy of religion and a radical expansion of its understanding of its central concept, namely the concept of religion itself. This chapter has thus been a further move in the direction of a more methodologically diverse and conceptually encompassing approach, focussing on contextualized understanding rather than, more narrowly, on the evaluation of 'truth claims'.

Moreover, by emphasizing phenomenological aspects of the ritual practices under discussion, including the grotesque imagery, thunderous drumming and intense mood, I hope to have brought out dimensions of ritual other than what Schilbrack has characterized as their cognitive or pedagogically oriented capabilities. Without needing to deny that religious rituals can, in some instances, constitute 'cognitive activities' and 'opportunities for inquiry', we should recognize that they can also be emotionally charged expressions of something deeply primordial and instinctual: they are capable of resonating with a sense of awe and wonder at, among other things, that which is sinister, threatening and terrible. And they are no less worthy of philosophical investigation for that.

In this chapter, then, we have seen ways of approaching, philosophically, certain neglected topics in the philosophy of religion. Also largely neglected by philosophers has been the abundance of traditions, practices and ways of thinking associated with so-called indigenous peoples. Some connections with that theme have been made both in the present chapter and in Chapter 5. It is to a more explicit and sustained consideration of indigenous traditions that we shall turn in Chapter 7.

7

'A Language in Which to Think of the World':

Animism, Philosophy and Indigenous Traditions

The phrase 'a language in which to think of the world' derives from a discussion by D. Z. Phillips of the notion of animism or, more specifically, of certain forms of animistic expression exemplified by particular Native Americans (Phillips 2001b: 158–9).[1] Commenting on an earlier essay by Mario von der Ruhr, Phillips endorses the contention that when Native Americans speak in terms that, for example, attribute the power of speech to trees and rocks, and ascribe emotions to the 'spirit of the land', the available interpretive options are not limited to a simplistic dichotomy between 'literal'

---

[1] I am aware of the disputes surrounding the appropriate terminology by which to refer to the pre-Columbian inhabitants of the Americas and their descendants. In the absence of any consensus on this issue, I follow certain other scholars (e.g. Nagel 1996: xi–xii) in using terms such as 'Native American', 'American Indian' and 'Amerindian' interchangeably.

and 'metaphorical' meaning (cf. von der Ruhr 1996). There is, Phillips concurs, a third possibility, which is to hear the forms of words at issue as presenting us with, precisely, 'a language in which to think of the world'. What this third interpretive option facilitates is an understanding of the animistic modes of expression as insinuating neither that trees and rocks speak in exactly the way that humans do, nor that they speak in a merely metaphorical sense (and hence, from a literal point of view, do not *really* speak at all). Rather, the modes of expression can be regarded as an entry point into a perspective on the world that offers alternative ways of conceptualizing living beings along with what, from a modern Western cultural standpoint, are liable to be construed as inert or inorganic components of the natural environment.

On the account to which I have just referred, the verbal and written affirmations of indigenous peoples can provide a means of accessing perspectives on the world that diverge from those with which modern Western readers may be most familiar.[2] And the philosophical approach exemplified by von der Ruhr and Phillips provides a means by which indigenous traditions may be brought within the purview of philosophy of religion; or rather, it provides a means of expanding that purview to better accommodate discussion of the traditions in question. It does this by seeking to do conceptual justice to the variety of perspectives that exist in the world rather than, as is all too often the case, fixating on only a narrow selection of religious concepts while, in many instances, abstracting those concepts from the very lived traditions in which they have their sense.

Extensive discussions of the forms of religion displayed by indigenous communities are virtually non-existent in the philosophy of religion, a rare exception being a book-length study by Arvind Sharma of what he terms 'primal religion'. Sharma describes philosophy of religion as undergoing a gradual 'deprovincialization' (2006: back cover), which has occurred as philosophers have examined the major religions of Asia as well as of the Western world. He adds, however, that despite being 'present in both the East

---

[2] Like 'Native Americans', 'indigenous peoples' remains a contested term. Though I shall not in this chapter be entering into the debate surrounding its use, I accept the point made by other commentators that, far from being treated as 'static and rigid', the meaning of 'indigenous' should be recognized as having a degree of context-dependence. Relevant contextual factors include the power relations between those who are categorized as indigenous on the one hand and the 'politically dominant group' within a given society on the other (Viljoen 2010: 78). For a variety of opinions on the term 'indigenous peoples', see Barnard (2006) plus the responses from seven other anthropologists and the rejoinder from Barnard that follow it in the same issue of the journal *Social Anthropology*.

and the West', a certain tradition – 'namely, the primal religious tradition' – remains neglected in those treatments, 'perhaps under the mistaken assumption that this religious tradition has little to offer by way of philosophical reflection' (ibid.).

Sharma, no doubt, harbours some questionable assumptions of his own. Among these is the assumption that it makes sense to think of indigenous religions as constituting a single religious tradition rather than a multiplicity of more or less variegated traditions. A further assumption on Sharma's part – embodied in the very structure of his book – is that discussion of indigenous religions can usefully be inserted into a preformed conceptual mould based on an existing list of categories. Instead of looking to see how the effort to engage philosophically with indigenous religions might transform the very parameters of the inquiry, Sharma attempts to shoehorn ideas drawn from indigenous sources into a framework borrowed from a general textbook on the philosophy of religion authored by John Hick (i.e. Hick 1990). Thus, while Sharma is to be commended for his intrepid spirit, the end result, as several commentators have noted, leaves much work to be done.[3]

In view of the paucity of material on indigenous religions within the philosophy of religion itself, one method of improving upon the kind of project typified by Sharma is to look towards debates in other disciplines. As we saw in Chapter 5, the work of anthropologists is a fertile resource in this regard, as are certain discussions in the field of religious studies. And among the topics to have generated vibrant debate in these disciplines since the 1990s is that of animism. Having, to a large extent, fallen out of favour among scholars of indigenous religions in the mid-twentieth century, talk of animism has gained fresh approval over recent decades as a means of identifying certain tendencies or 'orientations' that are 'immanent' in the ways in which many indigenous peoples relate to their environment.[4] Indeed,

---

[3] For critical appraisal of Sharma, see Grillo (2011), MacDonald (2011), Smith (2011). Grillo challenges the adoption of Hick's framework especially strongly: 'Using Hick's Christo-centric philosophy as the basis for establishing a comparative philosophy of religion replicates the fundamental error of early works in the history of religions: that is, it makes the implicit assumption that Christianity is the norm against which comparison with the "other" is made' (2011: 805).

[4] I am here borrowing the notions of orientation and immanence from Ingold (2000: 112). It should be noted that neither I nor most of the authors I am discussing in this chapter simply equate indigenous religion with animism. Not all indigenous religions are animistic and not all versions of animism are connected with indigenous religion. As we shall see, Edward Tylor *would* equate the two, but only inasmuch as he equates religion *in general* with animism.

some scholars have spoken enthusiastically of a 'new animism' that manifests in the 'worldviews and lifeways' not only of indigenous peoples but also of Neo-Pagans and environmental activists.[5]

In this chapter, I take animism as a central concept around which to develop philosophical engagement with indigenous religions. I begin by examining the origins of the concept of animism and its revival in recent and contemporary anthropology and religious studies. I then turn to the treatment of animism by a small number of philosophers, including Phillips and von der Ruhr, to whom I referred above. While the approach that regards animistic talk as illustrative of a particular perspective on the world is helpful as far as it goes, there is a danger of oversimplifying our understanding of that perspective if insufficient attention is paid to the variety of ways in which indigenous peoples interact with their environments. To guard against this danger, I examine the ongoing debate among anthropologists, historians and other scholars concerning the myth of the 'ecologically noble savage', a phrase first coined by Kent Redford (1991). As is often the case when a topic is scrutinized carefully, the conclusions to be drawn in relation to this debate are complex. But, as I hope to have brought out in this book as a whole, gesturing towards complexity is itself a helpful lesson for the philosophy of religion; doing so is apt to encourage – at least among those philosophers who wish to participate in the deprovincializing project – an aspiration for further methodological innovation, perhaps including a higher degree of interdisciplinary research.

The concept of animism: origins, decline and revival

The use of the term 'animism' to denote a religious orientation is normally traced back to Edward Tylor (1832–1917), who is widely esteemed as the founder, or at any rate one of the principal founders, of the discipline of anthropology in the nineteenth century (Bird-David 1999: 69; Stocking 2001: 105; Reid 2017: 363). Tylor himself derived the term 'animism' from earlier uses, notably its application in the eighteenth century by the German chemist and physician Georg Ernst Stahl, who invoked the notion of a 'sensitive soul' or *anima* pervading living organisms to account for the

---

[5] See, e.g., Bouissac (1989), Harvey (2017, esp. Ch. 5), Rountree (2012). The phrase 'animist worldviews and lifeways' is one that Harvey uses in various places (e.g. 2012: 194; 2017 *passim*).

presence of life and the onset of disease (see Ackerknecht 1982: 128).[6] Transposing the term from the medical to the religious and cultural sphere, Tylor deployed it to indicate the ascription of 'personality and life' not merely to animals and human beings but also to 'what we call inanimate objects', such as 'rivers, stones, trees, weapons, and so forth' (1920, vol. I: 477). For Tylor, animism was more than some relatively marginal religious attitude; construed concisely as 'the deep-lying doctrine of Spiritual Beings', it constitutes the essential characteristic of religion tout court (425). Tylor, famously, adopts 'belief in Spiritual Beings' as his 'minimum definition of Religion' (424). Hence, by identifying animism with the 'doctrine of Spiritual Beings', he effectively equates animism with religion, or at least with religion's 'essential source' (ibid.).

Animism was viewed by Tylor as the very 'groundwork of the Philosophy of Religion, from that of savages up to that of civilized men', adding that 'although it may at first seem to afford but a bare and meagre definition of a minimum of religion, it will be found practically sufficient; for where the root is, the branches will generally be produced' (426). Tylor is here using the term 'philosophy' in a broad sense, to mean a kind of system or worldview, 'of which belief is the theory and worship is the practice' (427). He is thus conceiving of philosophy of religion not as a branch of academic inquiry, but as an approach to the world that is distinctively religious or spiritual.[7] Despite acknowledging that animism, and hence religion, comprises practical as well as doxastic elements, Tylor's insistence that it is specifically *belief* in spiritual beings that is essential to religion has earned him a reputation for being 'intellectualistic' (Radin 1958: xi). He tends to treat religion, with animism as its foundation, as essentially a primitive – and ultimately a mistaken – theory about the world. Notwithstanding its tenacious presence in the more instinctive moments even of modern 'civilized' life, animism, for Tylor, represents a 'childish stage' of the human mind's development (Tylor 1920, vol. I: 286). According to the evolutionary model to which Tylor subscribed, this immature stage inevitably succumbs in the long run to scientific ways of thinking, which are deemed to be intellectually superior.

---

[6] Stahl (1737) is cited in Tylor (1920 [1871], vol. I: 425–6 n. 1). For more on Stahl's animism, see King (1964).
[7] We might say that, in Tylor's usage, 'of religion' constitutes the subjective or active genitive (implying the philosophy that *belongs to religion*) rather than the objective or passive genitive (implying that religion is what is being treated as an object of study *by philosophy*).

It is in large measure these associations with a condescending evolutionary conception of human cognitive development that led, over the course of the first half of the twentieth century, to a reluctance on the part of anthropologists, and indeed philosophers, to use the term 'animism'.[8] In more recent decades, however, 'animism' has been reclaimed as a non-pejorative designator, both by certain anthropologists and scholars of religion on the one hand and, on the other hand, by certain indigenous and other people who wish to identify themselves as animists. In some instances, to highlight the difference, Tylor's conception has been labelled 'old' animism in contrast to the revised and more politically respectable 'new' or 'neo-' animism,[9] though in many instances these qualifying prefixes are omitted.

Recent advocates of the viability of the concept of animism in the study of indigenous peoples frequently look to work in the mid-twentieth century by the anthropologist Irving Hallowell as a precursor and source of inspiration (e.g. Harvey 2017: 17). In his writings on the Ojibwe people of southern Canada, Hallowell is careful not to treat them as animists in what he regards as the 'dogmatic' sense, which would signify a people who indiscriminately 'attribute living souls to inanimate objects such as stones' (Hallowell 1960: 24–5). Rather, Hallowell views the Ojibwe as recognizing 'potentialities for animation in certain classes of objects under certain circumstances'; whether these potentialities are understood to have been actualized will depend on the forms of behaviour displayed by particular objects belonging to the relevant class. Thus, for example, the Ojibwe do not regard all stones as being alive, but they do regard some of them as being so, notably those that have been perceived to move apparently of their own accord (25). In some instances, the Ojibwe will even claim to be able to have a two-way conversation with a stone, thereby indicating 'that not only animate properties but even "person" attributes may be projected upon objects which to us clearly belong to a physical inanimate category' (26).

Hallowell's talk of attributes being *projected* might be taken to imply that he considers there to be something erroneous or purely imaginary about the Ojibwe's ascription of personal characteristics to what are, 'to us', inanimate objects. But on the whole Hallowell deliberately tries to avoid giving that

---

[8] 'To call any philosophy Animism is to condemn it. The word usually refers to an early level of man's thinking about the world, a level in which our distinction between animate and the inanimate had not yet been made' (Robinson 1949: 54). See also Bolle (1987), Mbiti (1990: 8).

[9] For 'new animism', see, inter alia, Århem (2016: 6); Franke (2010: 13); Tremlett, Sutherland and Harvey (2017: 4). For 'neo-animism', see, e.g., Howell (2013: 105).

impression, maintaining instead that a comprehensive understanding of another culture requires an effort to refrain from imposing on it a set of 'categorical abstractions derived from Western thought' (21). Rather, he insists, we should strive to adopt 'a world view perspective', which consists in seeing how the various conceptual strands of a given cultural system cohere together without privileging our own way of viewing things as necessarily normative.

Unlike Hallowell, certain theorists have followed Tylor in assuming that 'animistic thinking' incorporates 'fallacious reasoning' that leads to '"illogical" behaviour' such as the performance of sacrifices in the hope of persuading the natural environment to give one something in return (Humphrey 1976: 313). One way of trying to explain the origins of such purportedly misguided reasoning has been to devise evolutionary psychological theories, which speculate that, in the distant past, it would have been advantageous to human survival to ascribe life and anthropomorphic characteristics to various natural phenomena regardless of whether the phenomena really possess them. Supposedly, these ascriptions would have been advantageous because they instantiate a precautionary principle, encapsulated in the phrase 'better safe than sorry': assuming that something is alive or humanlike enables evasive action to be taken, whereas waiting until one is certain about its nature is liable, in many instances, to put one at risk (Guthrie 1993, esp. 4–5).[10]

Against this line of argument, it has been pointed out that the entities and phenomena to which animist peoples attribute life and personhood are not generally, let alone exclusively, those with which they are least familiar or about which they have the greatest degree of uncertainty. On the contrary, it tends to be precisely in relation to those features of the world that are best known to them that such peoples' expressions of animism are strongest. As the anthropologist Nurit Bird-David has contended, the evolutionary theory's supposition that human cognitive development has comprised a series of retrospective acknowledgements of earlier animistic mistakes remains dubious, for even on the most charitable reading it leaves unanswered the question of why these purported 'mistakes' are culturally affirmed and amplified by animist peoples (Bird-David 1999: 71). Worse than that, however, it insinuates that the cognitive capacities of indigenous people are

---

[10] As Daniel Dennett summarizes the idea: 'if you don't startle at dangerous motions, you'll soon be somebody else's supper' (2007: 109).

inferior to those of most animals, since it maintains that even amphibians are able to see their mistake after reacting to an inorganic object as though it possessed animate qualities (albeit that they are prone to react similarly next time) (ibid.).

Bird-David is among the anthropologists who, in the footsteps of Hallowell, view animism not as a childish or otherwise underdeveloped way of comprehending the world, but as embodying alternative ontological and epistemological perspectives (1999: 77–9).[11] Drawing upon her own fieldwork among the Nayaka, a small forager community in southern India, Bird-David contrasts animistic (or *relational*) epistemology with epistemology of a modern Western (or *modernist*) strain. To illustrate the difference between these, Bird-David characterizes the modernist approach as one that, drawing a sharp distinction between the knower and the known, tends to objectify that which is to be known and to analyse it into its component parts. When studying a forest, for example, botanists who deploy a modernist epistemology are apt to chop some specimen trees into pieces and divide the pieces into distinct types, which are then transported to a herbarium to be classified. By contrast, the Nayaka means of knowing would involve talking with trees, where 'talking with' encompasses activities that might include 'singing, dancing, or socializing in other ways'. 'To "talk with a tree" – rather than "cut it down" – is', Bird-David proposes, 'to perceive what *it* does as one acts towards it, being aware concurrently of changes in oneself and the tree. It is expecting response and responding, growing into mutual responsiveness and, furthermore, possibly into mutual responsibility' (1999: 77).

This notion of an epistemology, in the sense of a way of learning with and about one's environment, shades into the notion of an ontology, where the latter term is used to denote a way of conceptualizing the entities that constitute the world. Both the animistic epistemology and the animistic ontology are facets of a conception of community as comprising more than just the human inhabitants of a region: in effect, the region itself amounts to 'a local heterogeneous community whose members cooperate with or accommodate themselves to one another' (Bird-David 2017: 174). To designate the mode of existence characteristic of such communities, Bird-David coins the term *pluripresence*, by which she means to indicate a mutual

---

[11] See also various publications by Tim Ingold, esp. Ingold (2000). A concise discussion of Bird-David vis-à-vis Ingold is included in Århem (2016: 9–11).

togetherness shared by multiple beings of diverse species within a community small enough in geographical spread to facilitate 'the vivid availability' of all members to one another (2017: 21).[12]

As is suggested by her talk of cooperation and 'mutual responsibility', Bird-David perceives relational epistemology as also carrying certain ethical implications. Indeed, the idea that animism is tightly bound up with attitudes of solidarity with, and respect towards, nonhuman species and the environment as a whole is pervasive in the contemporary literature. It is frequently accompanied by the insinuation that animism, far from being of mere academic interest as one among many possible ways of relating to the world, is to be admired and celebrated as a way that is ethically and ecologically superior to others.[13] Though understandable, such admiration risks providing an oversimplified and hence distorted picture of the heterogeneous category of indigenous peoples, a risk that I shall explore later in this chapter. In the next two sections, however, I turn to some of the few instances in which animism and indigenous religiosity more generally have been discussed in specifically philosophical contexts.

Animism, indigeneity and the philosophy of religion

As I noted in this chapter's introduction, discussion of indigenous religions has for the most part been conspicuous by its absence in the philosophy of religion. When such religions have been referred to at all – either by the term 'indigenous' or by others, such as 'primal' or 'primitive' – it has often been precisely in order to clear the path for a discussion that ignores them. As we saw in Chapter 1, for instance, John Hick draws a distinction between two

---

[12] Bird-David refers to 'pluripresence' as a neologism (2017: xiv), but the word has in fact existed since the late eighteenth century, albeit with a different meaning. Boswell quotes Samuel Johnson as asserting that the Roman Catholic invocation of saints implies not their omnipresence (i.e. presence everywhere) but only their pluripresence (i.e. presence in multiple places at once) (Boswell 1831: 240).

[13] This celebratory posture is most obvious in the work of Graham Harvey, who not only speaks unapologetically as a proponent (rather than a mere scholar) of animism, but contends that the new animism, unlike the old, actively invites academics 'to participate more fully' in 'the living world' (2017: 212). Harvey's allegedly confessional stance has resulted in his being dubbed a 'new primitivist' (Platvoet 2004: 52) and a 'theological animist' (Cox 2007: 161–3). Ingold, too, often implies that animist ontologies and epistemologies afford not merely a different but a truer account of reality than do certain Western ones; see, e.g., Ingold (1999) and comments on Ingold in Århem (2016: 10).

broad categories of religion. On the one hand are those that Hick terms 'the great developed world faiths', which exhibit a prominent interest in personal 'salvation or liberation'; on the other hand are what Hick lumps together into the category of '"primitive" or "archaic" religion, which is more concerned with keeping things on an even keel, avoiding catastrophe' (1990: 3). Since it is the quest for salvation, characterized in terms of 'the transition from self-centeredness to Reality-centeredness' on which Hick is chiefly focused (ibid.), the indigenous religions, which he uncritically assumes to be unconcerned with issues of salvation, get left aside.[14] Subsequently, in his *An Interpretation of Religion* (2004), Hick acknowledges that he has given less attention to 'primal religion' than it deserves, though here he excuses this lacuna by remarking that the book aims to provide only a preliminary rather than a definitive inquiry. The onus, he says, is on those who 'find this approach inadequate or misleading' to develop their own (2004: xiii).

In other cases, consideration of indigenous religions has been omitted on account of their lacking a clear connection with the Western philosophical tradition. For instance, in laying out the parameters of their five-volume edited series on *The History of Western Philosophy of Religion*, Graham Oppy and Nick Trakakis note that they have based their decision to exclude entries on thinkers from 'the non-Western world', including 'the Asian, African and indigenous philosophical and religious traditions', 'primarily on the (admittedly not incontestable) view that [those traditions] have not had a great impact on the main historical narrative of the West' (2014: vii). Given the series' explicit focus on specifically Western philosophy of religion, this editorial decision is perhaps defensible. But the very fact that Western philosophy of religion has, according to these editors, managed to avoid engaging to any serious extent with Asian, African and indigenous traditions tells a poignant story in itself.

A further perceived obstacle to incorporating indigenous religions into philosophical discussions is the predominance of oral over literary modes of communication in indigenous societies. Thus, in a chapter on 'Religion and Global Ethics', Joseph Runzo-Inada, while recognizing the importance of indigenous religious ethics, especially in connection with environmental issues, opts to concentrate on 'the world religions' that, 'unlike indigenous

---

[14] More nuanced discussions of soteriology in relation to indigenous religions distinguish between 'this-worldly' and 'other-worldly' conceptions of salvation (Sharma 2006: 12), thereby making conceptual space for talk of indigenous soteriologies that aim 'at securing benefits in this world rather than in a life after death' (Cox 2007: 63).

oral traditions', 'have philosophical religious texts which facilitate comparisons in ethics' (2013: 700).

There have, of course, been exceptions to the general disregard of indigenous religions by philosophers, some of which I have mentioned already in this chapter. Aside from Sharma's monograph, one such exception takes the form of an exchange on the question 'Is Animism Alive and Well?' between Richard Eldridge (1996) and Mario von der Ruhr (1996) plus a subsequent endorsement of von der Ruhr's position by D. Z. Phillips (2001b: Ch. 6). The contributions of these philosophers are important inasmuch as they exhibit ways of avoiding the kinds of hasty marginalization of indigenous traditions exemplified by Hick, Runzo-Inada and Oppy and Trakakis. By offering potential points of connection with anthropological literature, some of which I briefly surveyed in the previous section, these philosophical treatments, while being limited in their own ways, open up possibilities of interdisciplinary inquiry that warrant critical attention and augmentation.

Central to the argument that Eldridge develops is the contention that while 'traditional, more animistic cultures and practices', on the one hand, and 'modern, scientific, materialist cultures and practices', on the other, both 'express persistent human interests and responses to reality', they nonetheless display significant differences (1996: 21). Following suggestions from figures such as Wittgenstein and the anthropologist Robin Horton, Eldridge makes a distinction analogous to the one that we have seen Bird-David making between modernist and animist ways of relating to the world. As Eldridge puts it, modern materialist cultures are disposed to encourage attempts to control nature, satisfy material desires and cultivate power, whereas traditional cultures generally accentuate 'the expression of a sense of human ensoulment and resonance with nature, thus leading to what Horton calls "an intensely poetic quality in everyday life" [Horton 1970: 170]' (Eldridge 1996: 21). Eldridge maintains that, despite the divergences between these general orientations, the poetic quality to which Horton alludes retains a place, perhaps an ineradicable place, in all human life, such that it may be apposite to speak of 'a natural poetry of being' (Eldridge 1996: 12).

Versions of the thought that vestiges of animistic or other supposedly premodern modes of response to the world persist in modern societies occur frequently in early literature on indigenous religions. Tylor himself was sympathetic to the idea that even 'full-grown civilized Europeans' are, for example, prone to react to inanimate objects as they might to purposive agents, especially in moments of passion, such as when, in anger, we lash out at an object that has caused us physical pain (Tylor 1920, vol. I: 286). Several decades later, Wittgenstein, in connection with a comparable observation of his own, proposed that reminding ourselves of these instinctive levels of reaction can satisfy (or perhaps supplant) our desire for an explanation of certain religious rites: the reminders help us to see that, analogously, rites may be expressing something deeply human without their needing to be based on a theory or belief (purportedly held by the participants) that the ritual action will bring about some practical result (Wittgenstein 1993: 137–8). In this respect, Wittgenstein's thought runs counter to that of Tylor, who would have regarded the instinctive reactions to which Wittgenstein is referring as themselves manifestations of a residual, and erroneous, belief.

Eldridge's intimation that there is something specifically poetic about animistic ways of thinking and behaving echoes (or anticipates) suggestions from Brian Clack, who borrows from Goethe the phrase 'poetry of life' (*die Poesie des Lebens*) to express the thought that much of what, in modern life, gets derided as superstition may be seen to possess 'a curious depth' (Clack 1995: 114).[15] One of Clack's examples, derived from the work of James Frazer, is that of the Cambodian King of Fire, who was said by the local community to own a sword containing a spirit 'who guards it constantly and works miracles with it' (Frazer 1911: 5). The legend surrounding the sword declares the sword's spirit to be that of a slave who, having accidentally spilt some of his own blood on the blade as it was being forged, 'died a voluntary death to expiate his involuntary offence' (ibid.). The destructive power of the sword is said to be such that the King's unsheathing it even partially would result in the sun becoming hidden and people and animals falling unconscious; if he were to withdraw it fully from the scabbard, 'the world would come to an end' (ibid.).[16] Commenting on this example, Clack observes that an excessively rationalistic interpretation would assume that a false conception of causality is in play, whereas adopting a different perspective might disclose something more profound. Instead of fixating on the error of supposing that a sword could have the magical power attributed to it, Clack recommends reflecting upon 'the fascination that envelops us when we entertain the possibility that it *might*'; in doing so, 'We may come to recognise the essentially poetic nature of such acts' (Clack 1995: 114).

---

[15] For Goethe's original use of the phrase, see Goethe (1998 [1833]: 20, maxim number 171).

[16] Frazer's account is based on reports from nineteenth-century French expeditions to the Central Highlands that cover the border area between modern-day Vietnam, Laos and Cambodia. For a more recent ethnographically informed account, see Salemink (2003, esp. Ch. 8).

Inviting us to perceive certain customs or practices under the aspect of poetry is a means of freeing us from the temptation to dismiss them as products of ignorance or confusion. Just as it would show a misunderstanding to conflate poetic utterances with, say, scientific hypotheses, so, according to the view exemplified by Eldridge and Clack, it would show a misunderstanding of practices imbued with animistic or magical elements to conflate them with straightforwardly instrumental styles of reasoning. What needs to be cultivated by the philosopher, or by any other prospective interpreter, is a sensitivity to the *distinctive character* of the modes of discourse in question and, as Hallowell among many others has urged, an alertness to the dangers of hearing that discourse through the potentially distorting filter of 'categorical abstractions' imposed from outside.[17]

For someone such as Mario von der Ruhr, who, like Eldridge and Clack, has been influenced by the philosophical thought of Wittgenstein, there is little here with which to take issue. Although von der Ruhr's response to Eldridge's discussion does contain several points of disagreement, he remains sympathetic to its overall tenor (von der Ruhr 1996: 27). In the following section, I shall not focus on the points of disagreement, since doing so would require entering into the minutiae of both Eldridge's and von der Ruhr's essays in more depth than is suitable for my purposes in this chapter. Rather, I shall concentrate on how von der Ruhr provides additional 'illustrative detail to bring out what might be meant by saying that an attitude towards nature is animistic' (27–8), and especially on the point, made by von der Ruhr and seconded by Phillips, that care is needed not to presume that the only alternative to a literalistic reading of what this could mean is a purely metaphorical one.

Beyond literalism and metaphor

As a point of contrast with suggestions outlined in the previous section, we might note that those who have been eager that animism *not* be thought of in terms of poetry include Tylor. He maintained that when 'the lower tribes of man' speak of the 'sun and stars, trees and rivers, winds and clouds' as

---

[17] For talk of the importance of noting '*the distinctive character*' (original emphasis) of different modes of discourse or 'linguistic practices', see the exposition of Wittgenstein's philosophical methods in Clack (1999: 51). For talk of 'categorical abstractions derived from Western thought', see Hallowell (1960: 21), which I quoted on page 169 above.

beings who not only have lives comparable to those of humans, but fulfil 'their special functions in the universe with the aid of limbs like beasts or of artificial instruments like men', the basis of these ideas ought not to be reduced 'to poetic fancy and transformed metaphor'; rather, the 'philosophy of nature' on which the ideas rest, though 'early and crude', is nonetheless 'thoughtful, consistent, and quite really and seriously meant' (1920, vol. I: 285). In assertions such as this we see a dichotomy between poetic or metaphorical meaning on the one hand and earnest or sincere meaning on the other. The dichotomy is questionable, given that there is no reason why a form of words could not be both metaphorical and seriously meant. Yet there is also an important point that Tylor is making, which is that it would indeed be misleading to regard articulations of animistic beliefs as 'merely' metaphorical if this were understood to mean that the beliefs are not genuinely held. What should be noted – and what Tylor does not quite acknowledge – is that a rejection of this reading of animism as mere metaphor need not entail a simplistic literalism, which assumes that rocks and trees and rivers are being spoken of as alive and conscious in exactly the same sense as human beings are. We should not take it for granted that we know perfectly well what it amounts to for animistic expressions to be 'really and seriously meant', and nor should we presume that this amounts to the same thing in every case. Seeing what it does amount to will require attention to the expressions themselves amid the broader cultural surroundings in which they have their place. I take this to be the central point that von der Ruhr is making in his essay, and his means of fleshing it out is to discuss certain exemplary passages from an anthology of Native American textual sources.

The passages adduced by von der Ruhr are ones that accentuate an attitude of reverence for the natural environment and disgust at its mistreatment by the white settlers of European descent. For example, he quotes a Wintu woman's lamentation that unlike the American Indians, who 'never hurt anything', white people plough up the land, displacing rocks and felling trees. The trees and rocks protest 'Don't. I am sore. Don't hurt me', but the white people persist in their destructive ways; as a consequence, 'The spirit of the land hates them' (Lee 1959: 163–4).[18] Complementing the Wintu

---

[18] Quoted in von der Ruhr (1996: 28) from McLuhan (1980: 15). Here and subsequently, in instances when I have consulted the original source, I shall cite it in the main text. Lee attributes this particular pronouncement to 'An old Wintu woman, speaking in prophetic vein' (1959: 163).

woman's lament is an affirmation by the Stoney Indian, Walking Buffalo (1871–1967), that trees talk to one another and to people, provided one is willing to listen. While the trees have taught him much – about the weather, animals and the 'Great Spirit' – the problem with the white people is that they refuse to listen, whether to Indians or 'to other voices in nature' (MacEwan 1969: 181).[19]

If remarks of the sort exemplified by the Wintu woman and by Walking Buffalo are heard in the light of a rudimentary division between literal (or 'realist') and metaphorical (or 'non-realist') meaning, then, von der Ruhr argues, they are prone to appear 'either ridiculous or cheap, *saying* either too much to be intelligible, or too little to convey the meaning intended' (1996: 30). They would appear ridiculous and extravagant if assumed to be asserting that trees and rocks ('literally', 'really') speak or cry out in pain just as human beings do; and they would appear cheap and insubstantial if assumed to be merely metaphorical, for they do not say enough to make clear what the force of the metaphor is supposed to be. Does, for example, talk of listening to the voices of trees come to anything more than the suggestion that one may discern that an animal is nearby, or that the wind is blowing, by listening to the leaves of a tree rustling? Von der Ruhr admits that the notion of metaphor that is pertinent to the literal–metaphorical dichotomy is, in itself, somewhat narrow, for it presupposes the translatability of metaphors into non-metaphorical terms without loss of meaning (1996: 44 n. 10). While this may be feasible in the case of some metaphors, it is unlikely to be feasible in the case of all. But, for the sake of argument, von der Ruhr is willing to go along with that conception of metaphors, since it is the one assumed by those theorists, such as Frazer and (as we have seen) Tylor, who suppose there to be a basic binary opposition here: either something is sincerely meant or it is merely metaphorical whimsy. We might note in passing that Wittgenstein, too, subscribed to a crude translatability conception of metaphors and similes at the time when he composed his 'Lecture on Ethics' towards the end of 1929. In that lecture, Wittgenstein asserts that 'a simile must be a simile for *something*. And if I can describe a fact by means of a simile I must also be able to drop the simile and to describe the fact without it' (1965: 15). In saying this, Wittgenstein assumes that in the absence of the supposedly requisite translatability, what was presumed to be a simile dissolves into nonsense. In his later work, however, Wittgenstein came to see

---

[19] Quoted in von der Ruhr (1996: 28) from McLuhan (1980: 23).

that there can be figurative forms of language – language used in a 'secondary sense' (1958, Part II: 216e) – that are neither straightforwardly translatable into nonfigurative terms nor nonsensical. They derive their meanings from their use in lived activities: '*Practice* gives the words their sense' (Wittgenstein 1998: 97e).

Beyond the reductive dichotomy between literality and metaphor, the third possibility that both von der Ruhr and Phillips want to foreground is that the remarks of Native Americans about trees and rocks and other features of the environment *show* us something: they 'reveal a distinctive attitude towards nature' in a form of words that could not simply be translated into other terms without falling short of expressing the attitude at issue (von der Ruhr 1996: 30). Again, in this respect they are comparable to the words of a poem: not in the sense that they could be dispensed with and replaced by a strictly 'literal' paraphrase, but precisely in the sense that they are indispensable. To quote Phillips again, 'we are offered a language in which to think of the world', a language through which we are enabled to comprehend how the earth and trees can be seen as having 'a certain spiritual status' that 'is internally related to, or constitutive of, what one takes the earth and the trees to be' (Phillips 2001b: 158–9). What this contention certainly does not entail is that the language or mode of discourse that we are being offered constitutes a conceptual scheme that is entirely incommensurable with any modern Western way of viewing the world. Mutual understanding between those who speak in animistic terms and those who do not is not being precluded. The point is that arriving at a deep understanding of the words at issue will not be achievable without acquiring far more than a superficial appreciation of the other's perspective on the world. The words themselves provide a point of entry into that perspective, but they must be situated within the broader framework of a form of life. To the extent that we are able to enter into the perspective in question – not in the sense of coming to share it ourselves but in the sense of coming to see more clearly what it would be to share it – we enrich our appreciation of how the world might be comprehended differently, how different concepts might be adopted or those that we already have might be embellished or modified. In short, we come to see different possibilities of sense or possibilities of meaning.

To fill out the framework in which the animistic talk of Native Americans occurs, von der Ruhr quotes further passages from the anthology upon which he is drawing. He quotes, for instance, Big Thunder (*c.* 1900) of the Abenaki nation, who refers to the Great Spirit as 'our father' and the earth as 'our mother'. The latter is a source of nourishment, for 'that which we put into the ground she returns to us, and healing plants she gives us likewise' (Curtis 1923: 11).[20] To elaborate this sense of the earth as mother, von der Ruhr quotes an Oglala Lakota chief named Luther Standing Bear (1868–1939) and a spiritual leader of the Wanapum people named Smohalla ('Dreamer', c. 1815–95). Standing Bear recounts how the Lakota people loved being close to the earth, to its 'mothering power'. 'The soil was soothing, strengthening, cleansing, and healing. That is why the old Indian still sits upon the earth instead of propping himself up and away from its life-giving forces' (Standing Bear 1933: 192).[21] Smohalla, in a passage that has been widely quoted elsewhere, rejects the forms of labour imposed upon his people by the Euro-Americans, labour that involves ploughing the land, digging for ore and cutting grass to make hay:

> You ask me to plow the ground. Shall I take a knife and tear my mother's breast? Then when I die she will not take me to her bosom to rest. You ask me to dig for stone. Shall I dig under her skin for her bones? . . . You ask me to cut grass and make hay. . . . How dare I cut off my mother's hair?
>
> McLuhan 1980: 56[22]

It is notable – again in passing – that the numerous places where this passage has been quoted include a work of analytic moral philosophy by Angelika Krebs, who cites it to illustrate the 'position' that nature in its entirety is sentient. To refute this 'position', Krebs observes that the ground does not groan or tremble when, for instance, farmers plough their fields, just as the sea does not respond in these ways when someone rows a boat upon it. Since, then, neither the land nor the sea displays the behavioural criteria necessary for the correct application of the concept of pain, Krebs concludes (without irony) that '[t]he claim that either feels pain is, thus, false' (Krebs 1999: 85). Regrettably, this use of an Amerindian's words, lacking any attempt to contextualize them within the broader worldview of the Wanapum or other indigenous peoples of the Columbia Plateau from which they originate, is not untypical of much Western philosophy. It is precisely this decontextualizing

---

[20] Quoted in von der Ruhr (1996: 31) from McLuhan (1980: 22).

[21] Quoted in von der Ruhr (1996: 31) from McLuhan (1980: 6).

[22] Quoted in von der Ruhr (1996: 31). McLuhan cites as her source Drake (1834), but neither this nor any other quotation from Smohalla occurs in that book. The earliest published occurrence of the passage is in Mooney (1896: 721), who derives it from a transcription by Major J. W. MacMurray dated 1884. That transcription, though not identical to the version that appears in McLuhan's anthology, differs only very slightly (e.g. 'tear my mother's breast' reads instead 'tear my mother's bosom'). See also Ramsey (1977: 13, 263).

propensity, which demonstrates a tin ear for language that is religiously or otherwise culturally inflected, that philosophers such as Phillips and von der Ruhr are resisting.

For von der Ruhr's part, he goes a long way towards contextualizing certain Native American expressions of an animistic bent by assembling illustrative textual excerpts. By integrating those excerpts into his overall discussion, von der Ruhr effectively does what he accuses James Frazer of not doing, namely expounding 'the "grammar" of the vocabulary' that is employed by the peoples being studied (von der Ruhr 1996: 35). Still, however, there is room for critical reflection upon the agenda that remains only implicit in von der Ruhr's selection of examples. No such selection can hope to be fully comprehensive, and hence there are choices to be made about, as it were, the story one wishes to tell by means of the examples. It is striking that von der Ruhr's examples of Native American modes of discourse are all derived from a single anthology. Although the compiler of that anthology, Teri McLuhan, has herself gathered the passages from diverse sources, she has patently done so with a specific purpose in mind. As an extract from a review in *The Toronto Star*, quoted on the opening page of the anthology, remarks, 'It's a religious and poetic work whose object is to draw attention to the lasting beauty and truth of the best of Indian tradition.'[23] And as McLuhan herself admits, 'This is not a scholarly book' (1980: 2); it makes no pretence to academic rigour. We should therefore expect to find in the anthology not a balanced assortment of excerpts, but rather, to borrow a phrase from Wittgenstein, 'a one-sided diet' (Wittgenstein 1958: §593).

In von der Ruhr's selection, the diet becomes even more one-sided: a distillation of a distillation, designed to illustrate the solemn and reverential attitude displayed by many Native Americans towards the environment they inhabit and with which they feel a deep affinity.[24] There is nothing wrong with seeking to bring out this particular aspect of Native American culture, and hence neither is there anything necessarily suspect about von der Ruhr's choice of examples. A danger of oversimplification and essentialization emerges, however, when the heterogeneity of Native American attitudes and ways of being is lost sight of and the recognition of plurality is replaced by a monolithic representation. 'For the Indian', von der Ruhr writes at one point,

---

[23] The review is from *The Toronto Star*, 19 December 1973, p. A8.
[24] In the case of Phillips' discussion (2001b: 157–9), there is yet another level of distillation, since he is selecting his examples third-hand from von der Ruhr (or fourth-hand, if we take into account the fact that von der Ruhr's source, namely McLuhan, has gleaned her examples from other publications).

'it was essential to be in close contact with the earth and everything on it' (1996: 31). While this may be a viable starting point for analysis, it is little more than that, and the notion of 'the Indian' that it invokes harbours an implicit idealization. Some Native Americans themselves have invoked such idealizations, just as they have endorsed a binary opposition between 'the Indian' or 'the Red man' on the one hand and 'the White man' on the other.[25] In the words of Vine Deloria Jr (1933–2005), a well-known Lakota author and campaigner for Native American rights, 'The Indian lived with his land. *The white destroyed his land. He destroyed the planet earth*' (2007: 186, original emphasis). In the light of the sustained persecution suffered by many Native Americans since the arrival of Europeans in the late fifteenth century, the motivation for such pronouncements is understandable. But the language is strategically rhetorical in nature, intended to advance the interests of indigenous peoples against non-indigenous encroachments. It is not the language of nonpartisan philosophical reflection.

In the next section, I develop further the point that nuance and complexity in the cultural ways of indigenous peoples needs to be recognized if our philosophical pictures of animistic forms of religiosity are not to degenerate into romanticized caricatures. To give focus to the discussion, I examine in particular debates surrounding the concept of the 'ecologically noble savage'.

Demythologizing the 'ecologically noble savage'

Though commonly associated with Jean-Jacques Rousseau (esp. his *Discourse on the Origin of Inequality* of 1755), the concept of the noble savage is traceable to a work on the Americas by the French lawyer and explorer Marc Lescarbot first published in 1609,[26] and the earliest occurrence of the term 'noble savage' in English is in John Dryden's Restoration drama *The Conquest*

---

[25] See, among many other examples, several of the speeches of Native Americans collected in Blaisdell (2000), such as the one in which Tecumseh of the Shawnee (dated October 1811) declares that 'The red man owns the country' and 'When the white man approaches you the earth shall swallow him up' (Blaisdell 2000: 58).

[26] See, e.g., Lescarbot (1928: 100): 'the savages have that noble quality, that they give liberally, casting at the feet of him whom they will honour the present that they give him.' Lescarbot immediately adds, however, that this apparent generosity is always motivated by the hope of receiving something in return. For the original French, see Lescarbot (1609: 598).

of Granada (1672).[27] Discussion of the concept has been revived and intensified in recent decades because of the prevalence both in anthropological literature and in popular culture of the contention, or the uncritical assumption, that the ways of life pursued by indigenous peoples are generally more conducive to environmental sustainability than are those of modern industrial societies. In the wake of a provocative article by conservation biologist Kent Redford (1991), this area of controversy became known as the 'ecologically noble savage debate' (Hames 2007; Porter 2014: xiv) owing to the perception by some that it hinges upon the viability of a certain version of the noble savage ideal, suitably reconfigured as an image of indigenous people ecologically attuned to their natural environment.

The debate has frequently been heated and politically charged, not least because of the close connections between claims that indigenous peoples are capable of managing natural habitats sustainably on the one hand and their demands for self-determination and land rights on the other. As one commentator has remarked, 'any evidence of ecologically unsound activities by indigenous and traditional peoples undermines their basic rights to land, resources, and cultural practice' (Posey 1993, quoted in Vickers 1994: 308). Promoters both of indigenous peoples' rights and of biodiversity conservation, including many spokespersons for indigenous communities themselves, have thus been keen to identify indigenous peoples as spiritually sensitive custodians of the environment.[28] Others have been concerned that this conception of indigenous peoples is not only inaccurate and simplistic but is ultimately detrimental to indigenous peoples' long-term interests, given that it is liable to foster the supposition that land rights ought to be contingent upon the demonstration of an overtly conservationist ethic (Stearman 1994: 351). What those on this latter side of the argument have contended is that in places where natural resources have been conserved by indigenous peoples, this is generally a mere epiphenomenon of factors such as 'low population density, simple technology, and lack of external markets to spur over-exploitation' (Hames 2007: 179–80; see also Hunn 1982; Alvard

---

[27] Dryden attributes to Almanzor, who fights for the Moors against the Spanish (but turns out to be the lost son of a Spanish duke), the words 'I am as free as Nature first made man / 'Ere the base Laws of Servitude began / When wild in woods the noble Savage ran' (1672: Part 1, Act 1). For discussion of the history of the notion of the noble savage, see Ellingson (2001), who argues that the very idea that belief in this notion was widespread in Enlightenment Europe is a more recent myth or 'construction'.

[28] Cf. United Nations: Department of Economic and Social Affairs (2009: 60): '[S]pirituality defines the relationships of indigenous peoples with their environment as custodians of the land.'

1993: 384). The conclusion, of course, need not be that there is no association between traditional indigenous ways of living and the conservation of biodiversity: it is just that the association rarely takes the form of a deliberate ethically motivated strategy on the part of the indigenous peoples. As Allyn Stearman observes of the Yuquí people of Bolivia, for instance, they cannot be described as possessing 'Resource management strategies', because they simply 'do not perceive a need for them' (1994: 348).

The relevance of this debate to the issues I have been examining is that it highlights a need on the part of those who wish to discuss indigenous forms of religion or spirituality, including philosophers of religion, to develop an awareness of broader issues of political and cultural representation. While it remains worthwhile to look for distinctive ways of relating to and thinking about the world in the words and actions of indigenous peoples (including ways of relating and thinking that may usefully be identified as animistic), the appreciation that we have of the messy complexities of human life is prone to be hampered if our observations are too narrowly focused. In addition, then, to assembling examples of statements that evoke a sense of benign reverence for the natural world, a more thoroughgoing 'grammatical' investigation of Native American ways of being should seek examples that disrupt facile or taken-for-granted assumptions.

Among the passages that von der Ruhr quotes, but which are amenable to divergent interpretations, is one in which Big Thunder describes the killing of a moose. Having referred to the Great Spirit as father and the earth as mother, Big Thunder proceeds to explain how, when hunting, it is not the Indian's arrow that engenders the death of the moose: 'it is nature that kills him.' This is because, with the arrow embedded in its side, the moose, 'like all living things ... goes to our mother to be healed'. By repeatedly rubbing its wound against the earth, it forces the arrow deeper into its flesh, 'till at last when he is nearly exhausted and I come up with him, the arrow may be driven clean through his body' (Curtis 1923: 11). Von der Ruhr quotes this passage to illustrate how the assertion that it is nature rather than the arrow that kills the moose avoids instantiating confusion over causal relations (von der Ruhr 1996: 36). We see in Big Thunder's description what he means by the assertion and how it coheres with the general attitude of respect towards the earth ('our mother') that he exhibits. For von der Ruhr's purposes, there is no need to explore the different moral reactions that the passage could elicit. But a fuller discussion might note, for example, the possibility of perceiving a certain cruelty in the thought that an animal, having gone 'to our mother to be healed', then finds itself caught in a spiral of increasing pain and ultimate death: the more it tries to relieve its agony by rubbing itself against the earth, the harsher its suffering becomes. The recognition of this cruel irony could be viewed as consonant with a sense of awe at the workings of nature: an acknowledgement that suffering and death are as much a part of reality as are joy and life. But the fact that any overt recognition of this irony is absent from Big Thunder's own account may arouse a certain uneasiness in some readers, a feeling that the notion of the earth's healing power is being construed in a manner that removes it from anything one had previously understood healing to consist in. These possibilities of alternative responses to a piece of quoted text in turn disclose possible ambivalences and complications in an animistic approach to life.

To further resist the temptation to romanticize or otherwise essentialize indigenous peoples, additional consideration might be given to the variety of ways in which, in practice, those peoples interact with one another and with their environment, including the animals and plants it comprises. Staying with the American context, studies have been carried out not only of contemporary indigenous communities but also, by means of archaeological methods, of early inhabitants over the long course of the pre-Columbian era. An especially protracted and turbulent debate concerns the question of whether, or to what extent, human hunting activities precipitated the prodigious extinction of large mammalian species towards the end of the Pleistocene Epoch around eleven thousand years ago. The mammals that vanished from North America within a period that some have estimated to be fewer than four centuries include various species of camel, elk-moose, giant beaver, ground sloth, horse, mammoth, mastodont, ox, peccary and tapir (Fiedel 2009: 21). Extinctions in South America at approximately the same time were even more numerous (Cione, Tonni and Soibelzon 2009). Several contributors to the debate maintain that climatic factors were decisive in occasioning the extinctions (Graham 1998: 69–70; Grayson and Meltzer 2002, 2003),[29] but major climatic changes had occurred at other times without causing such dramatic extinction rates (Fiedel 2009: 30). Moreover, the period of extinctions appears to have coincided precisely with the rapid colonization of the Americas by people who, soon after arriving from Siberia, developed weaponry that included the Clovis point, a

---

[29] For more circumspect assessments of the evidence, see Krech (1999: Ch. 1) and Kelly and Pasciunas (2007).

sharpened stone spearhead especially effective for killing large prey animals.[30]

While it would be anachronistic to identify indigenous Americans in the modern era with their paleolithic forebears, the evidence that early inhabitants of the Americas transformed the ecological balance by contributing significantly to the extinction of many large mammal species calls into question the glib assumption that pre-Columbian human populations invariably lived in harmony with an 'undisturbed wilderness' (Bakeless 1961: 201).

If we turn from studies of prehistoric peoples to more recent history, we see that the large-scale killing of prey species remained a common feature of indigenous life. The phenomenon of the buffalo jump, for example, appears to have persisted among Plains Indians for thousands of years up to the mid-nineteenth century, when the prevalence and efficiency of hunting on horseback with rifles made the practice largely redundant (Sponholz 1992: 47). The buffalo jump involved luring or driving entire herds of bison over steep cliff edges so that they would fall to their deaths. Parts of the bison could then be procured to be either eaten, in the case of the meat, or worn or traded in the case of the hides. But the animals were slain in such vast numbers – often hundreds at a time – that many carcasses were left to rot either without being touched at all or with only delicacies such as tongues or humps being removed (Verbicky-Todd 1984: 169).

It has been noted by scholars that traditional religious beliefs were bound up with the reluctance among Native Americans to allow any member of a hunted herd to survive. Shepard Krech underscores two beliefs in particular. One of these is the conception of bison as what Hallowell termed 'other-than-human persons';[31] the other is the idea that bison originate from beneath the earth and that, during the season when they migrate away from normal hunting areas, they have temporarily returned either to deep caverns or to grasslands at the bottom of lakes (Krech 1999: 147–8; Coates 2006: 15). The conceiving of bison as persons is relevant because it connects with the thought that any bison that escapes, either from a 'jump' or from other methods of mass slaughter, 'would warn others away' (Krech 1999: 147) much as a human person might under comparable circumstances, thereby threatening the

---

[30] Clovis points are so named because they were first discovered, in the late 1920s and 1930s, at a Paleoindian site several miles south of the city of Clovis in New Mexico (Boldurian and Cotter 1999: 10–13). Subsequent excavations have unearthed Clovis points at sites across North America, from Canada down to northern Mexico (O'Brien et al. 2015: 126). Similar points have been found in Central and South America (Haynes 2002: 11).

[31] For Hallowell's use of this phrase, see Hallowell (1960; 1992, esp. 64).

success of future hunts. Meanwhile, conceiving of the bison as originating underground and regularly residing underwater makes possible the expectation that they are unlimited in number and hence are ineradicable, regardless of how many are dispatched (Branch 1997, esp. 2–3). Also pertinent to Indian hunting practices is the widespread belief in the reincarnation or regeneration of animals after their physical demise. The Asinîskâwiðiniwak, or Rock Cree, of Northern Manitoba, for example, held that species such as moose, caribou and beaver are 'infinitely renewable resources whose numbers could neither be reduced by overkilling nor managed by selective hunting' (Brightman 1993: 280). As in many forager societies, including other Native American or First Nations peoples, the Rock Cree had no conception of waste because they considered that animal bodies are regenerated after death; hence 'animals could not be destroyed but only temporarily displaced' (288).

Deeply embedded in Rock Cree culture is the conviction that to kill an animal is a sacred act for which the animal will be grateful. The quarry is spoken of as a 'benefactor who "loves" the hunter and voluntarily surrenders its body', in return for which the hunter performs ritual displays of honour and respect (Brightman 1993: 287). Moreover, since it is deemed positively offensive to refrain from killing any animal that has offered itself, the practice of mass slaughter, too, was regarded as obligatory. Failure to fulfil the obligation would, in effect, constitute an expression of ingratitude (Krech 1999: 205; 2007: 12).[32] The concept of respect is thus a complex one that can take many forms. If assumptions were to be made that the respectful treatment of an animal precludes killing it or at least places an onus on the hunter to scrupulously utilize all parts of the carcass, or that respectful treatment entails the sparing of young or pregnant animals and prohibits the indiscriminate slaughter of large groups at one time, exceptions to each of these assumptions could be found across multiple Native American communities.

Further exploration of Native American conceptions of respect in relation to animals or 'other-than-human persons' or to the environment more generally would require consideration of various injunctions. These include injunctions to treat parts of a dead animal's body (such as bones, intestines, blood) in a prescribed manner; to wear the correct ritual charms and clothing when performing rites associated with the hunt; to avoid mocking animals; to display in trees the antlers, scapulae or skulls of land animals and

---

[32] The operative notion of an animal's 'offering' itself or making itself available is a flexible one in this context. It appears to encompass any instance in which an animal is amenable to be killed, regardless of whether it has or has not been deliberately hunted.

the skulls and wings of birds and to ensure that the bones of aquatic animals such as beavers are returned to the water.[33] 'Animals treated well in this manner will come to hunters who have demonstrated their friendship' (Krech 1999: 204). Further exploration of the topic would also require consideration of how indigenous understandings of respect have changed in response to the encounter with people of European extraction. It was undoubtedly the introduction of European trading markets that encouraged a dramatic escalation in the killing of fur-bearing animals such as beaver (Wynn 2012: 228–33). But it has also been the case that European understandings of conservation and sustainability have played a part in changing Native American conceptions of their environment.

My aim in this section has not been to execute an exhaustive investigation of the concept of respect among Native Americans, but to offer some reminders of the need to refrain from assuming too hastily that we already know what such a concept comes to in these societies. Von der Ruhr and Phillips perform an important philosophical task when they emphasize the possibility of interpreting animistic forms of language in ways that are neither crudely literalistic nor reductively metaphorical or merely figurative. Yet the examples chosen by these philosophers, and their respective discussions of those examples, run a serious risk of playing to prevalent stereotypes of the 'ecological Indian' or the 'ecologically noble savage'. Such stereotypes, as others have argued, 'are ultimately dehumanizing' on account of their obscuring 'both variation within human groups and commonalities between them' (Krech 1999: 26). The debates surrounding these stereotypes are multifaceted and often fraught. But closing one's mind to those debates is not an option if, in the philosophy of religion, one wishes to elucidate the diverse forms of language and forms of life of indigenous peoples without sacrificing attention to ambivalence and complexity.

Concluding remarks

Nothing in the foregoing section is intended to downplay the devastating consequences of European and Euro-American colonial activity for Native American populations and their environments. It should go without saying that, as Krech has put it, 'whatever the impact of Indians on the land and

---

[33] On the prescribed treatment of animals among the Mistassini Cree in particular, see Tanner (1979: Chs 6–8; 1988: 68–9).

resources, it didn't hold a candle to the long-term impact of people of European descent' (2007: 10). Regardless of whether indigenous communities, either in the Americas or elsewhere, can be shown to operate with a distinctively conservationist ethic, it remains the case that the conservation of biodiversity is likely to be best served by allowing such communities to retain control over their traditional territories (see Redford and Stearman 1993: 254; Stearman 1994: 353). But my purpose has not been to reach a decisive conclusion on that issue. Rather, it has been to expose some of the difficulties involved in giving any account of indigenous peoples and of the religious dimensions of their lives and forms of belief and language. These difficulties arise for anyone who wishes to engage philosophically with indigenous religions and thence to bring them, as it were, within the purview of philosophy of religion, as opposed to ignoring or marginalizing them as has habitually been done in much philosophy of religion hitherto. But philosophizing is never an easy matter.[34]

The work of some of the philosophers I have discussed in this chapter has revealed fruitful paths to pursue. Eldridge and Clack have, in different ways, contended that obstacles to appreciating the intelligibility of animistic ways of thinking may be diminished by, at least as a starting point, contemplating these ways as contributing to 'a natural poetry of being' (Eldridge) or 'poetry of life' (Clack). Certainly, such an approach can help to loosen the grip of stodgy literalistic and instrumentalist interpretive assumptions that we might otherwise be inclined to impose on the phenomena of animism – assumptions that get in the way of hearing animistic vocabulary as offering what Phillips calls 'a language in which to think of the world'. What both von der Ruhr and Phillips remind us is that poetry need not be thought of here in a reductive non-realist sense, as though a poem were merely a frothy way of saying what could just as readily and far more clearly be stated in non-poetic terms. If we were to reduce poetry to metaphor, and to subscribe to the dubious conception of metaphor as invariably amenable to literal paraphrase, then we might wish to dissociate animism from poetry on the grounds that, as Tylor legitimately insists, animistic discourse is generally 'thoughtful, consistent, and quite really and seriously meant' (1920, vol. I: 285). But once a richer understanding of poetic possibilities is introduced, the perceived need for this dissociation subsides.

---

[34] Cf. Rhees (1969: 171–2): '[I]f you want to pursue philosophy as something in which you can take it easy, then you should leave it alone. (Or in other words, if you try to do anything that way, you will not be doing philosophy.)'

Whatever we think of deploying the notion of the poetic in this context, the theme of contextualization remains vital, for it is by that means that we are enabled to hear – or to begin to hear – the significance of the language being used. Placing examples side by side, as von der Ruhr does, assists this process, building up a picture of what it means to speak of the earth as mother, Great Spirit as father, of trees and rocks as feeling sore and distressed and so on. Von der Ruhr thus gives us a lesson in what Phillips has dubbed the 'hermeneutics of contemplation' – the method of discerning possibilities of sense within modes of discourse and behaviour by contemplating their 'surroundings with sufficient philosophical attention' (Phillips 2001b: 86). The lesson is one that applies to philosophy of religion more broadly, as the pervasive debates between purportedly 'realist' and 'non-realist' theories of religious language all too readily try to bypass the need for attentiveness to language in use, preferring instead to ask questions about what some particular 'proposition' (such as 'God exists') means in isolation from any concrete situation in which it is expressed. The results of such abstractive methods of analysis are epitomized by the passage I cited from Angelika Krebs in which words of protest delivered by a Native American spiritual leader, having been dislocated from their cultural surroundings, are construed as a theoretical 'claim' that fails to satisfy the criteria for the application of a certain concept. These criteria, it is supposed, are available independently of close scrutiny of anything in the specific cultural or religious lives of the Indians who talk in these ways.

What I have urged in the latter portion of the chapter is the need to be wary of allowing an over-romanticized image – prevalent in both popular and academic culture – to dictate our selection and interpretation of examples. To do so in the study of indigenous religions is to impoverish our appreciation of the heterogeneousness of the category of indigeneity and of the multiple forms of life that have become associated with it. In the case of animistic worldviews, it is especially important to recognize the nuances pertaining to the concept of respect, for a culturally naïve understanding of this concept is apt to miss, for example, the extent to which the large-scale slaughter of animals can be, and has been, deemed not merely to be compatible with respect but to feature among its proper expressions. It is by attending to nuances such as these that moves can be made towards a deprovincialization and expansion of philosophy of religion that keeps its eye on the need, as Phillips so often put it, to do 'conceptual justice to the world in all its variety'.

8

Conclusions:
Loosening Up Our Lives

In a diary entry dated 6 May 1931, Wittgenstein reflects upon the philosophical and literary approach of the Danish philosopher Søren Kierkegaard. He notes that the approach involves representing a life and inviting the reader to consider how he or she relates to it – whether it entices one to live similarly or to adopt some alternative stance. According to Wittgenstein, it is as though Kierkegaard were saying, 'Through this representation I would like to, as it were, loosen up your life' (Wittgenstein 2003: 83, punctuation amended). This notion of loosening up one's life is central to Wittgenstein's own philosophy, too, and also to the radical pluralist approach to philosophy of religion that I have been prosecuting in this book. In my case, however, and in Wittgenstein's – unlike that of Kierkegaard – the aim is not to represent a life by assuming a persona and embodying the life through one's words. Still less is it to embody in this way what it would be to live a specifically Christian life. Instead, it is to look around at a wide array of forms of life and to describe features of them in a manner that brings out the variety, not in order to tempt the reader to adopt any one of those forms of life but rather to see them as possibilities – as possible ways of being human. It is by this method – by seeing that 'human life can be like that' (Phillips 2007b: 205) – that one's own preconceptions of what human life, and what human *religious* life in particular, 'must' be like are amenable to being loosened and destabilized. The result can be simultaneously unsettling and edifying.

In the contemporary world, pervaded by a diversity of religious and nonreligious perspectives, philosophy of religion has a vital role to play in helping to deepen our understanding of that diversity and to elucidate the particularities of the various systems of thought and practice. But philosophy of religion has been slow to step up to this task: while changes have occurred on the margins of this subdiscipline, the core textbooks and academic courses have, for the most part, remained constrained by a model according to which the rationality of theism is the central and abiding issue and 'theism' is construed, narrowly, in terms of intellectual assent to the proposition that God exists. Nonetheless, as I registered in Chapter 2, the chorus of voices on the margins – calling for an expansion of philosophy of religion to reflect the diversity of forms that religion takes – has steadily been growing. Even during the period that I have been working on this book, new collections of essays have been published whose starting point is a recognition of 'an identity crisis in contemporary philosophy of religion' (Kanaris 2018: back cover) and whose primary ambition is 'to identify new paths for philosophers of religion that are distinct from those traveled by theologians and other scholars of religion' (Draper and Schellenberg 2017: back cover). Such collections have contributed to the ongoing process of self-scrutiny, offering suggestions for innovation in relation to methodology or subject matter. An important feature of these suggestions is, precisely, the variety among them, for it is this variety of possibilities that challenges the assumption that there is a single orthodox approach to philosophy of religion that must be adhered to if any semblance of coherence and distinctiveness is to be retained.

The present book has been not only an addition to the calls for innovation, but also a demonstration of a particular approach with its own distinctive elements. Taking the recognition of religious diversity as the point of departure, the approach does not merely tinker with existing models of how philosophy of religion is done: it makes a decisive and radical break. Thus, in place of the standard repertoire of questions – about whether God exists, whether it is rational to believe that God exists, whether the properties classically attributed to God are individually and collectively coherent and so on – this book has examined an unconventional medley of issues. These include: the variegated concept of compassion, especially as it figures in Buddhist traditions; ways in which respect for the dead can be manifested in ritual practices, including mortuary cannibalism, and how such practices bear upon the understanding of what a human being is; the role of ritual performances involving divine possession and blood sacrifice in giving expression to a sense of awe at the grotesque and horrific dimensions of life; and the endeavour to make sense of animistic discourse without interpreting it in either simplistic literalist or reductive metaphorical terms, and also without perpetuating stereotypical assumptions about indigenous peoples' relationship to their environments. Far from supposing these issues to constitute a new paragon of what philosophers of religion ought to be concerned with, my aim has been to draw attention to the extent of possibilities. The issues discussed in this book are all of intrinsic philosophical interest and, importantly, of intrinsic human interest as well (a quality that is all too often lacking in many academic philosophical debates). They are also illustrative, rather than exhaustive, of the range of directions in which a radically pluralist philosophy of religion might go.

The selection of topics has not been purely arbitrary. Amid the diversity, a number of themes have been central. Crucial among these are the themes of attentiveness to heterogeneity and the thickening of description, each of which I shall concisely review below.

Attending to heterogeneity and thickening description

Attending to heterogeneity need not preclude also watching out for general tendencies and resemblances across ostensibly diverse phenomena and traditions, but it guards against the hankering after generality that runs the risk of submerging multiplicity beneath a homogeneous veneer. We saw this hankering at play in Chapter 1, in the respective theories of John Hick and John Cobb. Exemplifying widespread proclivities in the philosophy of religious diversity, Hick and Cobb both, in their separate ways, allow a personal ethical and theological agenda to guide their theoretical convictions. In Hick's case, the diverse ethical, soteriological and metaphysical dimensions of all the 'great' religions are reduced to a vapid notion of transformation from 'self-centredness' to 'Reality-centredness', and the Reality (or 'Real') in question is characterized in terms so diaphanous as to render it conceptually empty. In Cobb's case, the divine reality is supposed to have three aspects: cosmic, acosmic and theistic. But still the goal of diminishing disagreements between religions by nurturing progressive convergence militates against a due recognition of the diversity that exists within and beyond that threefold typology. The result, again, is conceptual homogenization for the sake of a personal theological enterprise.

In the further case of Victoria Harrison's internalist pluralism, which was also examined in Chapter 1, the driving motivation is, similarly, that of encouraging toleration and respect between religions, but without pretending that the differences between them are of little or no significance. Harrison's internalist theoretical framework, borrowed and adapted from Hilary Putnam, is not without interest. Involving, as it does, the contention that each religion (or 'faith-stance') constitutes a distinct conceptual scheme, it has the potential to open up discussion about the genuine similarities and divergences that characterize these various schemes. But even if one were to concur with the assumption that it is philosophy's prerogative to promote interreligious harmony, it remains unclear how the internalist picture of multiple more or less discrete conceptual schemes stands any chance of furthering that objective.

A radical pluralist approach is not opposed to the promotion of interreligious harmony, but its emphasis is on elucidation and understanding instead of rushing to impose upon the phenomena a general theory, such as the transcendental pluralism of Hick, the complementary pluralism of Cobb or the internalist pluralism of Harrison. Thus, while a consequence of the attention to particularities that typifies a radical pluralist approach may, in certain circumstances, be the improvement of harmonious and amicable interaction between members of different religions or of nonreligious groups, this is not an inevitable outcome. Indeed, a deeper understanding of a religious or nonreligious outlook may disclose precisely what it is about that outlook that its non-adherents find objectionable. The point, as far as a radical pluralist approach is concerned, is not to try to settle disputes but, where they exist, to contribute to a clarification of what those disputes are about.

The task of clarification by means of attention to heterogeneity goes hand in hand with the method of thick description; it is the thickening of description that provides the contextualization, which in turn affords an enriched comprehension of the phenomena under examination. As I admitted in Chapter 2, the appropriate thickness of a description is relative to the purpose for which the description is being supplied. But the move towards thickness is a move away from the kinds of thinly sketched examples that philosophers often concoct merely to embellish a thesis that they devised independently of the examples. Some instances of this were noted in my discussion of Harrison's use of examples in Chapter 1.

Works of narrative fiction and ethnography are among the sources from which thicker descriptive material can be derived, and this inevitably softens the boundary between a radical pluralist philosophy of religion on the one hand, and both cultural anthropology and narrative fiction on the other. This should not be a surprise, for works of anthropology and of narrative fiction (whether literary, cinematic or theatrical) can themselves be philosophical in certain respects. But the distinctively philosophical character of a radical pluralist approach hinges upon its engagement with existing philosophical claims or with implicit assumptions, including assumptions that the investigating philosopher is tempted to hold. The claims and assumptions can be many and varied, though they typically take the form of an overgeneralizing supposition. A radical pluralist approach seeks not to straightforwardly refute the suppositions in question, but to cast doubt upon their scope by drawing attention to apparent exceptions or complicating factors. To elaborate this point, it is relevant here to offer some reminders of how specific claims and assumptions have been targeted in the foregoing chapters.

Targeting overgeneralizing claims and assumptions

The target of Chapter 4 was the overgeneralizing contention that compassion lies at the heart of all major religions, with Buddhism being a paradigmatic case. Rather than trying to show that the contention is false, my aim in the chapter was to question whether it is really clear what it amounts to. The approach I adopted was not, in this instance, to furnish a sustained and thickly described example, but to adduce an assortment of examples to illustrate the multiplicity of ways in which the notion of compassion has been understood and articulated across several Buddhist traditions. Admittedly, more work would need to be done if one's aim were to deliver a thorough analysis of similarities and differences between the various instances of compassion; the project could also be extended farther by developing comparisons between Buddhist formulations of compassion and those in other religious and cultural settings. However, my purpose in Chapter 4, as in the book as a whole, was not to carry out a definitive survey, but to undertake an investigation that is broad-ranging enough to raise doubts about the substantiality of the target claim – initially as it applies to Buddhism, but also, by implication, as it applies beyond Buddhism as well.

In Chapter 5, a description of mortuary cannibalism among the Wari' of western Brazil was presented that is, I hope, sufficiently thick to put pressure on the suppositions that inform the chapter's targets. Those targets are, first, the philosophical thesis that a prohibition against eating people is in some sense internal to the concept of a human being, and, second, the widespread assumption that a proper display of respect for the dead precludes oral consumption as a means of disposing of the corpse. In keeping with the analogy that I drew in Chapter 2 between a critically descriptive philosophy of religion and the idea of cultural critique in anthropology, a study of Wari' mortuary cannibalism serves the critical function of defamiliarizing suppositions surrounding the concepts of a person and of respecting the dead in at least two ways. First, in accordance with what George Marcus and Michael Fischer call 'defamiliarization by epistemological critique' (1999: Ch. 6), such a study confronts readers from other, especially Western, cultures with unfamiliar – hence defamiliarized – ways of thinking and behaving. It thereby calls into question the inevitability or supposed necessity of the values and norms prevalent in Western cultural milieus or in the religious systems most familiar to those milieus. Second, what Marcus and Fischer refer to as 'defamiliarization by cross-cultural juxtaposition' (ibid.) is exemplified in the specific contrast between Wari' and Protestant missionary attitudes concerning the correct treatment of a corpse. For anyone who is tempted by the thought that cremation or burial *must* be the right or the most natural method of disposal, reflection upon the sort of funerary practices performed by the Wari' is apt to destabilize that temptation.

Needless to say, after reflection, one might remain convinced that cannibalism *is* incompatible with the respectful treatment of the dead. The critical point, however, is that this conviction no longer stands unchallenged. The 'mere' description of another way of doing things – another way of being human – has disclosed its culturally contingent status. Again, my treatment of the topic is far from comprehensive. Anyone wanting to know more about the intricacies of Wari' life and culture would need to consult the ethnographic sources that I cite in the chapter. But my aim was to supply enough detail to indicate the place that mortuary cannibalism had in the lives of the Wari' at the time when it was practised, and thus, by extension, to show that the eating of human beings as part of a funeral custom is a meaningful religious possibility. Some philosophers may insist that there is nevertheless a universally applicable answer to the question of what constitutes respectful treatment of the dead, an answer that applies to all human communities independently of historical, cultural or subcultural specificities. Nothing I have argued in this book categorically precludes such a universalizing answer, whether in this particular case or in others. But anyone who wishes to argue that, for example, mortuary cannibalism cannot be a respectful thing to do would have to find some means of showing why there is something suspect about describing the Wari' mortuary practices as exhibiting respect, even when viewed amid the relevant cultural surroundings.

A pervasive supposition, or syndrome of suppositions, that has been a target of my book as a whole concerns the issue of what topics are worthy of discussion in the philosophy of religion at all. Even those philosophers who presume to be taking account of religious diversity tend both to gravitate towards a relatively small ensemble of religious traditions and, among those traditions, to privilege expressions of religiosity that conform to the philosophers' ethical preferences and expectations. In short, philosophers of religion have, for the most part, treated the Abrahamic faiths, and to a lesser extent certain large-scale Asian religions (most notably Buddhism and Hinduism), as normative exemplars of what religion is, and have downplayed or ignored what they consider to be morally unpalatable manifestations of religious commitment. Thus topics such as blood sacrifice and divine possession, despite their ubiquity across multiple religious and cultural domains, have been marginalized, and small-scale indigenous traditions have been dismissed as archaic or primitive remnants of a 'pre-axial' age that had yet to reach intellectual maturity.[1] Contrary to these marginalizing and dismissive propensities, the radical pluralist approach that I have been exemplifying strives to foreground religion in its messy, and often controversial, complexity. To this end, Chapter 6 presented a thickly described and contextualized account of divine possession and animal sacrifice as they occur in a contemporary goddess-worshipping Hindu festival, and Chapter 7 examined the concept of animism as it has featured in both anthropological and philosophical discussions of indigenous religions.

Whatever we make of these aspects of religion personally – whether we find them in any way attractive or repellant – the effort to find ways of incorporating them into the philosophical conversation operates to expand our appreciation of religious possibilities, facilitating an enhanced conception of the highly ramified phenomena that form the subject matter of philosophy of religion.

---

[1] Cf. Maitzen (2017: 59): 'Intellectually mature human beings don't need the jumble of minor deities that their pre-Axial ancestors invented in a vain but understandable attempt to explain and control an unpredictable, dangerous world.'

Imagining philosophy of religion differently

Advancing proposals for what the future of philosophy of religion should be like has become somewhat fashionable over recent years, as is indicated by the number of books, articles, conferences and panel sessions with phrases such as 'the future of philosophy of religion' in their title or subtitle.[2] Pressure to diversify the curriculum is coming from both inside and outside philosophy of religion. Specialists in non-Western philosophical traditions are increasingly asking why the philosophy pursued in Western academic institutions, and in many institutions elsewhere in the world that have followed the Western paradigm, routinely disregards the non-Western traditions (see, e.g., Van Norden 2017). Similar questions are being asked of philosophy of religion in particular, with regard to its meagre coverage of religions that have historically predominated outside the Western world. The present book, without presuming to stipulate a single trajectory for the subdiscipline as a whole, has tendered some practical options for moving it in more cross-cultural, multireligious and interdisciplinary directions.

The radical pluralist approach advanced herein embodies one way of inheriting a broadly Wittgensteinian sensibility, mediated in part by the application of Wittgenstein's ideas to the philosophy of religion that was so persistently exhibited by D. Z. Phillips. Neither Wittgenstein nor Phillips had extensive conversance with non-Abrahamic traditions, though both of them took a critical interest in anthropological studies of ancient and small-scale religions (see esp. Wittgenstein 1993; Phillips 2001b), and Phillips frequently looked to works of narrative fiction and poetry as resources capable of elucidating religious forms of life that are commonly neglected by philosophers (Phillips 1982, 1986, 2006). Having picked up those methodological hints from Wittgenstein and Phillips, among others, I have sought to develop them along a far more robustly interdisciplinary path. For some philosophical readers, that path may appear unappealing because it strays so far from the one that philosophy of religion has standardly trodden. The interdisciplinary engagement may be perceived as threatening

---

[2] See, inter alia, Wildman (2010); Crockett, Putt and Robbins (2014); Schilbrack (2014a); Carroll (2016); McKim (2017); Grimshaw (2018). Relevant conferences include 'The Future of Continental Philosophy of Religion', Syracuse University, 7–9 April 2011, and the more circumspect 'Has Philosophy of Religion a Future?', McGill University, 25 April 2013.

a loss of disciplinary integrity. Others, more sympathetic to these adventures beyond traditional disciplinary boundaries, will view them as a fruitful stimulus for imagining philosophy of religion differently. Either way, I hope that enough has been done in this book to demonstrate the potential of a radical pluralist approach, as one among many approaches, for loosening up our lives, opening our minds and revitalizing the philosophical study of religion in the contemporary world.

References

Abhinavagupta. 1989 [10th–11th century CE]. *A Trident of Wisdom: Translation of Parātrīśikā-Vivaraṇa*, trans. Jaideva Singh. Albany, NY: State University of New York Press.

Ackerknecht, Erwin H. 1982. *A Short History of Medicine*, rev. edn. Baltimore, MD: Johns Hopkins University Press.

Adams, William Y. 1998. *The Philosophical Roots of Anthropology*. Chicago, IL: University of Chicago Press.

Akira, Hirakawa. 1990. *A History of Indian Buddhism: From Śākyamuni to Early Mahāyāna*, trans. and ed. Paul Groner. Honolulu, HI: University of Hawai'i Press.

Aldama, Frederick Luis, and Herbert Lindenberger. 2016. *Aesthetics of Discomfort: Conversations on Disquieting Art*. Ann Arbor, MI: University of Michigan Press.

Alexander, Tamar. 2003. Love and Death in a Contemporary *Dybbuk* Story: Personal Narrative and the Female Voice. In *Spirit Possession in Judaism: Cases and Contexts from the Middle Ages to the Present*, ed. Matt Goldish, 307–45. Detroit, MI: Wayne State University Press.

Alter, Andrew. 2008. *Dancing with Devtās: Drums, Power and Possession in the Music of Garhwal, North India*. Aldershot: Ashgate.

Alter, Nora M. 1995. Vietnamese Theatre of Resistance: Thich Nhat Hanh's Metaphysical Sortie on the Margins. In *Imperialism and Theatre: Essays on World Theatre, Drama, and Performance*, ed. J. Ellen Gainor, 1–18. London: Routledge.

Alvard, Michael S. 1993. Testing the 'Ecologically Noble Savage' Hypothesis: Interspecific Prey Choice by Piro Hunters of Amazonian Peru. *Human Ecology* 21 (4): 355–87.

Amaravati Sangha, trans. 2013. *Karaniya Metta Sutta: The Buddha's Words on Loving-Kindness. Access to Insight (Legacy Edition)*. Available online at: http://www.accesstoinsight.org/tipitaka/kn/khp/khp.9.amar.html (accessed 26 November 2016).

An Viên Television. 2014. Bồ tát Thích Quảng Đức – Trái Tim Bất Tử [Bodhisattva Thích Quảng Đức – Immortal Heart] [video file]. 26 April. Available online at: https://www.youtube.com/watch?v=Qz7fZNwOvH4 (accessed 28 October 2016).

ANI [Asian News International]. 2016. Kamakhya Temple Comes Alive with Deodhani Festival. 26 August. Available online at: https://www.aninews.in/news/national/politics/kamakhya-temple-comes-alive-with-deodhani-festival/ (accessed 23 September 2017).

Appleton, Naomi, and Sarah Shaw, trans. 2015. *The Ten Great Birth Stories of the Buddha: The Mahānipāta of the Jātakatthavaṇṇanā*, Vol. 2. Chiang Mai: Silkworm.

Ardley, Jane. 2002. *The Tibetan Independence Movement: Political, Religious and Gandhian Perspectives*. London: RoutledgeCurzon.

Arens, W. 1979. *The Man-Eating Myth: Anthropology and Anthropophagy*. New York: Oxford University Press.

Århem, Kaj. 2016. Southeast Asian Animism in Context. In *Animism in Southeast Asia*, ed. Kaj Århem and Guido Sprenger, 3–30. Abingdon: Routledge.

Armstrong, Karen. 2008. The Art of Compassion. In *Encyclopedia of Love in World Religions*, ed. Yudit Kornberg Greenberg, Vol. 1, 21–2. Santa Barbara, CA: ABC-CLIO.

Asaṅga. 2003 [4th century CE]. *The Summary of the Great Vehicle*, trans. John Keenan, 2nd edn. Berkeley, CA: Numata Center for Buddhist Translation and Research.

Associated Press. 2012. Tibetan Self-Immolators are Outcasts, Criminals and Mentally Ill, Claims China. *The Guardian*, 7 March. Available online at: https://www.theguardian.com/world/2012/mar/07/tibetan-immolators-outcasts-criminals-china (accessed 9 December 2016).

Avalon, Arthur [Sir John Woodroffe]. 1964 [1919]. *The Serpent Power: Being the Ṣaṭ-Cakra-Nirūpaṇa and Pādukā-Pañcaka*, 7th edn. Madras: Ganesh & Co.

Bagchi, P. C., ed. 1986. *Kaulajnana-nirnaya of the School of Matsyendranatha* [*c.* 11th century CE], trans. Michael Magee. Varanasi: Prachya Prakashan.

Bakeless, John. 1961 [1950]. *The Eyes of Discovery: The Pageant of North America as Seen by the First Explorers*. New York: Dover.

Bakhtin, Mikhail. 1984a [1963]. *Problems of Dostoevsky's Poetics*, ed. and trans. Caryl Emerson. Minneapolis, MN: University of Minnesota Press.

Bakhtin, Mikhail. 1984b [1965]. *Rabelais and His World*, trans. Hélène Iswolsky. Bloomington, IN: Indiana University Press.

Bakk, Karl R. 1989. *Man and His Deities*. Round Rock, TX: Parker.

Barnard, Alan. 2006. Kalahari Revisionism, Vienna and the 'Indigenous Peoples' Debate. *Social Anthropology* 14 (1): 1–16.

Barnhart, Joe E. 2005. Introduction: Hearing Voices. In *Dostoevsky's Polyphonic Talent*, ed. Joe E. Barnhart, ix–xx. Lanham, MD: University Press of America.

Barth, Fredrik. 1975. *Ritual and Knowledge among the Baktaman of New Guinea*. Oslo: Universitetsforlaget.

Bartholet, Jeffrey. 2012. Tibet's Man on Fire. *National Geographic*, 30 November. Available online at: http://news.nationalgeographic.com/news/2012/121130-tibet-burning-protest-china-world/ (accessed 10 December 2016).

Barton, John. 1996. Reading for Life: The Use of the Bible in Ethics and the Work of Martha C. Nussbaum. In *The Bible in Ethics: The Second Sheffield Colloquium*, ed. John W. Rogerson, Margaret Davies and M. Daniel Carroll R., 66–76. Sheffield: Sheffield Academic Press.

Barton, John. 2000. Disclosing Human Possibilities: Revelation and Biblical Stories. In *Revelation and Story: Narrative Theology and the Centrality of Story*, ed. Gerhard Sauter and John Barton, 53–60. Aldershot: Ashgate.

Barton, John. 2003. *Ethics and the Old Testament*, 2nd edn. London: SCM Press.

Basu, Helene. 2008. Drumming and Praying: Sidi at the Interface of Spirit Possession and Islam. In *Struggling with History: Islam and Cosmopolitanism in the Western Indian Ocean*, ed. Edward Simpson and Kai Kresse, 291–322. New York: Columbia University Press.

Battersby, Christine. 1978. Review of Stewart Sutherland, *Atheism and the Rejection of God*. *Philosophy* 53 (206): 566–70.

Bauckham, Richard. 1987. Theodicy from Ivan Karamazov to Moltmann. *Modern Theology* 4 (1): 83–97.

Bazin, Jean. 2003. Questions of Meaning. *Anthropological Theory* 3 (4): 418–34.

Bellette, A. F. 1978. Truth and Utterance in 'The Winter's Tale'. *Shakespeare Survey* 31: 65–75.

Benn, James A. 2007. *Burning for the Buddha: Self-Immolation in Chinese Buddhism*. Honolulu, HI: University of Hawai'i Press.

Benton, Catherine. 2006. *God of Desire: Tales of Kāmadeva in Sanskrit Story Literature*. Albany, NY: State University of New York Press.

Bergman, Ted L. L. 2003. *The Art of Humour in the 'Teatro Breve' and 'Comedias' of Calderón de la Barca*. Woodbridge: Tamesis.

Bermel, Albert. 1997. *Artaud's Theatre of Cruelty*. New York: Taplinger.

Biardeau, Madeleine. 1981. *L'hindouisme: Anthropologie d'une civilisation*. Paris: Flammarion.

Biardeau, Madeleine. 1989. *Hinduism: The Anthropology of a Civilization*, trans. Richard Nice. Delhi: Oxford University Press.

Biderman, Shlomo. 1978. Śaṅkara and the Buddhists. *Journal of Indian Philosophy* 6 (4): 405–13.

Bielefeldt, Carl. 2009. Expedient Devices, the One Vehicle, and the Life Span of the Buddha. In *Readings of the Lotus Sūtra*, ed. Stephen F. Teiser and Jacqueline I. Stone, 62–82. New York: Columbia University Press.

Biernacki, Loriliai. 2007. *Renowned Goddess of Desire: Women, Sex, and Speech in Tantra*. Oxford: Oxford University Press.

Biggs, Michael. 2006. Dying without Killing: Self-Immolations, 1963–2002. In *Making Sense of Suicide Missions*, ed. Diego Gambetta, 173–208. Oxford: Oxford University Press.

Bird-David, Nurit. 1999. 'Animism' Revisited: Personhood, Environment, and Relational Epistemology. *Current Anthropology* 40 (Supplement): 67–79.

Bird-David, Nurit. 2017. *Us, Relatives: Scaling and Plural Life in a Forager World*. Oakland, CA: University of California Press.

Blackburn, Simon. 1994. *The Oxford Dictionary of Philosophy*. Oxford: Oxford University Press.

Blackburn, Stuart H. 1988. *Singing of Birth and Death: Texts in Performance*. Philadelphia, PA: University of Pennsylvania Press.

Blaisdell, Bob, ed. 2000. *Great Speeches by Native Americans*. Mineola, NY: Dover.

Bodhi, Bhikkhu, trans. 2000. *The Connected Discourses of the Buddha: A Translation of the Saṃyutta Nikāya*. Somerville, MA: Wisdom.

Boldurian, Anthony T., and John L. Cotter. 1999. *Clovis Revisited: New Perspectives on Paleoindian Adaptations from Blackwater Draw, New Mexico*. Philadelphia, PA: University of Pennsylvania Museum.

Bolle, Kees W. 1987. Animism and Animatism. In *The Encyclopedia of Religion*, ed. Mircea Eliade, Vol. 1, 296–302. New York: Macmillan.

Booth, James. 1993. Self-Sacrifice and Human Sacrifice in Soyinka's *Death and the King's Horseman*. In *Research on Wole Soyinka*, ed. James Gibbs and Bernth Lindfors, 127–47. Trenton, NJ: Africa World Press.

Boswell, James. 1831 [1791]. *The Life of Samuel Johnson, LL.D.*, Vol. 2. London: Murray.

Bouissac, Paul. 1989. What Is a Human? Ecological Semiotics and the New Animism. *Semiotica: Journal of the International Association for Semiotic Studies* 77 (4): 497–516.

Branch, E. Douglas. 1997 [1929]. *The Hunting of the Buffalo*. Lincoln, NE: University of Nebraska Press.

Brightman, Robert. 1993. *Grateful Prey: Rock Cree Human–Animal Relationships*. Berkeley, CA: University of California Press.

Brottman, Mikita. 2001. *Meat is Murder! An Illustrated Guide to Cannibal Culture*, 2nd edn. London: Creation Books.

Brown, C. Mackenzie. 1998. *The Devī Gītā: The Song of the Goddess: A Translation, Annotation, and Commentary*. Albany, NY: State University of New York Press.

Buffetrille, Katia. 2012. Self-Immolation in Tibet: Some Reflections on an Unfolding History. *Revue d'Etudes Tibétaines* 25: 1–17.

Bühnemann, Gudrun. 2000. *The Iconography of Hindu Tantric Deities*, Vol. 1: *The Pantheon of the Mantramahodadhi*. Groningen: Forsten.

Burke, Edmund. 1759. *A Philosophical Enquiry into the Origin of Our Ideas of the Sublime and Beautiful*, 2nd edn. London: Dodsley.

Burley, Mikel. 2018a. Prioritizing Practice in the Study of Religion: Normative and Descriptive Orientations. *International Journal of Philosophy and Theology* 79 (4): 437–450.

Burley, Mikel. 2018b. Thickening Description: Towards an Expanded Conception of Philosophy of Religion. *International Journal for Philosophy of Religion* 83 (1): 3–19.

Burley, Mikel. Forthcoming. Ethnographically Informed Philosophy of Religion in a Study of Assamese Goddess Worship. In *Global-Critical Philosophy of Religion*, ed. Timothy D. Knepper and Gereon Kopf. Cham: Springer.

Burns, Robert. 1947. *Poems of Robert Burns*, ed. Henry W. Meikle and William Beattie. Harmondsworth: Penguin.

Buswell, Robert E., Jr, and Donald S. Lopez Jr. 2014. *The Princeton Dictionary of Buddhism*. Princeton, NJ: Princeton University Press.

Caldwell, Sarah. 1996. Bhagavati: Ball of Fire. In *Devī: Goddesses of India*, ed. John S. Hawley and Donna M. Wulff, 195–226. Berkeley, CA: University of California Press.

Carroll, Thomas D. 2016. The Problem of Relevance and the Future of Philosophy of Religion. *Metaphilosophy* 47 (1): 39–58.

Cartosio, Alessandro, and Irene Majo Garigliano, directors. 2014. *Ghora: Waiting for the Goddess* [film]. Available online at: https://vimeo.com/86702413.

Cassuto, Leonard. 1995. Jack London's Class-Based Grotesque. In *Literature and the Grotesque*, ed. Michael J. Meyer, 113–28. Amsterdam: Rodopi.

Cavell, Stanley. 1979 [1971]. *The World Viewed: Reflections on the Ontology of Film*, enlarged edn. Cambridge, MA: Harvard University Press.

Cavell, Stanley. 2002. *Must We Mean What We Say? A Book of Essays*, 2nd edn. Cambridge: Cambridge University Press.

China Tibet Online. 2012. How the Dalai Clique Incites Self-Immolation. 20 March. Available online at: http://chinatibet.people.com.cn/96069 /7762820.html (accessed 9 December 2016).

Choudhury, Shankhadeep. 2002. Nepal King Offers Animal Sacrifice in Kamakhya. *Times of India*, 27 June. Available online at: http://timesofindia. indiatimes.com/india/Nepal-King-offers-animal-sacrifice-in-Kamakhya/ articleshow/14279990.cms (accessed 23 September 2017).

Chun, S. Min. 2014. *Ethics and Biblical Narrative: A Literary and Discourse-Analytical Approach to the Story of Josiah*. Oxford: Oxford University Press.

Cione, Alberto L., Eduardo P. Tonni and Leopoldo Soibelzon. 2009. Did Humans Cause the Late Pleistocene-Early Holocene Mammalian Extinctions in South America in a Context of Shrinking Open Areas? In *American Megafaunal Extinctions at the End of the Pleistocene*, ed. Gary Haynes, 125–44. n.p.: Springer.

Clack, Brian R. 1995. D. Z. Phillips, Wittgenstein and Religion. *Religious Studies* 31 (1): 111–20.

Clack, Brian R. 1999. *An Introduction to Wittgenstein's Philosophy of Religion*. Edinburgh: Edinburgh University Press.

Clark, Stephen R. L. 1977. *The Moral Status of Animals*. Oxford: Oxford University Press.

Clayton, John. 2006. *Religions, Reasons and Gods: Essays in Cross-Cultural Philosophy of Religion*. Cambridge: Cambridge University Press.

Coates, Peter. 2006. The Human and Natural Environment. In *A New Introduction to American Studies*, ed. Howard Temperley and Christopher Bigsby, 7–28. Harlow: Pearson.

Cobb, John B., Jr. 1975. *Christ in a Pluralistic Age*. Philadelphia, PA: Westminster Press.

Cobb, John B., Jr. 1982. *Beyond Dialogue: Toward a Mutual Transformation of Christianity and Buddhism*. Philadelphia, PA: Fortress Press.

Cobb, John B., Jr. 1990a. Beyond 'Pluralism'. In *Christian Uniqueness Reconsidered: The Myth of a Pluralistic Theology of Religions*, ed. Gavin D'Costa, 81–95. Maryknoll, NY: Orbis Books.

Cobb, John B., Jr. 1990b. Dialogue. In Leonard Swidler, John B. Cobb Jr., Paul F. Knitter and Monika K. Hellwig, *Death or Dialogue? From the Age of Monologue to the Age of Dialogue*, 1–18. London: SCM Press.

Cobb, John B., Jr. 1993. Order Out of Chaos: A Philosophical Model of Interreligious Dialogue. In *Inter-Religious Models and Criteria*, ed. J. Kellenberger, 71–86. New York: St Martin's Press.

Cobb, John B., Jr. 1999 [1987]. Global Theology in a Pluralistic Age. In his *Transforming Christianity and the World: A Way beyond Absolutism and Relativism*, ed. Paul F. Knitter, 49–60. Maryknoll, NY: Orbis Books.

Cobb, John B., Jr. 2002. *Postmodernism and Public Policy: Reframing Religion, Culture, Education, Sexuality, Class, Race, Politics, and the Economy*. Albany, NY: State University of New York Press.

Cohen, Emma. 2008. What Is Spirit Possession? Defining, Comparing, and Explaining Two Possession Forms. *Ethnos* 73 (1): 101–126.

Cohen, Richard S. 2001. Shakyamuni: Buddhism's Founder in Ten Acts. In *The Rivers of Paradise: Moses, Buddha, Confucius, Jesus, and Muhammad as Religious Founders*, ed. David Noel Freedman and Michael J. McClymond, 121–232. Grand Rapids, MI: Eerdmans.

Collins, Steven. 1998. *Nirvana and Other Buddhist Felicities: Utopias of the Pali Imaginaire*. Cambridge: Cambridge University Press.

Conklin, Beth A. 1995. 'Thus are Our Bodies, Thus was Our Custom': Mortuary Cannibalism in an Amazonian Society. *American Ethnologist* 22 (1): 75–101.

Conklin, Beth A. 2001. *Consuming Grief: Compassionate Cannibalism in an Amazonian Society*. Austin, TX: University of Texas Press.

Conze, Edward, trans. 1975. *The Large Sutra on Perfect Wisdom, with the Divisions of the Abhisamayālaṅkāra*. Berkeley, CA: University of California Press.

Corfield, Justin. 2013. *Historical Dictionary of Ho Chi Minh City*. London: Anthem Press.

Cormier, Harvey. 2015. What Is the Use of Calling Putnam a Pragmatist? In *The Philosophy of Hilary Putnam*, ed. Randall E. Auxier, Douglas R. Anderson and Lewis Edwin Hahn, 801–19. Chicago, IL: Open Court.

Cottingham, John. 2005. *The Spiritual Dimension: Religion, Philosophy and Human Value*. Cambridge: Cambridge University Press.

Coulson, Jessie. 1962. *Dostoevsky: A Self-Portrait*. London: Oxford University Press.

Cowper, H. S. 1906. *The Art of Attack: Being a Study in the Development of Weapons and Appliances of Offence, from the Earliest Times to the Age of Gunpowder*. Ulverston: Holmes.

Cox, James L. 2007. *From Primitive to Indigenous: The Academic Study of Indigenous Religions*. Aldershot: Ashgate.

Crockett, Clayton, B. Keith Putt and Jeffrey W. Robbins, eds. 2014. *The Future of Continental Philosophy of Religion*. Bloomington, IN: Indiana University Press.

Csordas, Thomas J. 1999. Embodiment and Cultural Phenomenology. In *Perspectives on Embodiment: The Intersections of Nature and Culture*, ed. Gail Weiss and Honi Fern Haber, 143–62. New York: Routledge.

Curtis, Natalie. 1923. *The Indians' Book: An Offering by the American Indians of Indian Lore, Musical and Narrative, to form a Record of the Songs and Legends of Their Race*, 2nd edn. New York: Harper.

Curtler, Hugh Mercer. 1997. *Resdiscovering Values: Coming to Terms with Postmodernism*. Armonk, NY: Sharpe.

Czachesz, István. 2012. *The Grotesque Body in Early Christian Discourse: Hell, Scatology, and Metamorphosis*. Sheffield: Equinox.

Das, Paromita. 2007. *History and Archaeology of North-East India: 5th Century to 1826 A.D.: With Special Reference to Guwahati*. New Delhi: Agam Kala Prakashan.

Davis, Caroline Franks. 1989. *The Evidential Force of Religious Experience*. Oxford: Oxford University Press.

D'Costa, Gavin. 1990. Preface. In *Christian Uniqueness Reconsidered: The Myth of a Pluralistic Theology of Religions*, ed. Gavin D'Costa. Maryknoll, viii–xxii. NY: Orbis Books.

D'Costa, Gavin. 1996. The Impossibility of a Pluralist View of Religions. *Religious Studies* 32 (2): 223–32.

D'Costa, Gavin. 2016. Changing the Typology? Why Pluralism Should be Renamed Post-Christian Inclusivism. In *Twenty-First Century Theologies of Religions: Retrospection and Future Prospects*, ed. Elizabeth J. Harris, Paul Hedges and Shanthikumar Hettiarachchi, 128–41. Leiden: Brill.

de la Mare, Walter. 1941. *Collected Poems*. New York: Holt.

Deloria, Vine, Jr. 2007 [1970]. *We Talk, You Listen: New Tribes, New Turf.* Lincoln, NE: University of Nebraska Press.

Dennett, Daniel C. 2007. *Breaking the Spell: Religion as a Natural Phenomenon.* London: Penguin.

Denzin, Norman K. 1978 [1970]. *The Research Act: A Theoretical Introduction to Sociological Methods*, 2nd edn. New York: McGraw-Hill.

Denzin, Norman K. 2001. *Interpretive Interactionism*, 2nd edn. Thousand Oaks, CA: Sage.

Denzin, Norman K., and Yvonna S. Lincoln, eds. 2017. *The Sage Handbook of Qualitative Research*, 5th edn. Thousand Oaks, CA: Sage.

Descombes, Vincent. 2002. A Confusion of Tongues. *Anthropological Theory* 2 (4): 433–46.

Devsharma, Dharanikanta. 2014. *The Holy Shrine of Kamakhya.* Guwahati: Mahamaya Prakashan.

Diamond, Cora. 1978. Eating Meat and Eating People. *Philosophy* 53 (206): 465–79.

Diamond, Cora. 1982. Anything but Argument? *Philosophical Investigations* 5 (1): 23–41.

Diamond, Cora. 1988. Losing Your Concepts. *Ethics* 98 (2): 255–77.

Dickinson, Emily. 1998. *The Poems of Emily Dickinson: Variorum Edition*, ed. R. W. Franklin, 3 vols. Cambridge, MA: Harvard University Press.

Diemberger, Hildegard. 2005. Female Oracles in Modern Tibet. In *Women in Tibet*, ed. Janet Gyatso and Hanna Havnevik, 113–68. London: Hurst & Co.

Dimock, Edward C., Jr. 1962. The Goddess of Snakes in Medieval Bengali Literature. *History of Religions* 1 (2): 307–21.

Dold, Patricia. 2004. The Mahavidyas at Kamarupa: Dynamics of Transformation in Hinduism. *Religious Studies and Theology* 23 (1): 89–122.

Dold, Patricia A. 2011. Pilgrimage to Kāmākhyā through Text and Lived Religion: Some Forms of the Goddess at an Assamese Temple Site. In *Studying Hinduism in Practice*, ed. Hillary P. Rodrigues, 46–61. Abingdon: Routledge.

Dold, Patricia A. 2013. Re-Imagining Religious History through Women's Song Performance at the Kāmākhyā Temple Site. In *Re-imagining South Asian Religions: Essays in Honour of Professors Harold G. Coward and Ronald W. Neufeldt*, ed. Pashaura Singh and Michael Hawley, 115–54. Leiden: Brill.

Dole, Gertrude. 1962. Endocannibalism among the Amahuaca Indians. *Transactions of the New York Academy of Sciences* 24 (Series 2) (5): 567–73.

Dorjee, Tenzin. 2012. My Take: Why the Dalai Lama Cannot Condemn Tibetan Self-Immolations. *CNN Belief Blog*, 18 July. Available online at: http://religion.blogs.cnn.com/2012/07/18/my-take-why-the-dalai-lama-cannot-condemn-tibetan-self-immolations/ (accessed 12 November 2016).

Dostoevsky, Fyodor. 1912 [1880]. *The Brothers Karamazov*, trans. Constance Garnett. London: Heinemann.

Drake, Samuel G. 1834. *Biography and History of the Indians of North America*, 3rd edn. Boston, MA: Perkins and Hilliard, Gray & Co.

Draper, Paul, and J. L. Schellenberg, eds. 2017. *Renewing Philosophy of Religion: Exploratory Essays*. Oxford: Oxford University Press.

Drury, M. O'C. 1984. Conversations with Wittgenstein. In *Recollections of Wittgenstein*, ed. Rush Rhees, 97–171. Oxford: Oxford University Press.

Dryden, John. 1672. *The Conquest of Granada by the Spaniards*. London: Herringman.

Dunn, Oliver, and James E. Kelley, Jr. 1989. Editors' Introduction. In *The Diario of Christopher Columbus's First Voyage to America, 1492–1493: Abstracted by Fray Bartolomé de las Casas*, 3–14. Norman, OK: University of Oklahoma Press.

Efird, David, and David Worsley. 2015. Critical Review of Eleonore Stump's *Wandering in Darkness: Narrative and the Problem of Suffering*. *Philosophical Quarterly* 65 (260): 547–58.

Eggeling, Julius, trans. 1894. *Satapatha-Brâhmana according to the Text of the Mâdhyandina School* [*c*. 6th century BCE], Part 3. Oxford: Clarendon Press.

Eisenstadt, S. N. 1986. Introduction: The Axial Age Breakthroughs – Their Characteristics and Origins. In *The Origins and Diversity of Axial Age Civilizations*, ed. S. N. Eisenstadt, 1–25. Albany, NY: State University of New York Press.

Eldridge, Richard. 1996. Is Animism Alive and Well? In *Can Religion Be Explained Away?*, ed. D. Z. Phillips, 3–25. Basingstoke: Macmillan.

Eliade, Mircea. 1969. *Yoga: Immortality and Freedom*, trans. Willard R. Trask, 2nd edn. Princeton, NJ: Princeton University Press.

Ellingson, Ter. 2001. *The Myth of the Noble Savage*. Berkeley, CA: University of California Press.

Everett, Daniel L., and Barbara Kern. 1997. *Wari': The Pacaas Novos Language of Western Brazil*. London: Routledge.

Fales, Evan. 2013. Theodicy in a Vale of Tears. In *The Blackwell Companion to the Problem of Evil*, ed. Justin P. McBrayer and Daniel Howard-Snyder, 349–62. Malden, MA: Wiley-Blackwell.

Fausto, Carlos. 2007. Feasting on People: Eating Animals and Humans in Amazonia. *Current Anthropology* 48 (4): 497–514.

Fiedel, Stuart. 2009. Sudden Deaths: The Chronology of Terminal Pleistocene Megafaunal Extinction. In *American Megafaunal Extinctions at the End of the Pleistocene*, ed. Gary Haynes, 21–37. n.p.: Springer.

Filippi, Gian Giuseppe. 2008. Oracles and Shamans in Arunachal Pradesh. *Central Asiatic Journal* 52 (1): 11–35.

Flood, Gavin. 2006. *The Tantric Body: The Secret Tradition of Hindu Religion*. London: I.B. Tauris.

Florida, R. E. 1998–99. A Response to Damien Keown's *Suicide, Assisted Suicide and Euthanasia: A Buddhist Perspective. Journal of Law and Religion* 13 (2): 413–16.

Franke, Anselm. 2010. Much Trouble in the Transportation of Souls, or: The Sudden Disorganization of Boundaries. In *Animism*, Vol. 1, ed. Anselm Franke, 11–53. Berlin: Sternberg Press.

Frazer, Sir James George. 1911. *The Golden Bough: A Study in Magic and Religion*, 3rd edn, Part 1: *The Magic Art and the Evolution of Kings*, Vol. 2. London: Macmillan.

Freeman, Derek. 1983. *Margaret Mead and Samoa: The Making and Unmaking of an Anthropological Myth*. Cambridge, MA: Harvard University Press

Freeman, Derek. 1999. *The Fateful Hoaxing of Margaret Mead: A Historical Analysis of Her Samoan Research*. Boulder, CO: Westview Press.

Frye, Stanley, trans. 2006. *Sutra of the Wise and the Foolish*, 3rd edn. Dharamsala: Library of Tibetan Works and Archives.

Fuller, C. J. 2004. *The Camphor Flame: Popular Hinduism and Society in India*, rev. edn. Princeton, NJ: Princeton University Press.

Gates, Henry Louis, Jr. 1981. Being, the Will, and the Semantics of Death. *Harvard Educational Review* 51 (1): 163–73.

Geertz, Clifford. 1973. Thick Description: Toward an Interpretive Theory of Culture. In his *The Interpretation of Cultures: Selected Essays*, 3–30. New York: Basic Books.

George, Olakunle. 1999. Cultural Criticism in Wole Soyinka's *Death and the King's Horseman. Representations* 67: 67–91.

Gibbs, James. 1986. *Wole Soyinka*. Basingstoke: Macmillan.

Gibbs, James. 1993. The Masks Hatched Out. In *Research on Wole Soyinka*, ed. James Gibbs and Bernth Lindfors, 51–79. Trenton, NJ: Africa World Press.

Gibson, Alexander Boyce. 1973. *The Religion of Dostoevsky*. London: SCM Press.

Gikandi, Simon. 2003. Introduction. In Wole Soyinka, *Death and the King's Horseman*, vii–xxiv. New York: Norton.

Gilman, James. 2007. *Faith, Reason, and Compassion: A Philosophy of the Christian Faith*. Lanham, MD: Rowman & Littlefield.

Giri, Ananta Kumar, and John Clammer, eds. 2014. *Philosophy and Anthropology: Border Crossings and Transformations*. London: Anthem Press.

Gleeson, Andrew. 2012. *A Frightening Love: Recasting the Problem of Evil*. Basingstoke: Palgrave Macmillan.

Goethe, Johann Wolfgang von. 1998 [1833]. *Maxims and Reflections*, trans. Elisabeth Stopp, ed. Peter Hutchinson. London: Penguin.

Goldman, Laurence R. 1999. From Pot to Polemic: Uses and Abuses of Cannibalism. In *The Anthropology of Cannibalism*, ed. Laurence R. Goldman, 1–26. Westport, CT: Bergin and Garvey.

Gombrich, Richard F. 2000 [1981]. A New Theravadin Liturgy. In *The Life of Buddhism*, ed. Frank E. Reynolds and Jason A. Carbine, 180–94. Berkeley, CA: University of California Press.

Gombrich, Richard F. 2006. *How Buddhism Began: The Conditioned Genesis of the Early Teachings*, 2nd edn. Abingdon: Routledge.

Gombrich, Richard F. 2009 [1995]. *Buddhist Precept and Practice: Traditional Buddhism in the Rural Highlands of Ceylon*. Abingdon: Routledge.

Goodman, Charles. 2009. *Consequences of Compassion: An Interpretation and Defense of Buddhist Ethics*. Oxford: Oxford University Press.

Gordon-Grube, Karen. 1988. Anthropophagy in Post-Renaissance Europe: The Tradition of Medicinal Cannibalism. *American Anthropologist* 90 (2): 405–9.

Goswami, Indira. 2006. *The Man from Chinnamasta*, trans. Prashant Goswami. New Delhi: Katha.

Goswami, Kali Prasad. 1998. *Kāmākhyā Temple: Past and Present*. New Delhi: APH.

Goswami, Kali Prasad. 2000. *Devadāsī: Dancing Damsel*. New Delhi: APH.

Goswami, M. C. 1960. An Annual Shamanistic Dance (Deodha Nach) at Kamakhya, Assam. *Journal of the University of Gauhati (Science)* 11 (2): 37–58.

Goswami, Priyan. 2015. *Kamakhya: The Mother Goddess*. Guwahati: Orchid.

Grady, M.-C. 1898. 坐化 [zuò huà], La transformation assise [The Seated Transformation]. *T'oung pao* 9 (1): 230–2.

Graham, Russell W. 1998. The Pleistocene Terrestrial Mammal Fauna of North America. In *Evolution of Tertiary Mammals of North America*, Vol. 1: *Terrestrial Carnivores, Ungulates, and Ungulatelike Mammals*, ed. Christine M. Janis, Kathleen M. Scott and Louis L. Jacobs, 66–71. Cambridge: Cambridge University Press.

Grayson, Donald K., and David J. Meltzer. 2002. Clovis Hunting and Large Mammal Extinction: A Critical Review of the Evidence. *Journal of World Prehistory* 16 (4): 313–59.

Grayson, Donald K., and David J. Meltzer. 2003. A Requiem for North American Overkill. *Journal of Archaeological Science* 30 (5): 585–93.

Grieve, Gregory Price. 2012. Do Human Rights Need a Self? Buddhist Literature and the Samsaric Subject. In *Theoretical Perspectives on Human Rights and Literature*, ed. Elizabeth Swanson Goldberg and Alexandra Schultheis Moore, 247–60. New York: Routledge.

Griffin, David Ray. 2005a. John Cobb's Whiteheadian Complementary Pluralism. In *Deep Religious Pluralism*, ed. David Ray Griffin, 39–66. Louisville, KY: Westminster John Knox Press.

Griffin, David Ray. 2005b. Religious Pluralism: Generic, Identist, and Deep. In *Deep Religious Pluralism*, ed. David Ray Griffin, 3–38. Louisville, KY: Westminster John Knox Press.

Griffith-Dickson, Gwen. 2005. *The Philosophy of Religion*. London: SCM Press.

Griffiths, Paul J. 1990. The Uniqueness of Christian Doctrine Defended. In *Christian Uniqueness Reconsidered: The Myth of a Pluralistic Theology of Religions*, ed. Gavin D'Costa, 157–73. Maryknoll, NY: Orbis Books.

Grillo, Laura S. 2011. The Urgency of Widening the Discourse of Philosophy of Religion: A Discussion of *A Primal Perspective on the Philosophy of Religion* by Arvind Sharma. *Journal of the American Academy of Religion* 79 (4): 803–13.

Grimshaw, Mike. 2018. The Future of the Philosophy of Religion Is the Philosophy of Culture – and *vice versa*. *Palgrave Communications* 4 (72): 1–9.

Guthrie, Stewart. 1993. *Faces in the Clouds: A New Theory of Religion*. Oxford: Oxford University Press.

Gužauskytė, Evelina. 2014. *Christopher Columbus's Naming in the 'Diarios' of the Four Voyages (1492–1504): A Discourse of Negotiation*. Toronto, ON: University of Toronto Press.

Halberstam, David. 2008. *The Making of a Quagmire: America and Vietnam during the Kennedy Era*, rev. edn, ed. Daniel J. Singal. Lanham, MD: Rowman & Littlefield.

Hallowell, A. Irving. 1960. Ojibwa Ontology, Behavior, and World View. In *Culture in History: Essays in Honor of Paul Radin*, ed. Stanley Diamond, 19–52. New York: Columbia University Press.

Hallowell, A. Irving. 1992. *The Ojibwa of Berens River, Manitoba: Ethnography into History*, ed. Jennifer S. H. Brown. Fort Worth, TX: Harcourt Brace Jovanovich College.

Hames, Raymond. 2007. The Ecologically Noble Savage Debate. *Annual Review of Anthropology* 36: 177–90.

Hamilton, Clarence H. 1950. The Idea of Compassion in Mahāyāna Buddhism. *Journal of the American Oriental Society* 70 (3): 145–51.

Haq, Kaiser. 2015. *The Triumph of the Snake Goddess*. Cambridge, MA: Harvard University Press.

Harpham, Geoffrey Galt. 2006. *On the Grotesque: Strategies of Contradiction in Art and Literature*, 2nd edn. Aurora, CO: Davies.

Harrison, Paul. 1987. Who Gets to Ride in the Great Vehicle? Self-Image and Identity among the Followers of the Early Mahāyāna. *Journal of the International Association of Buddhist Studies* 10 (1): 67–89.

Harrison, Victoria S. 2000. *The Apologetic Value of Human Holiness: Von Balthasar's Christocentric Philosophical Anthropology*. Dordrecht: Kluwer.

Harrison, Victoria S. 2006. Internal Realism and the Problem of Religious Diversity. *Philosophia* 34 (3): 287–301.

Harrison, Victoria S. 2008. Internal Realism, Religious Pluralism and Ontology. *Philosophia* 36 (1): 97–110.

Harrison, Victoria S. 2012. An Internalist Pluralist Solution to the Problem of Religious and Ethical Diversity. *Sophia* 51 (1): 71–86.

Harrison, Victoria S. 2013. Religious Diversity. In *The Routledge Companion to Theism*, ed. Charles Taliaferro, Victoria S. Harrison and Stewart Goetz, 477–90. New York: Routledge.

Harrison, Victoria S. 2015. Religious Pluralism. In *The Routledge Handbook of Contemporary Philosophy of Religion*, ed. Graham Oppy, 257–69. Abingdon: Routledge.

Hartshorne, Charles. 1988. Śaṅkara, Nāgārjuna, and Fa Tsang, with Some Western Analogues. In *Interpreting across Boundaries: New Essays in Comparative Philosophy*, ed. Gerald James Larson and Eliot Deutsch, 98–115. Princeton, NJ: Princeton University Press.

Harvey, Graham. 2012. Things Act: Casual Indigenous Statements about the Performance of Object-Persons. In *Vernacular Religion in Everyday Life: Expressions of Belief*, ed. Marion Bowman and Ülo Valk, 194–210. Sheffield: Equinox.

Harvey, Graham. 2017. *Animism: Respecting the Living World*, 2nd edn. London: Hurst.

Harvey, Peter. 1998–99. A Response to Damien Keown's *Suicide, Assisted Suicide and Euthanasia: A Buddhist Perspective*. *Journal of Law and Religion* 13 (2): 407–12.

Harvey, Peter. 2000. *An Introduction to Buddhist Ethics: Foundations, Values and Issues*. Cambridge: Cambridge University Press.

Haynes, Gary. 2002. *The Early Settlement of North America: The Clovis Era*. Cambridge: Cambridge University Press.

Hedges, Paul. 2010. *Controversies in Interreligious Dialogue and the Theology of Religions*. London: SCM Press.

Heim, S. Mark. 1995. *Salvations: Truth and Difference in Religion*. Maryknoll, NY: Orbis Books.

Herodotus. 1859 [*c.* 440 BCE]. *The History* [*Historiae*], trans. George Rawlinson, Vol. 3. London: Murray.

Hick, John. 1973. *God and the Universe of Faiths*. London: Macmillan.

Hick, John. 1976. *Death and Eternal Life*. London: Collins.

Hick, John. 1980. *God Has Many Names: Britain's New Religious Pluralism*. London: Macmillan.

Hick, John. 1990. *Philosophy of Religion*, 4th edn. Upper Saddle River, NJ: Prentice-Hall.

Hick, John. 1993. *Disputed Questions in Theology and the Philosophy of Religion*. Basingstoke: Macmillan.

Hick, John. 1995. *The Rainbow of Faiths: Critical Dialogues on Religious Pluralism*. London: SCM Press.

Hick, John. 2004. *An Interpretation of Religion: Human Responses to the Transcendent*, 2nd edn. Basingstoke: Palgrave Macmillan.

Hick, John. 2010. *Dialogues in the Philosophy of Religion*. Basingstoke: Palgrave Macmillan.

Himmelman, P. Kenneth. 1997. The Medicinal Body: An Analysis of Medicinal Cannibalism in Europe, 1300–1700. *Dialectical Anthropology* 22 (2): 183–203.

Hopkins, E. W. 1913. Sanskrit Kabăiras or Kubăiras and Greek Kabeiros. *Journal of the American Oriental Society* 33: 55–70.

Horton, Robin. 1970. African Traditional Thought and Western Science. In *Rationality*, ed. Bryan R. Wilson, 131–71. Oxford: Blackwell.

Howell, Signe. 2013. Metamorphosis and Identity: Chewong Animistic Ontology. In *The Handbook of Contemporary Animism*, ed. Graham Harvey, 101–12. Durham: Acumen.

Hrdlička, Ales. 1907. Cannibalism. In *Handbook of American Indians North of Mexico*, ed. Frederick Webb Hodge, Part 1, 200–1. Washington, DC: Government Printing Office.

Huemer, Wolfgang. 2013. The Character of a Name: Wittgenstein's Remarks on Shakespeare. In *Wittgenstein Reading*, ed. Sascha Bru, Wolfgang Huemer and Daniel Steuer, 23–37. Berlin: De Gruyter.

Hugo, Victor. n.d. [1827]. *Cromwell*. Paris: Hetzel.

Hulme, Peter. 1986. *Colonial Encounters: Europe and the Native Caribbean, 1492–1797*. London: Methuen.

Humphrey, Nicholas. 1976. The Social Function of Intellect. In *Growing Points in Ethology*, ed. P. P. G. Bateson and R. A. Hilde, 303–17. Cambridge: Cambridge University Press.

Hunn, Eugene S. 1982. Mobility as a Factor Limiting Resource Use in the Columbia Plateau of North America. In *Resource Managers: North American and Australian Hunter-Gatherers*, ed. Nancy M. Williams and Eugene S. Hunn, 17–43. Boulder, CO: Westview Press.

Hurvitz, Leon, trans. 1976. *Scripture of the Lotus Blossom of the Fine Dharma: Translated from the Chinese of Kumārajīva* [4th–5th century CE]. New York: Columbia University Press.

Hutchison, John A. 1991. *Paths of Faith*, 4th edn. New York: McGraw-Hill.

Ingalls, Daniel H. H. 1954. Śaṁkara's Arguments against the Buddhists. *Philosophy East and West* 3 (4): 291–306.

Ingold, Tim. 1999. Comments. *Current Anthropology* 40 (Supplement): 81–2.

Ingold, Tim. 2000. *The Perception of the Environment: Essays on Livelihood, Dwelling and Skill*. London: Routledge.

International Campaign for Tibet [ICT]. 2012. Harrowing Images and Last Message from Tibet of First Lama to Self-Immolate. 1 February. Available online at: https://www.savetibet.org/harrowing-images-and-last-message-from-tibet-of-first-lama-to-self-immolate/ (accessed 8 December 2016).

International Campaign for Tibet [ICT]. 2018. Self-Immolations by Tibetans. 10 December. Available online at: https://www.savetibet.org/resources/fact-sheets/self-immolations-by-tibetans/ (accessed 18 December 2018).

Ives, Christopher. 1992. *Zen Awakening and Society*. Honolulu, HI: University of Hawai'i Press.

Jackson, John L., Jr. 2013. *Thin Description: Ethnography and the African Hebrew Israelites of Jerusalem*. Cambridge, MA: Harvard University Press.

Jaspers, Karl. 1953 [1949]. *The Origin and Goal of History*, trans. Michael Bullock. New Haven, CT: Yale University Press.

Jenkins, Stephen. 2011. On the Auspiciousness of Compassionate Violence. *Journal of the International Association of Buddhist Studies* 33 (1–2): 299–331.

Jha, Makhan. 1991. *Social Anthropology of Pilgrimage*. New Delhi: Inter-India Publications.

Jones, Howard. 2003. *Death of a Generation: How the Assassinations of Diem and JFK Prolonged the Vietnam War*. Oxford: Oxford University Press.

Kakati, Bani Kanta. 1941. *Assamese, Its Formation and Development*. Gauhati: Government of Assam.

Kakati, Bani Kanta. 1948. *The Mother Goddess Kāmākhyā: Or Studies in the Fusion of Aryan and Primitive Beliefs of Assam*. Gauhati: Lawyer's Book Stall.

Kalu Rinpoche. 1986. *The Dharma that Illuminates All Beings like the Light of the Sun and the Moon*. Albany, NY: State University of New York Press.

Kanaris, Jim, ed. 2018. *Reconfigurations of Philosophy of Religion: A Possible Future*. Albany, NY: State University of New York Press.

Kant, Immanuel. 1998 [1787]. *Critique of Pure Reason*, trans. Paul Guyer and Allen W. Wood. Cambridge: Cambridge University Press.

Katō, Bunnō, Yoshirō Tamura and Kōjirō Miyasaka, trans. 1975. *The Threefold Lotus Sutra* [*c.* 1st century BCE to 3rd century CE], trans. revised by W. E. Soothill, Wilhelm Schiffer and Pier P. Del Campana. New York: Weatherhill.

Kayser, Wolfgang. 1963. *The Grotesque in Art and Literature*, trans. Ulrich Weisstein. Bloomington, IN: Indiana University Press.

Kelly, Robert L., and Mary M. Prasciunas. 2007. Did the Ancestors of Native Americans Cause Animal Extinctions in Late-Pleistocene North America? And Does It Matter If They Did? In *Native Americans and the Environment: Perspectives on the Ecological Indian*, ed. Michael E. Harkin and David Rich Lewis, 95–122. Lincoln, NE: University of Nebraska Press.

Keown, Damien. 1992. *The Nature of Buddhist Ethics*. New York: St Martin's Press.

Keown, Damien. 1998–99. Suicide, Assisted Suicide and Euthanasia: A Buddhist Perspective. *Journal of Law and Religion* 13 (2): 385–405.

Kessler, Gary E. 1999. *Philosophy of Religion: Toward a Global Perspective*. Belmont, CA: Wadsworth.

Kierkegaard, Søren. 1939 [1843]. *Fear and Trembling: A Dialectical Lyric*, trans. Robert Payne. London: Oxford University Press.

Kieschnick, John. 1997. *The Eminent Monk: Buddhist Ideals in Medieval Chinese Hagiography*. Honolulu, HI: University of Hawai'i Press.

King, Lester S. 1964. Stahl and Hoffmann: A Study in Eighteenth Century Animism. *Journal of the History of Medicine and Allied Sciences* 19 (2): 118–30.

Kinsley, David. 1986. *Hindu Goddesses: Visions of the Divine Feminine in the Hindu Religious Tradition*. Berkeley, CA: University of California Press.

Kinsley, David. 1997. *Tantric Visions of the Divine Feminine: The Ten Mahāvidyās*. Berkeley, CA: University of California Press.

Kirchin, Simon. 2013. Thick Concepts and Thick Descriptions. In *Thick Concepts*, ed. Simon Kirchin, 60–77. Oxford: Oxford University Press.

Knepper, Timothy D. 2013. *The Ends of Philosophy of Religion: Terminus and Telos*. New York: Palgrave Macmillan.

Knepper, Timothy D. 2014. The End of Philosophy of Religion? *Journal of the American Academy of Religion* 82 (1): 120–49.

Knitter, Paul F., ed. 2005. *The Myth of Religious Superiority: Multifaith Explorations of Religious Pluralism*. Maryknoll, NY: Orbis.

Krebs, Angelika. 1999. *Ethics of Nature: A Map*. Berlin: De Gruyter.

Krech, Shepard, III. 1999. *The Ecological Indian: Myth and History*. New York: Norton.

Krech, Shepard, III. 2007. Beyond *The Ecological Indian*. In *Native Americans and the Environment: Perspectives on the Ecological Indian*, ed. Michael E. Harkin and David Rich Lewis, 3–31. Lincoln, NE: University of Nebraska Press.

Ladipo, Duro. 1964. *Three Yoruba Plays: Ọba Koso, Ọba Mọrọ, Ọba Waja*. English adaptations by Ulli Beier. Ibadan: Mbari.

Lamarque, Peter, and Stein Haugom Olsen. 1994. *Truth, Fiction, and Literature: A Philosophical Perspective*. Oxford: Clarendon Press.

Lambek, Michael. 1989. From Disease to Discourse: Remarks on the Conceptualization of Trance and Spirit Possession. In *Altered States of Consciousness and Mental Health: A Cross-Cultural Perspective*, ed. Colleen A. Ward, 36–61. Newbury Park, CA: Sage.

Lamotte, Étienne. 1965. Le Suicide religieux dans le bouddhisme ancien. *Bulletin de la Classe des Lettres et des Sciences morales et politiques* 5ᵉ Série 51: 156–68.

Lamotte, Étienne. 1987. Religious Suicide in Early Buddhism. *Buddhist Studies Review* 4 (2): 105–18.

Lasaulx, Ernst von. 1956. *Neuer Versuch einer alten auf die Wahrheit der Thatsachen gegründeten Philosophie der Geschichte*. München: Literarisch-Artistische Anstalt.

Las Casas, Bartolemé de. 1989 [1530]. *The Diario of Christopher Columbus's First Voyage to America, 1492–1493: Abstracted by Fray Bartolomé de las Casas*, ed. Oliver Dunn and James E. Kelley, Jr. Norman, OK: University of Oklahoma Press.

Law, Robin. 1985. Human Sacrifice in Pre-Colonial West Africa. *African Affairs* 84 (334): 53–87.

Lee, Dorothy. 1959. *Freedom and Culture*. Englewood Cliffs, NJ: Prentice-Hall.

Lescarbot, Marc. 1609. *Histoire de la Nouvelle France*. Paris: Milot.

Lescarbot, Marc. 1928 [1609]. *Nova Francia: A Description of Acadia, 1606*, trans. P. Erondelle. New York: Harper.

Lestringant, Frank. 1997. *Cannibals: The Discovery and Representation of the Cannibal from Columbus to Jules Verne*, trans. Rosemary Morris. Berkeley, CA: University of California Press.

Lin, Wei. 2003. Padmasambhava and His Eight Manifestations. In John C. Huntington and Dina Bangdel, *The Circle of Bliss: Buddhist Meditational Art*, 150–2. Columbus, OH: Columbus Museum of Art.

Ling, Trevor. 1993. Introduction. In *Buddhist Trends in Southeast Asia*, ed. Trevor Ling, 1–5. Singapore: Institute of Southeast Asian Studies.

Livingston, Paisley, and Carl Plantinga, eds. 2009. *The Routledge Companion to Philosophy and Film*. Abingdon: Routledge.

Logan, Pamela. 2002. *Tibetan Rescue: The Extraordinary Quest to Save the Sacred Art Treasures of Tibet*. Boston, MA: Tuttle.

MacDonald, Mary N. 2011. The Primitive, the Primal, and the Indigenous in the Study of Religion. *Journal of the American Academy of Religion* 79 (4): 814–26.

MacEwan, Grant. 1969. *Tatanga Mani: Walking Buffalo of the Stonies*. Edmonton, AB: Hurtig.

Mahanta, Khagen Chandra. 1997. Shamanistic Dance and Treatment of Disease in Assam. In *Contemporary Society: Tribal Studies*, Vol. 1: *Structure and Process*, ed. Georg Pfeffer and Deepak Kumar Behera, 309–19. New Delhi: Concept.

Mahanta, Khagen Chandra. 2008. *North East India: The Horizon of Anthropology*. Delhi: Kalpaz.

Maity, P. K. 1966. *Historical Studies in the Cult of the Goddess Manasā: A Socio-Cultural Study*. Calcutta: Punthi Pustak.

Maity, P. K. 1989. *Human Fertility Cults and Rituals of Bengal: A Comparative Study*. New Delhi: Abhinav.

Maitzen, Stephen. 2017. Against Ultimacy. In *Renewing Philosophy of Religion: Exploratory Essays*, ed. Paul Draper and J. L. Schellenberg, 48–62. Oxford: Oxford University Press.

Majo Garigliano, Irene. 2015. *The Brahmans of the Kāmākhyā Temple Complex (Assam). Customary Rights, Relations with Pilgrims and Administrative Power*. PhD thesis, Sapienza Università di Roma.

Makley, Charlene. 2015. The Sociopolitical Lives of Dead Bodies: Tibetan Self-Immolation Protest as Mass Media. *Cultural Anthropology* 30 (3): 448–76.

Marcus, George E., and Michael M. J. Fischer. 1999. *Anthropology as Cultural Critique: An Experimental Moment in the Human Sciences*, 2nd edn. Chicago, IL: University of Chicago Press [1st edn, 1986].

Markham, Clements. 1910. A List of the Tribes of the Valley of the Amazons, including Those on the Banks of the Main Stream and of All the Tributaries. *Journal of the Royal Anthropological Institute of Great Britain and Ireland* 40 (January–June): 73–140.

Mbiti, John S. 1990. *African Religions and Philosophy*, 2nd edn. Oxford: Heinemann.

McClymond, Kathryn. 2008. *Beyond Sacred Violence: A Comparative Study of Sacrifice*. Baltimore, MD: Johns Hopkins University Press.

McFarlane, Stewart. 2006. Skilful Means, Moral Crises and Conflict Resolution. In *Buddhism and Peace: Theory and Practice*, ed. Chanju Mun, 157–67. Honolulu, HI: Blue Pine.

McKim, Robert. 2017. The Future of Philosophy of Religion, the Future of the Study of Religion, and (Even) the Future of Religion. In *Renewing Philosophy of Religion: Exploratory Essays*, ed. Paul Draper and J. L. Schellenberg, 112–30. Oxford: Oxford University Press.

McLuhan, T. C. 1980 [1972]. *Touch the Earth: A Self-Portrait of Indian Existence*. London: Abacus.

Meacock, Heather. 2000. *An Anthropological Approach to Theology: A Study of John Hick's Theology of Religious Pluralism, towards Ethical Criteria for a Global Theology of Religions*. Lanham, MD: University Press of America.

Mead, Margaret. 1928. *Coming of Age in Samoa: A Psychological Study of Primitive Youth for Western Civilisation*. New York: Morrow.

Meindl, Dieter. 1996. *American Fiction and the Metaphysics of the Grotesque*. Columbia, MO: University of Missouri Press.

Merleau-Ponty, Maurice. 1973. *The Prose of the World*. Evanston, IL: Northwestern University Press.

Mevissen, Gerd J. R. 2000. Īṣat-paṅgu Śanaiścara, the Lame Planetary God Saturn and His *vāhana*.s. In *South Asian Archaeology 1997: Proceedings of the Fourteenth International Conference of the European Association of South Asian Archaeologists, held in the Istituto Italiano per l'Africa e l'Oriente, Palazzo Brancaccio, Rome, 7–14 July 1997*, Vol. 3, ed. Maurizio Taddei and Giuseppe De Marco, 1267–97. Rome: Istituto Italiano per l'Africa e l'Oriente.

Miles, William F. S. 1994. *Hausaland Divided: Colonialism and Independence in Nigeria and Niger*. Ithaca, NY: Cornell University Press.

Mishra, Nihar Ranjan. 2004. *Kamakhya: A Socio-Cultural Study*. New Delhi: D.K. Printworld.

Mooney, James. 1896. *The Ghost-Dance Religion and the Sioux Outbreak of 1890*. Washington, DC: Government Printing Office.

Morriston, Wes. 2017. Protest and Enlightenment in the Book of Job. In *Renewing Philosophy of Religion: Exploratory Essays*, ed. Paul Draper and J. L. Schellenberg, 223–42. Oxford: Oxford University Press.

Möser, Justus. 1766. *Harlequin: Or, a Defence of Grotesque Comic Performances*, trans. Joachim Andreas Friedrich Warnecke. London: Nicoll.

Motohashi, Ted. 1999. The Discourse of Cannibalism in Early Modern Travel Writing. In *Travel Writing and Empire: Postcolonial Theory in Transit*, ed. Steve Clark, 83–99. London: Zed Books.

Msiska, Mpalive-Hangson. 2007. *Postcolonial Identity in Wole Soyinka*. Amsterdam: Rodopi.

Mukhopadhyay, Subrata Kumar. 1994. *Cult of Goddess Sitala in Bengal: An Enquiry into Folk Culture*. Calcutta: Firma KLM.

Mulhall, Stephen. 2007. Film as Philosophy: The Very Idea. *Proceedings of the Aristotelian Society* 107: 279–94.

Mulhall, Stephen. 2009. *The Wounded Animal: J. M. Coetzee and the Difficulty of Reality in Literature and Philosophy*. Princeton, NJ: Princeton University Press.

Mulhall, Stephen. 2016. *On Film*, 3rd edn. Abingdon: Routledge.

Nagel, Joane. 1996. *American Indian Ethnic Renewal: Red Power and the Resurgence of Identity and Culture*. Oxford: Oxford University Press.

Ñāṇamoli, Bhikkhu, and Bhikkhu Bodhi, trans. 2009. *The Middle Length Discourses of the Buddha: A Translation of the Majjhima Nikāya*, 4th edn. Somerville, MA: Wisdom.

Nattier, Jan. 2003. *A Few Good Men: The Bodhisattva Path according to 'The Inquiry of Ugra (Ugraparipṛcchā)'*. Honolulu, HI: University of Hawai'i Press.

Nhat Hanh, Thich. 1967. 'In Search of the Enemy of Man': From a Letter by Thich Nhat Hanh addressed to the Rev. Dr. Martin Luther King, Jr., June 1, 1965. In his *Vietnam: Lotus in a Sea of Fire*, 106–7. New York: Hill and Wang.

Nhat Hanh, Thich. 1995. *Living Buddha, Living Christ*. New York: Riverhead.

Noble, Louise. 2004. The *Fille Vièrge* as Pharmakon: The Therapeutic Value of Desdemona's Corpse. In *Disease, Diagnosis, and Cure on the Early Modern Stage*, ed. Stephanie Moss and Kaara L. Peterson, 135–50. Aldershot: Ashgate.

Noble, Louise. 2011. *Medicinal Cannibalism in Early Modern English Literature and Culture*. Basingstoke: Palgrave Macmillan.

Norris, Christopher. 2002. *Hilary Putnam: Realism, Reason and the Uses of Uncertainty*. Manchester: Manchester University Press.

Novic, Elisa. 2016. *The Concept of Cultural Genocide: An International Law Perspective*. Oxford: Oxford University Press.

Nussbaum, Martha C. 1992. *Love's Knowledge: Essays on Philosophy and Literature.* Oxford: Oxford University Press.

Nyanaponika Thera. 1958. *The Four Sublime States.* Kandy: Buddhist Publication Society.

Obeyesekere, Ranjini, trans. 2009. *Yasodharā, the Wife of the Bōdhisattva.* Albany, NY: State University of New York Press.

O'Brien, Michael J., Briggs Buchanan, Matthew T. Boulanger, Alex Mesoudi, Mark Collard, Metin I. Eeren, R. Alexander Bentley and R. Lee Lyman. 2015. Transmission of Cultural Variants in the North American Paleolithic. In *Learning Strategies and Cultural Evolution during the Paleolithic,* ed. Alex Mesoudi and Kenichi Aoki, 121–43. Tokyo: Springer.

Ohnuma, Reiko. 2000. Internal and External Opposition to the Bodhisattva's Gift of His Body. *Journal of Indian Philosophy* 28 (1): 43–75.

Ohnuma, Reiko. 2007. *Head, Eyes, Flesh, and Blood: Giving Away the Body in Indian Buddhist Literature.* New York: Columbia University Press.

Ojaide, Tanure. 1992–93. Teaching Wole Soyinka's *Death and the King's Horseman* to American College Students. *College Literature* 19–20 (3–1): 210–14.

Oldenberg, Hermann. 1988 [1894]. *The Religion of the Veda,* trans. Shridhar B. Shrotri. Delhi: Motilal Banarsidass.

Oliver, Simon. 2010. Analytic Theology. *International Journal of Systematic Theology* 12 (4): 464–475.

O'Neill, Onora. 1980. Review of Stephen Clark, *The Moral Status of Animals. Journal of Philosophy* 77 (7): 440–6.

O'Neill, Onora. 1986. The Power of Example. *Philosophy* 61 (235): 5–29.

Oppy, Graham. 2014. *Reinventing Philosophy of Religion: An Opinionated Introduction.* Basingstoke: Palgrave Macmillan.

Oppy, Graham. 2015. Review of John Cottingham, *Philosophy of Religion: Towards a More Humane Approach. Notre Dame Philosophical Reviews* (2015.04.11). Available online at: http://ndpr.nd.edu/news/philosophy-of-religion-towards-a-more-humane-approach/ (accessed 13 June 2017).

Oppy, Graham, and N. N. Trakakis. 2014. Editorial Introduction. In *The History of Western Philosophy of Religion,* Vol. 5: *Twentieth-Century Philosophy of Religion,* ed. Graham Oppy and N. N. Trakakis, vii–ix. Abingdon: Routledge.

Padma, Sree. 2013. *Vicissitudes of the Goddess: Reconstructions of the Gramadevata in India's Religious Traditions.* Oxford: Oxford University Press.

Padoux, André. 1987. Tantrism: An Overview. In the *Encyclopedia of Religion,* ed. Mircea Eliade, Vol. 14, 272–4. New York: Macmillan.

Padoux, André. 1990. *Vāc: The Concept of the Word in Selected Hindu Tantras,* trans. Jacques Gontier. Albany, NY: State University of New York Press.

Perloff, Marjorie. 2014. Wittgenstein's Shakespeare. In *Will the Modernist: Shakespeare and the European Historical Avant-Gardes,* ed. Giovanni Cianci and Caroline Patey, 107–24. Oxford: Peter Lang.

Philipse, Herman. 2012. *God in the Age of Science? A Critique of Religious Reason*. Oxford: Oxford University Press.

Phillips, D. Z. 1970. *Faith and Philosophical Enquiry*. London: Routledge and Kegan Paul.

Phillips, D. Z. 1982. *Through a Darkening Glass: Philosophy, Literature, and Cultural Change*. Oxford: Blackwell.

Phillips, D. Z. 1986. *R. S. Thomas: Poet of the Hidden God*. Allison Park, PA: Pickwick.

Phillips, D. Z. 1990. The Presumption of Theory. In *Value and Understanding: Essays for Peter Winch*, ed. Raimond Gaita, 216–41. Abingdon: Routledge.

Phillips, D. Z. 1992. Philosophy and the Heterogeneity of the Human. In his *Interventions in Ethics*, 251–71. Albany, NY: State University of New York Press.

Phillips, D. Z. 1999. *Philosophy's Cool Place*. Ithaca, NY: Cornell University Press.

Phillips, D. Z. 2000. *Recovering Religious Concepts: Closing Epistemic Divides*. Basingstoke: Macmillan.

Phillips, D. Z. 2001a. Rejoinder. In *Encountering Evil: Live Options in Theodicy*, ed. Stephen T. Davis, 174–80. Louisville, KY: Westminster John Knox Press.

Phillips, D. Z. 2001b. *Religion and the Hermeneutics of Contemplation*. Cambridge: Cambridge University Press.

Phillips, D. Z. 2003. Afterword: Rhees on Reading *On Certainty*. In Rush Rhees, *Wittgenstein's 'On Certainty': There – Like Our Life*, ed. D. Z. Phillips, 133–82. Oxford: Blackwell.

Phillips, D. Z. 2004a. Antecedent Presumption, Faith and Logic. In *Newman and Faith*, ed. Ian Ker and Terrence Merrigan, 1–24. Louvain: Peeters Press.

Phillips, D. Z. 2004b. *Religion and Friendly Fire: Examining Assumptions in Contemporary Philosophy of Religion*. Aldershot: Ashgate.

Phillips, D. Z. 2006. *From Fantasy to Faith: Morality, Religion and Twentieth-Century Literature*, 2nd edn. London: SCM Press.

Phillips, D. Z. 2007a. Locating Philosophy's Cool Place – A Reply to Stephen Mulhall. In *D. Z. Phillips' Contemplative Philosophy of Religion: Questions and Responses*, ed. Andy F. Sanders, 29–54. Aldershot: Ashgate.

Phillips, D. Z. 2007b. Philosophy's Radical Pluralism in the House of Intellect – A Reply to Henk Vroom. In *D. Z. Phillips' Contemplative Philosophy of Religion: Questions and Responses*, ed. Andy F. Sanders, 197–211. Aldershot: Ashgate.

Plank, Katarina. 2016. Burning Buddhists: Self-Immolation as Political Protest. In *Sacred Suicide*, ed. James R. Lewis and Carole M. Cusack, 173–91. Abingdon: Routledge.

Platvoet, Jan G. 2004. Beyond 'Primitivism': 'Indigenous Religions'. *AASR Bulletin* 21: 47–52.

Pliny [the Elder]. 1855–57 [77–79 CE]. *The Natural History of Pliny* [*Naturalis Historia*], trans. John Bostock and H. T. Riley, 6 vols. London: Bohn.

Pojman, Louis, and Michael Rea, eds. 2012. *Philosophy of Religion: An Anthology*, 6th edn. Boston, MA: Wadsworth.

Porter, Joy. 2014. *Native American Environmentalism: Land, Spirit, and the Idea of Wilderness*. Lincoln, NE: University of Nebraska Press.

Posey, Darrell A. 1993. Do Amazonian Indians Conserve Their Environment? And Who Are We to Know If They Do or Do Not? *Abstracts: American Anthropological Association: 92nd Annual Meeting, Washington, DC, November 17–21, 1993*, 473.

Powers, John. 2000. *A Concise Encyclopedia of Buddhism*. Oxford: Oneworld.

Prescott, William H. 1873. *History of the Conquest of Mexico*, Vol. 1, ed. John Foster Kirk. Philadelphia, PA: Lippincott.

Preus, J. Samuel. 1987. *Explaining Religion: Criticism and Theory from Bodin to Freud*. New Haven, CT: Yale University Press.

Prothero, Stephen. 2012. My Take: Dalai Lama Should Condemn Tibetan Self-Immolations. *CNN Belief Blog*, 12 July. Available online at: http://religion.blogs.cnn.com/2012/07/12/my-take-dalai-lama-should-condemn-tibetan-self-immolations/ (accessed 12 November 2016).

Purdum, Elizabeth D., and J. Anthony Paredes. 1989. Rituals of Death: Capital Punishment and Human Sacrifice. In *Facing the Death Penalty: Essays on a Cruel and Unusual Punishment*, ed. Michael L. Radelet, 139–55. Philadelphia, PA: Temple University Press.

Putnam, Hilary. 1981. *Reason, Truth and History*. Cambridge: Cambridge University Press.

Putnam, Hilary. 1987. *The Many Faces of Realism*. LaSalle, IL: Open Court.

Putnam, Hilary. 1992a. *Realism with a Human Face*, ed. James Conant. Cambridge, MA: Harvard University Press.

Putnam, Hilary. 1992b. *Renewing Philosophy*. Cambridge, MA: Harvard University Press.

Putnam, Hilary. 1994a. Comments and Replies. In *Reading Putnam*, ed. Peter Clark and Bob Hale, 242–95. Oxford: Blackwell.

Putnam, Hilary. 1994b. Sense, Nonsense, and the Senses: An Inquiry into the Powers of the Human Mind. *Journal of Philosophy* 91 (9): 445–517.

Pye, Michael. 2003. *Skilful Means: A Concept in Mahayana Buddhism*, 2nd edn. London: Routledge.

Race, Alan. 1993. *Christians and Religious Pluralism: Patterns in the Christian Theology of Religions*, 2nd edn. London: SCM Press [1st edn, 1983].

Radin, Paul. 1958. Introduction to the Torchbook Edition. In Edward Burnett Tylor, *Religion in Primitive Culture*, ix–xvii. New York: Harper.

Ram, Kalpana. 2013. *Fertile Disorder: Spirit Possession and Its Provocation of the Modern*. Honolulu, HI: University of Hawai'i Press.

Ramos, Imma. 2017. *Pilgrimage and Politics in Colonial Bengal: The Myth of the Goddess Sati*. Abingdon: Routledge.

Ramsey, Jarold, ed. 1977. *Coyote Was Going There: Indian Literature of the Oregon Country*. Seattle, WA: University of Washington Press.

Rangdröl, Tsele Natsok. 1993. Clarifying the True Meaning. In Yeshe Tsogyal, *The Lotus-Born: The Life Story of Padmasambhava*, 7–25. Boston, MA: Shambhala.

Rastogi, Navjivan. 1979. *The Krama Tantricism of Kashmir: Historical and General Sources*, Vol. 1. Delhi: Motilal Banarsidass.

Rea, Michael C. 2009. Introduction. In *Analytic Theology: New Essays in the Philosophy of Theology*, ed. Oliver D. Crisp and Michael C. Rea, 1–30. Oxford: Oxford University Press.

Read, Piers Paul. 1974. *Alive: The Story of the Andes Survivors*. London: Alison Press.

Read, Rupert, and Jerry Goodenough, eds. 2005. *Film as Philosophy: Essays on Cinema after Wittgenstein and Cavell*. Basingstoke: Palgrave Macmillan.

Redford, Kent H. 1991. The Ecologically Noble Savage. *Cultural Survival Quarterly* 15 (1): 46–8.

Redford, Kent H., and Allyn M. Stearman. 1993. Forest Dwelling Native Amazonians and the Conservation of Biodiversity: Interests in Common or in Collision? *Conservation Biology* 7 (2): 248–55.

Reid, Julia. 2017. Archaeology and Anthropology. In *The Routledge Research Companion to Nineteenth-Century British Literature and Science*, ed. John Holmes and Sharon Ruston, 357–71. Abingdon: Routledge.

Remshardt, Ralf. 2004. *Staging the Savage God: The Grotesque in Performance*. Carbondale, IL: Southern Illinois University Press.

Rhees, Rush. 1969. *Without Answers*. London: Routledge and Kegan Paul.

Rhees, Rush. 1994. The Fundamental Problems of Philosophy. *Philosophical Investigations* 17 (4): 573–86.

Ricoeur, Paul. 1965. *De l'interprétation: essai sur Freud*. Paris: du Seuil.

Ricoeur, Paul. 1970. *Freud and Philosophy: An Essay on Interpretation*, trans. Denis Savage. New Haven, CT: Yale University Press.

Ricoeur, Paul. 1971. Foreword. In Don Ihde, *Hermeneutic Phenomenology: The Philosophy of Paul Ricoeur*, xiii–xvii. Evanston, IL: Northwestern University Press.

Rivière, P. G. 1980. Review of W. Arens, *The Man-Eating Myth: Anthropology and Anthropophagy*. *Man*, n.s., 15 (1): 203–5.

Robinson, Elmo A. 1949. Animism as a World Hypothesis. *Philosophical Review* 58 (1): 53–63.

Robinson, Richard H., Willard L. Johnson and Thanissaro Bhikkhu. 2005. *Buddhist Religions: A Historical Introduction*, 5th edn. Belmont, CA: Wadsworth.

Rocher, Gregory de. 1979. *Rabelais's Laughers and Joubert's 'Traité du Ris'*. University, AL: University of Alabama Press.

Rountree, Kathryn. 2012. Neo-Paganism, Animism, and Kinship with Nature. *Journal of Contemporary Religion* 27 (2): 305–20.

Rousseau, Jean-Jacques. 1994 [1755]. *Discourse on the Origin of Inequality*, trans. Franklin Philip. Oxford: Oxford University Press.

Roving Report. 2016. Kamakhya Temple Comes Alive with Deodhani Festival [video file]. 25 August. Available online at: https://www.youtube.com/watch?v=CIoHCcQ-iDI (accessed 27 June 2017).

Rowe, William L. 1984. Evil and the Theistic Hypothesis: A Response to Wykstra. *International Journal for Philosophy of Religion* 16 (2): 95–100.

Rowe, William L. 2004. Evil Is Evidence against Theistic Belief. In *Contemporary Debates in Philosophy of Religion*, ed. Michael L. Peterson and Raymond J. VanArragon, 3–13. Malden, MA: Blackwell.

Rowe, William L., and William J. Wainwright, eds. 1973. *Philosophy of Religion: Selected Readings*. New York: Harcourt Brace Jovanovich.

Ruhmkorff, Samuel. 2013. The Incompatibility Problem and Religious Pluralism beyond Hick. *Philosophy Compass* 8 (5): 510–22.

Runzo-Inada, Joseph. 2013. Religion and Global Ethics. In *The Routledge Companion to Philosophy of Religion*, ed. Chad Meister and Paul Copan, 2nd edn, 700–11. Abingdon: Routledge.

Ruskin, John. 1881. *The Stones of Venice*, Vol. 3: *The Fall*. New York: Wiley.

Ryle, Gilbert. 1968. Thinking and Reflecting. *Royal Institute of Philosophy Lectures* 1: 210–26.

Ryle, Gilbert. 2009 [1968]. The Thinking of Thoughts: What is 'Le Penseur' Doing? In his *Collected Papers*, Vol. 2: *Collected Essays 1929–1968*, 494–510. Abingdon: Routledge.

Sahlins, Marshall. 1979. Cannibalism: An Exchange. *New York Review of Books* 26 (4): 46–7. Available online at: https://www.nybooks.com/articles/1979/03/22/cannibalism-an-exchange/#fnr-10 (accessed 19 December 2018).

Salemink, Oscar. 2003. *The Ethnography of Vietnam's Central Highlanders: A Historical Contextualization, 1850–1990*. London: RoutledgeCurzon.

Sanders, Andy F., ed. 2007. *D. Z. Phillips' Contemplative Philosophy of Religion: Questions and Responses*. Aldershot: Ashgate.

Sanderson, Alexis. 2013. Pleasure and the Emotions in Tantric Śaiva Soteriology. Public Lecture, University of Hamburg, 18 June [Handout]. Available online at: https://oxford.academia.edu/AlexisSanderson (accessed 15 September 2017).

Śāntideva. 1995 [8th century CE]. *The Bodhicaryāvatāra*, trans. Kate Crosby and Andrew Skilton. Oxford: Oxford University Press.

Sargeant, Winthrop, trans. 2009 [1984]. *The Bhagavad Gītā: Twenty-Fifth-Anniversary Edition*, ed. Christopher Key Chapple. Albany, NY: State University of New York Press.

Sarma, Hemanta Kumar. 1992. *Socio-Religious Life of the Assamese Hindus: A Study of the Fasts and Festivals of Kamrup District*. Delhi: Daya Publishing House.

Sarma, Nabin Chandra. 1988. *Essays on the Folklore of North-Eastern India*. Pathsala: Bani Prokash.

Sax, William S. 2011. A Himalayan Exorcism. In *Studying Hinduism in Practice*, ed. Hillary P. Rodrigues, 146–57. Abingdon: Routledge.

Schilbrack, Kevin, ed. 2002. *Thinking through Myths: Philosophical Perspectives*. London: Routledge.

Schilbrack, Kevin. 2004a. Introduction: On the Use of Philosophy in the Study of Rituals. In *Thinking through Rituals: Philosophical Perspectives*, ed. Kevin Schilbrack, 1–30. New York: Routledge.

Schilbrack, Kevin, ed. 2004b. *Thinking through Rituals: Philosophical Perspectives*. New York: Routledge.

Schilbrack, Kevin. 2014a. The Future of Philosophy of Religion. *Sophia* 53 (3): 383–8.

Schilbrack, Kevin. 2014b. *Philosophy and the Study of Religions: A Manifesto*. Malden, MA: Wiley-Blackwell.

Schilbrack, Kevin. 2015. Should Philosophy of Religion Do More? A Response to Critics. *Journal of the American Academy of Religion* 83 (1): 254–60.

Schilbrack, Kevin. 2016. Religious Practices and the Formation of Subjects. Paper presented at Boston University Institute for Philosophy and Religion, 21 September 2016 [video file]. Available online at: http://www.bu.edu/ipr/video-schilbrack/ (accessed 4 August 2017).

Schilbrack, Kevin. 2017. Critical Realism and the Academic Study of Religion [audio file]. *Critical Realism Network*, 20 April. Available online at: https://www.youtube.com/watch?v=RFgNuzZSh70 (accessed 25 June 2017).

Schmidt-Leukel, Perry. 2005. Exclusivism, Inclusivism, Pluralism: The Tripolar Typology – Clarified and Reaffirmed. In *The Myth of Religious Superiority: Multifaith Explorations of Religious Pluralism*, ed. Paul F. Knitter, 13–27. Maryknoll, NY: Orbis.

Schmidt-Leukel, Perry. 2017. *Religious Pluralism and Interreligious Theology: The Gifford Lectures – An Extended Edition*. Maryknoll, NY: Orbis.

Sen, Sukumar. 1953. *Vipradāsa's Manasā-Vijaya*. Calcutta: Asiatic Society.

Shakya, Tsering. 2012a. Self-Immolation: The Changing Language of Protest in Tibet. *Revue d'Etudes Tibétaines* 25: 19–39.

Shakya, Tsering. 2012b. Transforming the Language of Protest [28 March 2012]. Hot Spots, *Cultural Anthropology* website, 8 April. Available online at:

https://culanth.org/fieldsights/94-transforming-the-language-of-protest (accessed 21 October 2016).

Sharer, Robert J., with Loa P. Traxler. 2006. *The Ancient Maya*, 6th edn. Stanford, CA: Stanford University Press.

Sharma, Arvind. 1995. *The Philosophy of Religion: A Buddhist Perspective*. Delhi: Oxford University Press.

Sharma, Arvind. 2006. *A Primal Perspective on the Philosophy of Religion*. Dordrecht: Springer.

Shastri, Biswanarayan. 1989. Kāmākhyā. In *History and Archaeology: Prof. H. D. Sankalia Felicitation Volume*, ed. Bhaskar Chatterjee, 122–9. Delhi: Ramanand Vidya Bhawan.

Shastri, B. N. [Biswanarayan], trans. 2008. *The Kālikāpurāṇa*, ed. Surendra Pratap. Delhi: Nag.

Shaw, Sarah. 2006. *Buddhist Meditation: An Anthology of Texts from the Pāli Canon*. Abingdon: Routledge.

Shweder, Richard A. 2005. Cliff Notes: The Pluralisms of Clifford Geertz. In *Clifford Geertz by His Colleagues*, ed. Richard A. Shweder and Byron Good, 1–9. Chicago, IL: University of Chicago Press.

Siegel, Morris. 1941. Religion in Western Guatemala: A Product of Acculturation. *American Anthropologist*, n.s., 43 (1): 62–76.

Sircar, D. C. 1973. *The Śākta Pīṭhas*, 2nd edn. Delhi: Motilal Banarsidass.

Skilleås, Ole Martin. 2001. *Philosophy and Literature: An Introduction*. Edinburgh: Edinburgh University Press.

Skilling, Peter. 2013. Vaidalya, Mahāyāna, and Bodhisatva in India: An Essay towards Historical Understanding. In *The Bodhisattva Ideal: Essays on the Emergence of Mahāyāna*, 69–162. Kandy: Buddhist Publication Society.

Smallshaw, Sebastian. 2015. Schubert Manuscripts and 'Acts of Piety': Sourcing a Wittgenstein Anecdote. *Wittgenstein Initiative* [16 March]. Available online at: http://wittgenstein-initiative.com/wittgenstein-schubert/ (accessed 19 December 2018).

Smart, Ninian. 1960. *World Religions: A Dialogue*. London: SCM Press.

Smart, Ninian. 1973. *The Science of Religion and the Sociology of Knowledge: Some Methodological Questions*. Princeton, NJ: Princeton University Press.

Smart, Ninian. 1995. The Philosophy of Worldviews, or the Philosophy of Religion Transformed. In *Religious Pluralism and Truth: Essays on the Cross-Cultural Philosophy of Religion*, ed. Thomas Dean, 17–31. Albany, NY: State University of New York Press.

Smart, Ninian. 1996. *Dimensions of the Sacred: An Anatomy of the World's Beliefs*. Berkeley, CA: University of California Press.

Smart, Ninian. 1998. *The World's Religions*, 2nd edn. Cambridge: Cambridge University Press.

Smart, Ninian. 1999. *Worldviews: Crosscultural Explorations of Human Beliefs*, 3rd edn. Englewood Cliffs, NJ: Prentice Hall.

Smith, Frederick M. 2006. *The Self Possessed: Deity and Spirit Possession in South Asian Literature and Civilization*. New York: Columbia University Press.

Smith, Huston. 1991 [1958]. *The World's Religions: Our Great Wisdom Traditions*. New York: HarperSanFrancisco.

Smith, Jeremy H. 2011. Primal Religious Experience as Philosophical Evidence: A Response to Arvind Sharma's *A Primal Perspective on the Philosophy of Religion*. *Journal of the American Academy of Religion* 79 (4): 827–41.

Soyinka, Wole. 1975. *Death and the King's Horseman*. London: Methuen.

Soyinka, Wole. 1978. *Myth, Literature and the African World*. Cambridge: Cambridge University Press.

Soyinka, Wole. 1982. Theatre in African Traditional Cultures: Survival Patterns. In *African History and Culture*, ed. Richard Olaniyan, 237–49. Lagos: Longman Nigeria.

Soyinka, Wole. 1988 [1979]. Who's Afraid of Elesin Oba? In his *Art, Dialogue and Outrage: Essays on Literature and Culture*, 110–31. Ibadan: New Horn Press.

Spencer, Jon Michael. 1990. *Protest and Praise: Sacred Music of Black Religion*. Minneapolis, MN: Fortress Press.

Sponholz, Ed. 1992. Head-Smashed-In Buffalo Jump: A Centre for Cultural Preservation and Understanding. In *Buffalo*, ed. John E. Foster, Dick Harrison and I. S. MacLaren, 45–59. Edmonton, AB: University of Alberta Press.

Stahl, Georg Ernst. 1737. *Theoria medica vera: physiologiam et pathologiam*, 2nd edn. Halle: Literis Orphanotrophei.

Standing Bear, Luther. 1933. *Land of the Spotted Eagle*. Boston, MA: Houghton-Mifflin.

Stearman, Allyn MacLean. 1994. 'Only Slaves Climb Trees': Revisiting the Myth of the Ecologically Noble Savage in Amazonia. *Human Nature* 5 (4): 339–57.

Steinmetz, Rudolf S. 1896. Endokannibalismus. *Mittheilungen der anthropologischen Gesellschaft in Wien* 26: 1–60.

Stocking, George W. 2001. *Delimiting Anthropology: Occasional Essays and Reflections*. Madison, WI: University of Wisconsin Press.

Stoller, Paul. 1984. Horrific Comedy: Cultural Resistance and the Hauka Movement in Niger. *Ethos* 12 (2): 165–88.

Stoller, Paul. 1995. *Embodying Colonial Memories: Spirit Possession, Power, and the Hauka in West Africa*. New York: Routledge.

Strauss, Victor von. 1870. *Laò-Tsè's Taò Tĕ Kīng: Aus dem Chinesischen ins Deutsche übersetzt, eingeleitet und commentirt*. Leipzig: Verlag von Friedrich Fleischer.

Strong, John S. 2015. *Buddhisms: An Introduction*. London: Oneworld.

Students for a Free Tibet. 2019. About. Available online at: https://studentsforafreetibet.org/about/ (accessed 17 April 2019).

Stump, Eleonore. 2010. *Wandering in Darkness: Narrative and the Problem of Suffering*. Oxford: Oxford University Press.

Styan, J. L. 1968. *The Dark Comedy: The Development of Modern Comic Tragedy*, 2nd edn. Cambridge: Cambridge University Press.

Sumegi, Angela. 2008. *Dreamworlds of Shamanism and Tibetan Buddhism: The Third Place*. Albany, NY: State University of New York Press.

Surin, Kenneth. 1986. *Theology and the Problem of Evil*. Eugene, OR: Wipf and Stock.

Sutherland, Gail Hinich. 1991. *The Disguises of the Demon: The Development of the Yakṣa in Hinduism and Buddhism*. Albany, NY: State University of New York Press.

Sutherland, Stewart R. 1977. *Atheism and the Rejection of God: Contemporary Philosophy and 'The Bothers Karamazov'*. Oxford: Blackwell.

Swinburne, Richard. 2004. *The Existence of God*, 2nd edn. Oxford: Clarendon Press.

Swinburne, Richard. 2008. *Was Jesus God?* Oxford: Oxford University Press.

TA [Tibet Archive]. 2012. 1998 Tibetan Self Immolation by Thupten Ngodup to Expose China's Brutality in Tibet [video file]. 29 March. Available online at: https://www.youtube.com/watch?v=0ldl4bhQv18 (accessed 14 December 2016).

Tanner, Adrian. 1979. *Bringing Home Animals: Religious Ideology and Mode of Production of the Mistassini Cree Hunters*. New York: St Martin's Press.

Tanner, Adrian. 1988. The Significance of Hunting Territories Today. In *Native People, Native Lands: Canadian Indians, Inuit and Metis*, ed. Bruce Alden Cox, rev. edn, 60–74. Ottawa, ON: Carleton University Press.

Tatz, Mark, trans. 1994. *The Skill in Means (Upāyakauśalya) Sūtra* [c. 1st century BCE]. Delhi: Motilal Banarsidass.

Ṭhānissaro Bhikkhu (Geoffrey DeGraff). 2010. *Skill in Questions: How the Buddha Taught*. Valley Center, CA: Metta Forest Monastery. Available online at: http://www.dhammatalks.org/Archive/Writings/skillInQuestions_v140109.pdf (accessed 10 December 2016).

Thomson, Philip. 1972. *The Grotesque*. London: Methuen.

Tillich, Paul. 1951. *Systematic Theology*, Vol. 1. Chicago, IL: University of Chicago Press.

Times Now. 2013. Times Now Special: The Dalai Lama (Full Interview) [video file]. 25 March. Available online at: https://www.youtube.com/watch?v=-XXZslT3mmE (accessed 10 December 2016).

Tokumitsu, Miya. 2015. The Migrating Cannibal: Anthropophagy at Home and at the Edge of the World. In *The Anthropomorphic Lens: Anthropomorphism, Microcosmism and Analogy in Early Modern Thought and Visual Arts*, ed.

Walter S. Melion, Bret Rothstein and Michel Weemans, 93–116. Leiden: Brill.

Trakakis, Nick. 2008. *The End of Philosophy of Religion*. London: Continuum.

Tremlett, Paul-François, Liam T. Sutherland and Graham Harvey. 2017. Introduction: Why Tylor, Why Now? In *Edward Burnett Tylor, Religion and Culture*, ed. Paul-François Tremlett, Graham Harvey and Liam T. Sutherland, 1–7. London: Bloomsbury.

Tsering, Tashi. 2011. Tibet is Burning [video file]. 11 December. Available online at: https://www.youtube.com/watch?v=vwff-xmnBiA (accessed 22 October 2016).

Tsering, Tempa. 1997. Culturecide? Tibetocide? De-Shangrialised? *Tibetan Bulletin* 1 (1): 18–20.

Tsogyal, Yeshe. 1993. *The Lotus-Born: The Life Story of Padmasambhava*, trans. Erik Pema Kunsang, ed. Marcia Binder Schmidt. Boston, MA: Shambhala.

Tsong-kha-pa. 2004 [*c.* 1402 CE]. *The Great Treatise on the Stages of the Path to Enlightenment*, trans. Lamrim Chenmo Translation Committee, Vol. 2. Ithaca, NY: Snow Lion.

Tsonis, Jack. 2012. Review of Robert N. Bellah and Hans Joas, eds. *The Axial Age and Its Consequences*. *Alternative Spirituality and Religion Review* 3 (2): 262–7.

Tsonis, Jack. 2014. The Deep History of Ritual and Mythology: New Terrain in the Study of Religion. *Journal of Religious History* 38 (1): 115–31.

Tylor, Edward B. 1920 [1871]. *Primitive Culture: Researches into the Development of Mythology, Philosophy, Religion, Language, Art, and Custom*, 2 vols, 6th edn. London: Murray.

United Nations: Department of Economic and Social Affairs. 2009. *State of the World's Indigenous Peoples*. New York: United Nations.

Urban, Hugh B. 2003. 'India's Darkest Heart': Kālī in the Colonial Imagination. In *Encountering Kālī: In the Margins, at the Center, in the West*, ed. Rachel Fell McDermott and Jeffrey J. Kripal, 169–95. Berkeley, CA: University of California Press.

Urban, Hugh B. 2010. *The Power of Tantra: Religion, Sexuality and the Politics of South Asian Studies*. London: I.B. Tauris.

Urban, Hugh B. 2015. Desire, Blood, and Power: Georges Bataille and the Study of Hindu Tantra in Northeastern India. In *Negative Ecstasies: Georges Bataille and the Study of Religion*, ed. Jeremy Biles and Kent L. Brintnall, 68–80. New York: Fordham University Press.

Urban, Hugh B. 2018. Dancing for the Snake: Possession, Gender, and Identity in the Worship of Manasā in Assam. *Journal of Hindu Studies* 11 (3): 304–27.

Van Norden, Bryan W. 2017. *Taking Back Philosophy: A Multicultural Manifesto*. New York: Columbia University Press.

Väyrynen, Pekka. 2013. *The Lewd, the Rude and the Nasty: A Study of Thick Concepts in Ethics*. Oxford: Oxford University Press.

Verbicky-Todd, Eleanor. 1984. *Communal Buffalo Hunting among the Plains Indians: An Ethnographic and Historic Review*. Edmonton, AB: Archaeological Survey of Alberta.

Vickers, William T. 1994. From Opportunism to Nascent Conservation: The Case of the Siona-Secoya. *Human Nature* 5 (4): 307–37.

Vilaça, Aparecida. 2000. Relations between Funerary Cannibalism and Warfare Cannibalism: The Question of Predation. *Ethnos* 65 (1): 83–106.

Vilaça, Aparecida. 2010. *Strange Enemies: Indigenous Agency and Scenes of Encounters in Amazonia*. Durham, NC: Duke University Press.

Vilaça, Aparecida. 2016. *Praying and Preying: Christianity in Indigenous Amazonia*. Oakland, CA: University of California Press.

Viljoen, Frans. 2010. Reflections on the Legal Protection of Indigenous Peoples' Rights in Africa. In *Perspectives on the Rights of Minorities and Indigenous Peoples in Africa*, ed. Solomon Dersso, 75–93. Pretoria: Pretoria University Law Press.

von der Ruhr, Mario. 1996. Is Animism Alive and Well? A Response to Professor Eldridge. In *Can Religion Be Explained Away?*, ed. D. Z. Phillips, 26–45. Basingstoke: Macmillan.

Walshe, Maurice, trans. 1995. *The Long Discourses of the Buddha: A Translation of the Dīgha Nikāya*. Somerville, MA: Wisdom.

Walter, Damian. 2001. The Medium of the Message: Shamanism as Localised Practice in the Nepal Himalayas. In *The Archaeology of Shamanism*, ed. Neil S. Price, 105–19. London: Routledge.

Warder, A. K. 1990. *Indian Kāvya Literature*, Vol. 2. Delhi: Motilal Banarsidass.

Warner, Cameron David. 2012. The Blazing Horror of Now [26 March 2012]. Hot Spots, *Cultural Anthropology* website, 8 April. Available online at: https://culanth.org/fieldsights/115-the-blazing-horror-of-now (accessed 15 October 2016).

Wartenberg, Thomas E. 2007. *Thinking on Screen: Film as Philosophy*. Abingdon: Routledge.

Whalen-Bridge, John. 2015. *Tibet on Fire: Buddhism, Protest, and the Rhetoric of Self-Immolation*. Basingstoke: Palgrave Macmillan.

Whaling, Frank. 1979. Śaṅkara and Buddhism. *Journal of Indian Philosophy* 7 (1): 1–42.

Whitehead, Alfred North. 1978 [1929]. *Process and Reality: An Essay in Cosmology*, ed. David Ray Griffin and Donald W. Sherburne. New York: Free Press.

Wieman, Henry Nelson. 1946. *The Source of Human Good*. Chicago, IL: University of Chicago Press.

Wildman, Wesley J. 2010. *Religious Philosophy as Multidisciplinary Comparative Inquiry: Envisioning a Future for the Philosophy of Religion*. Albany, NY: State University of New York Press.

Willerslev, Rane. 2009. The Optimal Sacrifice: A Study of Voluntary Death among the Siberian Chukchi. *American Ethnologist* 36 (4): 693–704.

Williams, Adebayo. 1993. Ritual and the Political Unconscious: The Case of *Death and the King's Horseman. Research in African Literatures* 24 (1): 67–79.

Williams, Bernard. 1985. *Ethics and the Limits of Philosophy*. London: Fontana.

Williams, Paul. 2009. *Mahāyāna Buddhism: The Doctrinal Foundations*, 2nd edn. Abingdon: Routledge.

Winch, Peter. 1964. Understanding a Primitive Society. *American Philosophical Quarterly* 1 (4): 307–24.

Winch, Peter. 1996. Doing Justice or Giving the Devil His Due. In *Can Religion Be Explained Away?*, ed. D. Z. Phillips, 161–74. Basingstoke: Macmillan.

Winternitz, Maurice. 1983 [1912]. Buddhist Literature. In his *A History of Indian Literature: Buddhist Literature and Jaina Literature*, trans. V. Srinivasa Sarma, Vol. 2, 1–407. Delhi: Motilal Banarsidass.

Winzeler, Robert L. 2008. *Anthropology and Religion: What We Know, Think, and Question*. Lanham, MD: AltaMira Press.

Wittgenstein, Ludwig. 1958. *Philosophical Investigations*, trans. G. E. M. Anscombe, 2nd edn. Oxford: Blackwell.

Wittgenstein, Ludwig. 1965. A Lecture on Ethics. *Philosophical Review* 74 (1): 3–12.

Wittgenstein, Ludwig. 1966. *Lectures and Conversations on Aesthetics, Psychology and Religious Belief*, ed. Cyril Barrett. Oxford: Blackwell.

Wittgenstein, Ludwig. 1969. *The Blue and Brown Books: Preliminary Studies for the 'Philosophical Investigations'*, 2nd edn. Oxford: Blackwell.

Wittgenstein, Ludwig. 1979. *Remarks on Frazer's 'Golden Bough'*, ed. Rush Rhees, trans. A. C. Miles and Rush Rhees. Retford: Brynmill.

Wittgenstein, Ludwig. 1980. *Culture and Value*, ed. G. H. von Wright and Heikki Nyman, trans. Peter Winch. Oxford: Blackwell.

Wittgenstein, Ludwig. 1981. *Zettel*, ed. G. E. M. Anscombe and G. H. von Wright, trans. G. E. M. Anscombe, 2nd edn. Oxford: Blackwell.

Wittgenstein, Ludwig. 1993. Remarks on Frazer's *Golden Bough*. In *Philosophical Occasions, 1912–1951*, ed. James C. Klagge and Alfred Normann, 118–55. Indianapolis, IN: Hackett.

Wittgenstein, Ludwig. 1998. *Culture and Value*, ed. G. H. von Wright and Heikki Nyman, rev. by Alois Pichler, trans. Peter Winch. Oxford: Blackwell.

Wittgenstein, Ludwig. 2003. *Public and Private Occasions*, ed. James C. Klagge and Alfred Nordmann. Lanham, MD: Rowman & Littlefield.

Wittgenstein, Ludwig. 2009 [1953]. *Philosophical Investigations*, 4th edn, trans. G. E. M. Anscombe, P. M. S. Hacker and Joachim Schulte. Malden, MA: Wiley-Blackwell.

Woeser, Tsering. 2016. *Tibet on Fire: Self-Immolations against Chinese Rule*, trans. Kevin Carrico. London: Verso.

Wood, William. 2015. Review Essay Roundtable on Kevin Schilbrack, *Philosophy and the Study of Religions: A Manifesto. Journal of the American Academy of Religion* 83 (1): 248–53.

Wu, Tien-wei. 1983. *Lin Biao and the Gang of Four: Contra-Confucianism in Historical and Intellectual Perspective*. Carbondale, IL: Southern Illinois University Press.

Wynn, Graeme. 2012. On the Margins of Empire (1760–1840). In *The Illustrated History of Canada: 25th Anniversary Edition*, ed. Craig Brown, 181–276. Montreal, QC, and Kingston, ON: McGill-Queen's University Press.

Wynn, Mark R. 2005. *Emotional Experience and Religious Understanding: Integrating Perception, Conception and Feeling*. Cambridge: Cambridge University Press.

Wynn, Mark R. 2009. *Faith and Place: An Essay in Embodied Religious Epistemology*. Oxford: Oxford University Press.

Wynn, Mark R. 2013. *Renewing the Senses: A Study of the Philosophy and Theology of the Spiritual Life*. Oxford: Oxford University Press.

Ziporyn, Brook. 2000. *Evil and/or/as the Good: Omnicentrism, Intersubjectivity, and Value Paradox in Tiantai Buddhist Thought*. Cambridge, MA: Harvard-Yenching Institute.

Index